IMAGES
of America

PLANTATION

I0806271

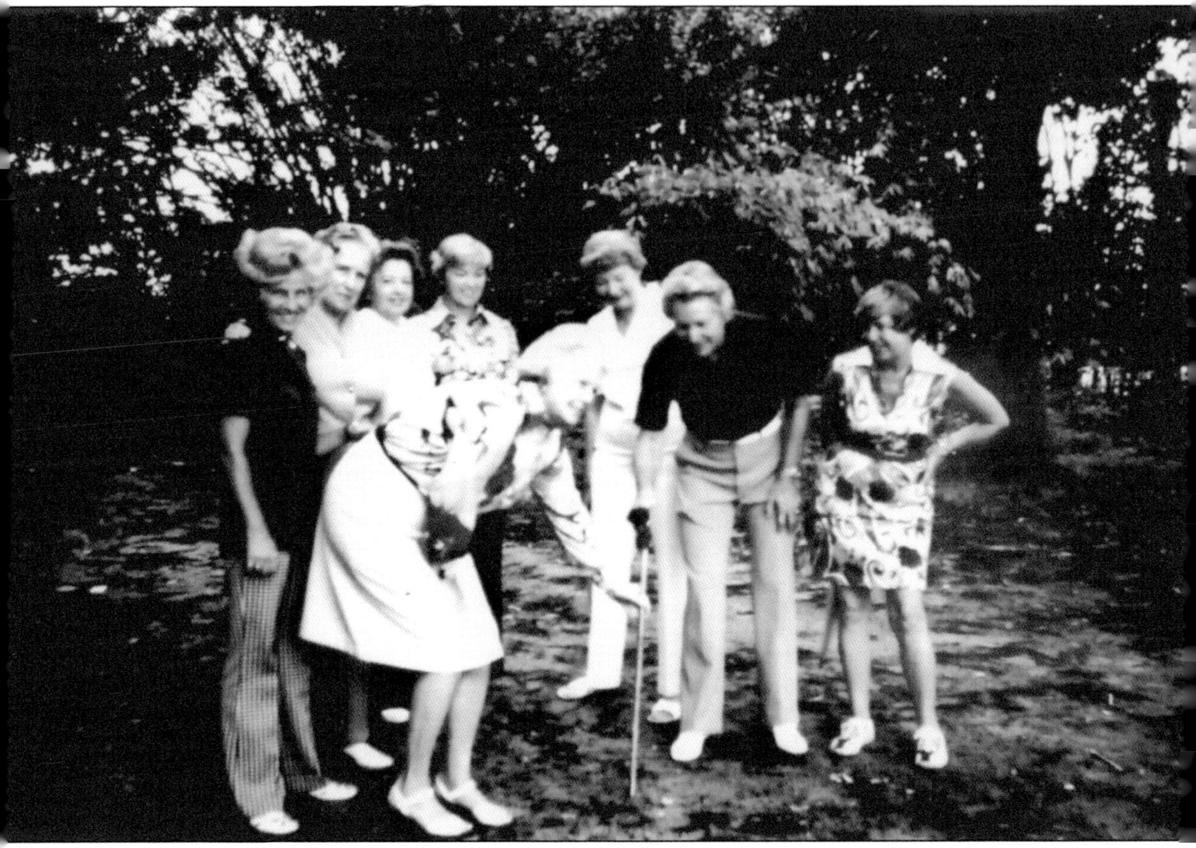

In February 1978, the Plantation Historical Society attempted to move Fred Peters's house to the south side of Peters Road. The house was to function as the historical museum. Society members Dorothy O'Hare and Robert Blakely (holding the stake) and, from left to right, Phyllis Napp, Genevieve Veltri, Diane Blakely, Ginny Allen, Lois Brickhouse, and Jean Hanes are pictured at what was to be the house's new location.

On the Cover: The Plantation Volunteer Fire Department was incorporated in 1957. The photograph of Engine No. 1 was taken March 1, 1959. Engine No. 1 is a 500-gallon front-mount pumper and is still a commissioned piece of apparatus housed at the Plantation Historical Museum. Pictured are, from left to right, John P. Knuck, J. Bryan Dye, Bernard Wilhelm, John Tiedemann, Bob Blakeley, Bill Babel, Chief Fred Peters, and assistant chief Les Bitting Sr. From left to right on top of the truck are Norm Neimeyer, Frank Campbell, and Herb Seeger.

IMAGES
of America

PLANTATION

Shirley Schuler

ARCADIA
PUBLISHING

ISBN 978-0-7385-9415-6

Published by Arcadia Publishing
Charleston, South Carolina

Printed in the United States of America

Library of Congress Control Number: 2012934475

For all general information, please contact Arcadia Publishing:
Telephone 843-853-2070
Fax 843-853-0044
E-mail sales@arcadiapublishing.com
For customer service and orders:
Toll-Free 1-888-313-2665

Visit us on the Internet at www.arcadiapublishing.com

This book is dedicated to the women who had the vision to preserve the history of the City of Plantation for future generations.

Contents

ACKNOWLEDGMENTS

In 1974, a small group of women formed the Plantation Historical Society to preserve the history and archives of the Plantation community. The first meeting was held in the Veltri home, and Genevieve Veltri was elected the first president. Also present were Ginny Allen, Helen Bigney, Carol Barton, Lois Brickhouse, Betty Cobb, Beverly Grant, Marilyn King, Phyllis Napp, and Dottie O'Hare. Without this foundation and the support of the society members who followed, this project would not have been possible.

The Plantation Historical Society is grateful to all the former and current residents, local businesses, clubs, and organizations that continue to contribute to the museum's local history collection. The society encourages anyone with historical photographs and artifacts relevant to the history of Plantation to contact the Plantation Historical Museum.

In order to complete this book, the following individuals assisted with the collection and organization of images, fact-checking, and proofreading: John Feeney and Rosemary Schafer (Plantation Historical Museum staff); Ken Boyce, Ginny Chiapel, and Cheryl Greenberg (City of Plantation Parks and Recreation); Sally Finlen (Plantation Library Board); Monika Knapp (the Helen B. Hoffman Plantation Library); Ginette Fogel (City of Plantation graphic designer/administrator); and Priscilla Richards (City of Plantation administration).

Special acknowledgment must be given to the mayors and city council members, past and present, for their support of the preservation of the City of Plantation's history.

Unless otherwise indicated, all images were provided by the Plantation Historical Museum.

INTRODUCTION

The City of Plantation is fast approaching its diamond anniversary—60 years as a prosperous, thriving, and successful municipality. We have come so far in the last decade that it is hard to remember what Plantation was like in its early days. Around the time the city was incorporated, Plantation was a vast wilderness, as indicated by its motto *E Vasitate Haec Urbs*, meaning "Out of the Wilderness, This City." There were less than 1,000 residents, only one police officer, and a group of residents volunteering to serve as firefighters. There was one school, Berenice T. Peters Elementary School, named for the wife of the city's founder, Frederick C. Peters, and there was only one park facility, the Plantation Community Center at Kennedy Park.

Today, Plantation has 85,000 residents. Its police department is nearly 200 strong, and its volunteer fire department is the largest and most successful volunteer department in the state of Florida. There are 10 public schools to educate children from kindergarten to the 12th grade and numerous day care, charter, and private schools.

Plantation boasts one of the lowest millage rates in Broward County and a strong mayor-form government that is committed to quality redevelopment within its business districts and neighborhood stabilization with world-class recreation facilities. Nationally recognized companies, such as DHL, American Express, National Beverage, Cigna Health, University of Miami, Bascom Palmer Eye Institute, and Motorola all call Plantation home.

In keeping with Frederick Peters's original master plan, Plantation's elected officials have made its parks and recreation system a top priority in every budget. There are currently 42 parks throughout the city, totaling more than 600 acres of open space. Holiday events, parades, and city camps are highlights throughout the year, providing memories that last a lifetime and traditions passed down from generation to generation.

The earliest (400 BC–1700 AD) known inhabitants of the western area of what became Broward County were a nomadic hunting-and-gathering people that the Spanish called the Tequesta. What little we know of the Tequesta comes from the excavation of mounds found where they camped.

By 1800, most of the indigenous Indians had disappeared from Florida. Other native tribes from Georgia, Alabama, and Louisiana migrated south to Florida. These groups merged together to become the Seminoles (from the Spanish *cimarrones*, or "free people"), taking refuge in the Everglades and offering protection and shelter to escaped African slaves, absorbing them into the tribe.

Conflict over land between the Seminoles and the white settlers resulted in the Seminole Wars, which lasted from 1835 to 1842. At the conclusion of the wars, the Seminoles who remained in South Florida retreated deeper into the swamps. In 1845, Florida became a state, and by the late 1890s, the Seminoles were engaged in trade with the white settlers.

In 1896, Henry Flagler's Florida East Coast Railway reached Fort Lauderdale, bringing with it an influx of people and a desire for usable land. Napoleon Bonaparte Broward was governor of Florida from January 3, 1905, to January 5, 1909. He had made draining the Everglades a major campaign theme, comparing the future potential of canal systems in South Florida to those in Holland. In 1906, the first attempt was made to drain the Everglades.

Named for the former Florida governor, Broward County was created by the Florida legislature in 1915 by combining portions of Dade and Palm Beach Counties. The project designed to drain the Everglades and construct canals connected to Lake Okeechobee continued, touching off a land boom. Prices for swampland climbed higher and higher until, like a balloon, the land boom burst. Fortunes were lost overnight. As a final blow, a hurricane hit Broward and Dade Counties in September 1926, causing some of the worst property damage in US history and slowing the development of South Florida.

One of Plantation's founders, Frederick C. Peters, moved his family to south Dade County from Missouri in 1931 to escape the harsh winters. Peters's interest in agriculture started with potatoes and was followed by an interest in cattle, which led him to seek undeveloped, inexpensive grazing land for his prized Polled Herefords.

The land between Palm Beach and Dade Counties was isolated and far west of any development and was linked by what is now US Highway 441 or State Road 7. Signs advertised land for "$10 down, $10 a month." In 1939, Frederick C. Peters purchased 10,000 acres for $25 per acre from the Everglades Plantation Company. Although not yet incorporated, the area was nicknamed Plantation. Peters hired Les E. Bitting to move his cattle to his new pastures.

Peters built a summer home on his farm in 1944 on the north side of what is now Peters Road. An Agricultural Experiment Station of the University of Florida was also established on the farm. Peters hired Russell T. Pancoast to develop a master plan for the city and C. Kay Davis to develop a water control system. Miami Beach builder Chauncey "Bob" Clark, with his brother Stewart, formed a building company called Plantation Homes Inc., and began construction of the first homes in Plantation on East Acre Drive in 1947.

With the canal system incomplete, flooding from two hurricanes nearly ended Peters and Clark's dream. Developer Chauncey Clark risked financial ruin by repairing and restoring every home that was damaged at his own expense. The community survived, and by 1949, there were 40 homes in east Plantation.

In 1949, resident Dr. Abram Hoffman formed the Plantation Homeowners' Association, creating an unofficial government for the growing city. The newly founded Plantation Woman's Club welcomed newcomers to the area. There were still no streetlights, telephones, newspapers, or mail delivery. Broward Boulevard extended to Royal Palm Court, and wrought-iron gates and a stone entry wall, the inspiration for today's brick entry walls, marked the entrance to Plantation where the turnpike now crosses Broward Boulevard.

By 1950, the population had reached 200. The Plantation Golf Course and Country Club, which was developed to encourage the Broward County Commission to extend Broward Boulevard westward, opened on December 15, 1950.

With a population of less than 500 and a budget of under $2,000, the residents of Plantation incorporated on April 30, 1953. Incorporation gave them control over growth and prevented other cities from annexing their land. The Plantation Homeowner's Association appointed Ellsworth D. Gage as the mayor, and Walter Bartels, Paul Stoner, Winslow Freeman, George Bartold, and Wilfred Perry were appointed to the city council. None of the early city officials drew salaries. S. Robinson Estey became the first elected mayor in 1955 and served until 1959. The Plantation Police Department was organized in 1955, with one officer to patrol the whole city. Plantation residents founded the Plantation Volunteer Fire Department in 1957, which continues to operate as a volunteer department today. In 1958, the mailing address changed from Fort Lauderdale to Plantation.

Initially, schoolchildren were bused to Fort Lauderdale to attend school, and organized sports activities were conducted at Holiday Park. Fred Peters gave 10 acres of land to the school board and Plantation's first school, the Berenice Todd Peters Elementary School, was dedicated in 1959. A summer recreation program began in 1955. In the spring of 1958, a pony league for boys ages 13–15 started.

By the end of the decade, the city's budget was over $170,000. There were no ad valorem taxes; funds were collected through building and license fees and utility taxes. The operating cost of the police department ($24,000) was paid from cigarette taxes. James Ward was elected mayor in 1959 and served until 1971.

The 1960s were a decade of growth for the city. Land was annexed and Plantation's boundaries stretched from State Road 7 west to Flamingo Road and from Sunrise Boulevard south to State Road 84. City officials wanted to ensure that the aesthetics of Plantation reflected Fred Peters, Russell Pancoast, and Chauncey Clark's vision, so zoning ordinances were created to require landscaped spaces around buildings and prohibit identical homes from being built within 600 feet of one another. Hurricane Donna hit the area in September 1960, and residents were relieved to find that the pumps and canals provided effective drainage. In July 1963, the monthly salary of a council member was $100, with the mayor's salary set at $200 a month.

Primarily a family-oriented community, residents worked with the city to form a Police Athletic League (PAL), a recreation department, and a library. The Plantation Junior Woman's Club started with 74 charter members on March 9, 1960.

In 1963, the City of Plantation marked a decade of progress with a weeklong gala celebration starting May 11. Festivities included a parade along Broward Boulevard, the dedication of the Plantation Community Center on Palm Tree Road, a family-style street dance at the Plantation Village shopping center on East Acre Drive, accordion concerts, a Baby Buggy contest, and a fireworks display held at Plantation Field on Northwest 70th Avenue near Sunrise Boulevard.

Frederick C. Peters passed away suddenly at the Miami Heart Institute on July 18, 1964, survived by his wife and sons. His "Dream City" continued to grow, but retained its small-town personality.

Longtime residents remember the "noon whistle" that blew every day except on Sunday at 12:00 sharp. Although no longer in use, the whistle is still on the property at Fire Station No. 1. Plantation's unique "blue bag" garbage collection system started in 1969 under Mayor Jim Ward. Residents still participate in a "pay as you throw" user fee–based collection program by purchasing the "blue bags" at local stores.

By 1970, the city's population was 23,000, and Jack Carter served as mayor from 1971 to 1975. Gulfstream Land and Development Company purchased 5,400 acres for the master-planned community of Jacaranda in 1970, ushering in a building boom that brought award-winning residential communities, the Jacaranda Golf Course and Country Club, and commercial development. Plantation continued to experience growth with the annexation of Melaleuca Isles and Plantation Acres in 1973. By the end of the decade, Plantation's population had more than doubled. In 1975, Frank Veltri was elected mayor and would serve six consecutive four-year terms until his retirement in 1999.

The 1970s were a decade of celebrations: a new city hall was dedicated (1973), Deicke Auditorium opened (1973), residents celebrated the country's bicentennial (1976), and the city's 25th birthday was observed (1978). In the summer of 1978, the Westfield Mall, formerly the Broward Mall, opened and remains one of the busiest retail destinations in the county today.

The 1980s began with the completion of the 77-acre Plantation Central Park recreation complex. When it opened, the park featured softball, football, and soccer fields; a track; an Olympic pool; tennis center; a gymnasium with indoor basketball; a game room; weight room; and classrooms. As the population grew to 50,000 so did the number of city facilities, which included fire stations, Pine Island Park, Veterans Park, and a new police station.

Plantation was designated by the National Arbor Day Foundation as a Tree City in 1980 and has maintained this designation every year since. The Tree City USA program provides direction, technical assistance, public attention, and national recognition for urban and community forestry programs. As part of the Tree City USA program, the landscape department developed the Plantation Landscaping Award for Nurturing Our Town (PLANT) Awards to show special appreciation and recognition to businesses, institutions, and properties for their outstanding landscape designs and maintenance programs.

The members of the Plantation Volunteer Fire Association celebrated their 25th anniversary in 1982. The first female firefighter joined that same year. There were now five fire stations and 12 engines. In 1989, Mayor Frank Veltri appointed Robert S. Pudney as the first paid fire chief.

In 1988, the Fashion Mall opened with Lord & Taylor and Macy's as its anchor stores. The shopping mall closed in 2006 due to hurricane damage, and the property currently awaits redevelopment. That same year, the Fountains Shopping Center was also opened on University Drive. Today, it is a thriving part of the Midtown District.

Plantation's population reached 65,000 in 1990, with Mayor Veltri still at the helm. With the completion of Interstate 595 in 1991, the city was now at the crossroads of Broward's expressway system. Plantation's central location and its direct access to the Fort Lauderdale–Hollywood

International Airport and Port Everglades attracted major employers to the area. Cornerstone Corporate Center consists of office buildings surrounding an 11-acre lake. Kemper National Services also moved its operations to the area that would become the Midtown District.

Plantation's services continued to expand in order to meet the needs of a growing community. In 1995, the city started its own emergency medical service providing care and transportation of the sick and injured within the city. The Fire Administration Building and Firefighter's Memorial Park were dedicated in 1998. The Plantation Volunteer Fire Department is the largest volunteer fire department in Florida. The Plantation Police Department added a K-9 unit consisting of six dogs and their handlers in 1999. The Plantation Historical Museum expanded in 1991, creating a home for the city's first fire engine. The City of Plantation Parks and Recreation Department opened Tara Park and the Volunteer Park Community Center in Plantation Acres and Sunset Park, with seven lighted baseball diamonds (two of which are major league regulation size) and four unlit T-ball fields. Central Park added a training pool, water play area, and roller hockey rinks, and the tennis center was renamed in honor of Mayor Frank Veltri.

Hurricane Andrew struck South Florida at Homestead on August 24, 1992. The storm sheared Broward County, causing approximately $20 million in damage. In the decade after the storm, there was a sudden housing boom in the county, as residents from Dade who lost their homes migrated to the western areas of Broward, including Plantation.

The fire at the Plantation Towne Mall on September 7, 1996, would be recorded as the largest fire in Plantation's history and one of the largest tactical operations in the history of Broward County. The fire would consume 56,000 square feet of the 133,000-square-foot enclosed mall. The shopping mall was rebuilt as Plantation Towne Square and anchored by a new Publix store.

Frank Veltri, the longest serving mayor of Plantation who led the city throughout 24 years of expansion and progress, retired at the end of his sixth term in 1999.

Rae Carole Armstrong, who became Plantation's first female mayor, succeeded him. Her public career started in 1983 when she was elected as Plantation's first female council member.

With the city's population at 85,000 and nearing build-out, it was time to focus on business district redevelopment and neighborhood improvement. The following years have seen diverse community programs, creative parks projects, attention to sustainable practices, and innovative economic development opportunities.

Plantation celebrated its golden anniversary in 2003, marking 50 years of community with a weeklong celebration.

Hurricane Wilma struck October 24, 2005, becoming the fourth most costly storm in US history. Massive property damage and extensive power outages challenged both residents and community leaders.

Another milestone was met on November 4, 2006, when the volunteer fire department hosted its 50th barbecue, an annual tradition in Plantation. Former mayor and past fire chief Frank Veltri made a special appearance at the event; on November 30, 2006, at age 94, he passed away.

After 12 years as mayor and a total of 28 years of service to the city, Mayor Armstrong made the decision to retire in March 2011.

Now looking to the future with the election of Diane Veltri Bendekovic as mayor in March 2011, redevelopment continues in the business corridors of Plantation's Gateway, Midtown, and the Technology Park. The city has repeatedly been named one of the nation's 100 Best Communities for Young People by America's Promise Alliance.

Through the cooperation of city officials and employees, residents, businesses, community clubs, and volunteer organizations, the City of Plantation has become a modern municipality with a unique hometown atmosphere where the "grass is greener."

One

The Early Years

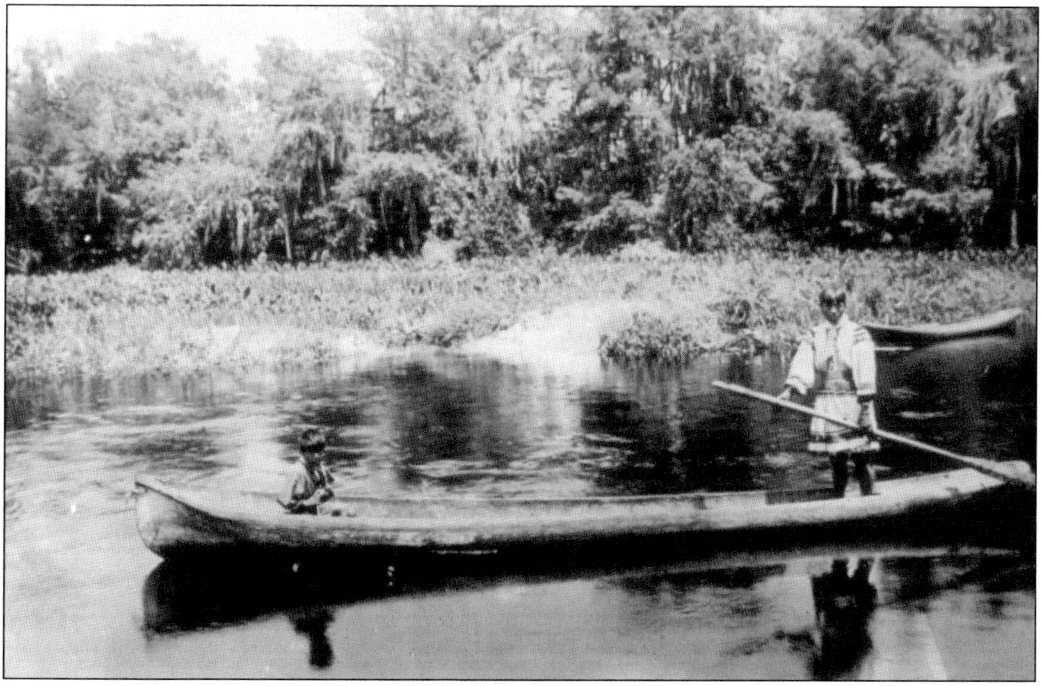

In the early 1900s, the Plantation area was covered with two to three feet of water at least three months of the year. Rev. William Osceola, a Seminole Indian pastor, remembered Seminole Indians hunting, fishing, and camping for weeks at a time in this area.

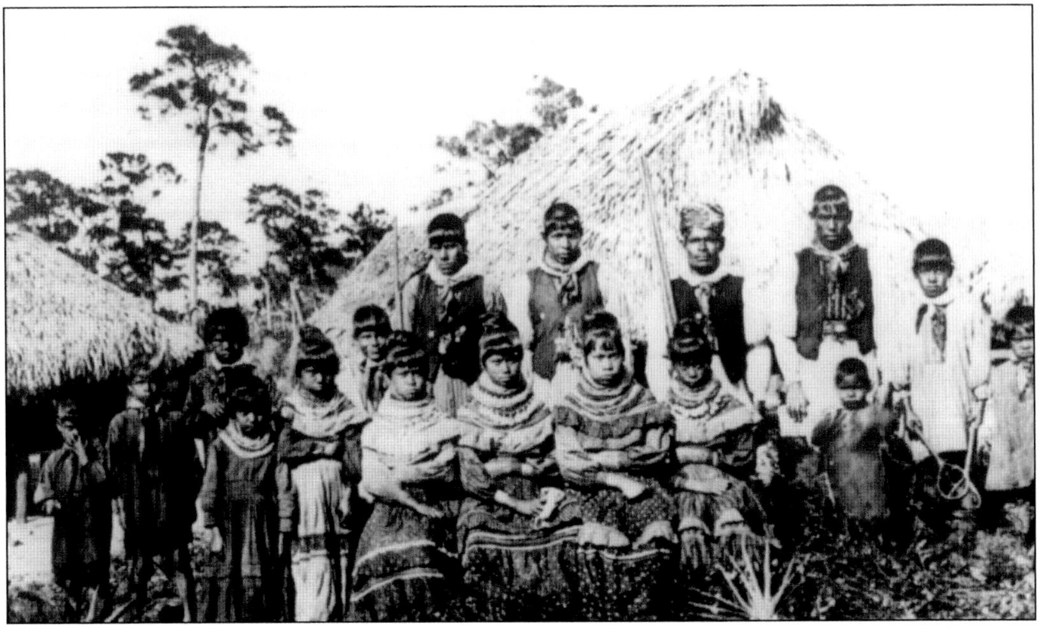

Pictured is the last encampment of Seminoles on the Pine Island Ridge in western Broward County in the 1890s. This area served as Seminole headquarters during the second and third Seminole Wars. (Courtesy of Florida Memory Project.)

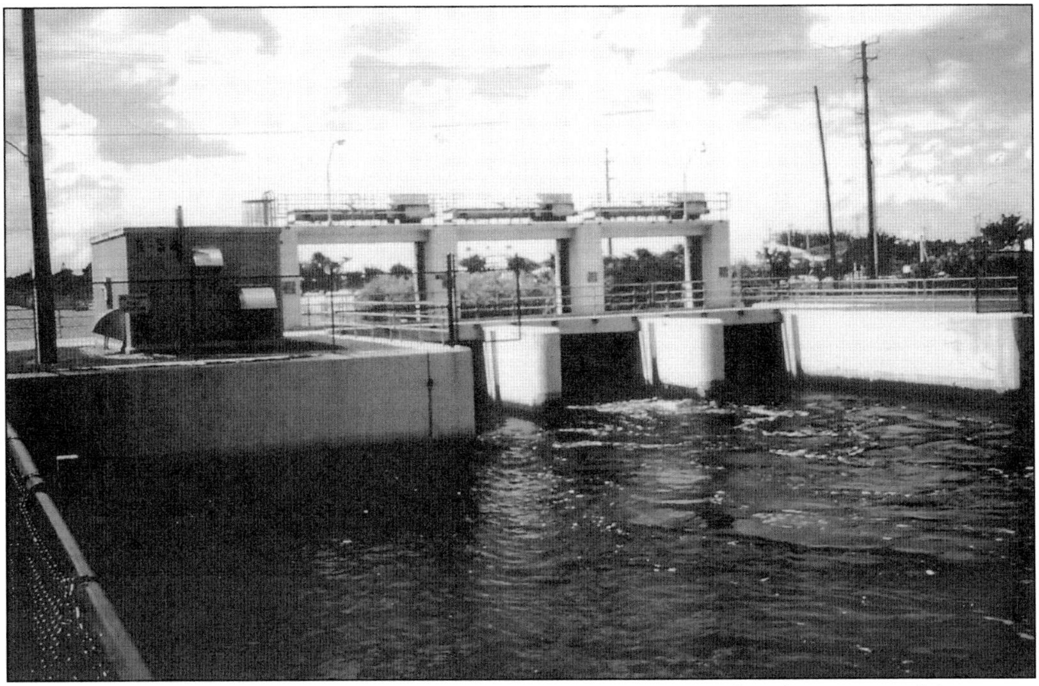

The Sewell Lock was built in 1911 on the North New River Canal and was opened for use in 1912 to accommodate barges carrying freight along the New River. Owned and operated by the South Florida Water Management District, the lock was the first built on the New River and is the best preserved of all the surviving South Florida locks. On February 17, 1978, it was listed in the National Register of Historic Places. This photograph shows the lock in the late 1990s.

In 1906, Capt. Walter Holloway, US Army Corps of Engineers, made the first attempt to drain the Everglades in the area. The first waterway dug was appropriately named the Holloway Canal, which runs north and south from the New River to the C-13 Canal on the south side of Sunrise Boulevard. (Courtesy of Broward County Historical Commission.)

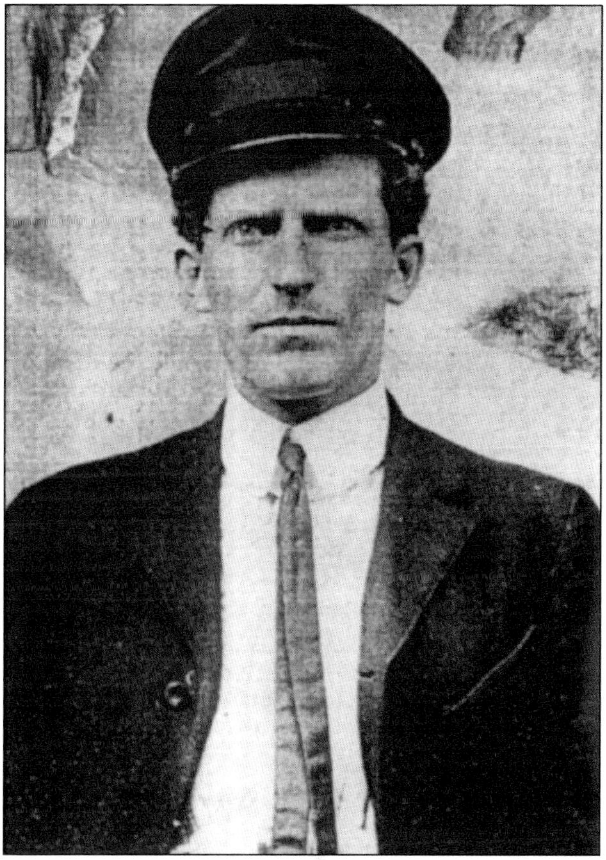

A Kansas wheat farmer, Charles DeWeddle purchased land during the Everglades Land Lottery in March 1911 in Fort Lauderdale. The land, part of the Everglades Plantation Development, was located in what is now the Plantation Isles development. Shown camping on their new property are, from left to right, Daniel DeWeddle, Charles DeWeddle Jr., Frank DeWeddle, Charles DeWeddle, Maria Forslin DeWeddle, Gertrude DeWeddle, and Noah Selman DeWeddle.

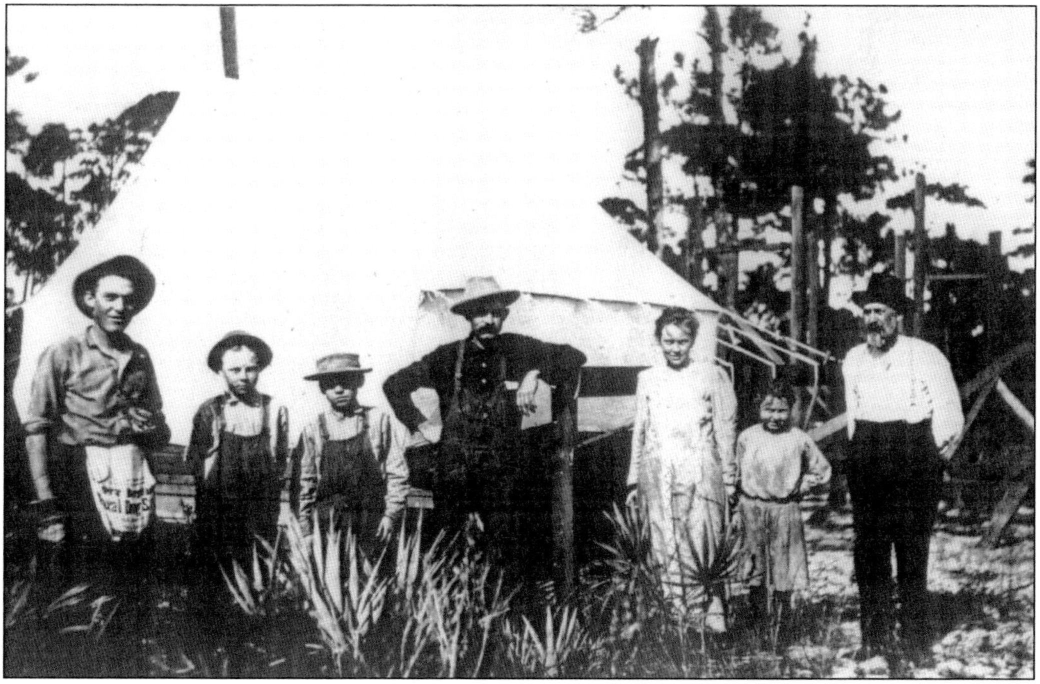

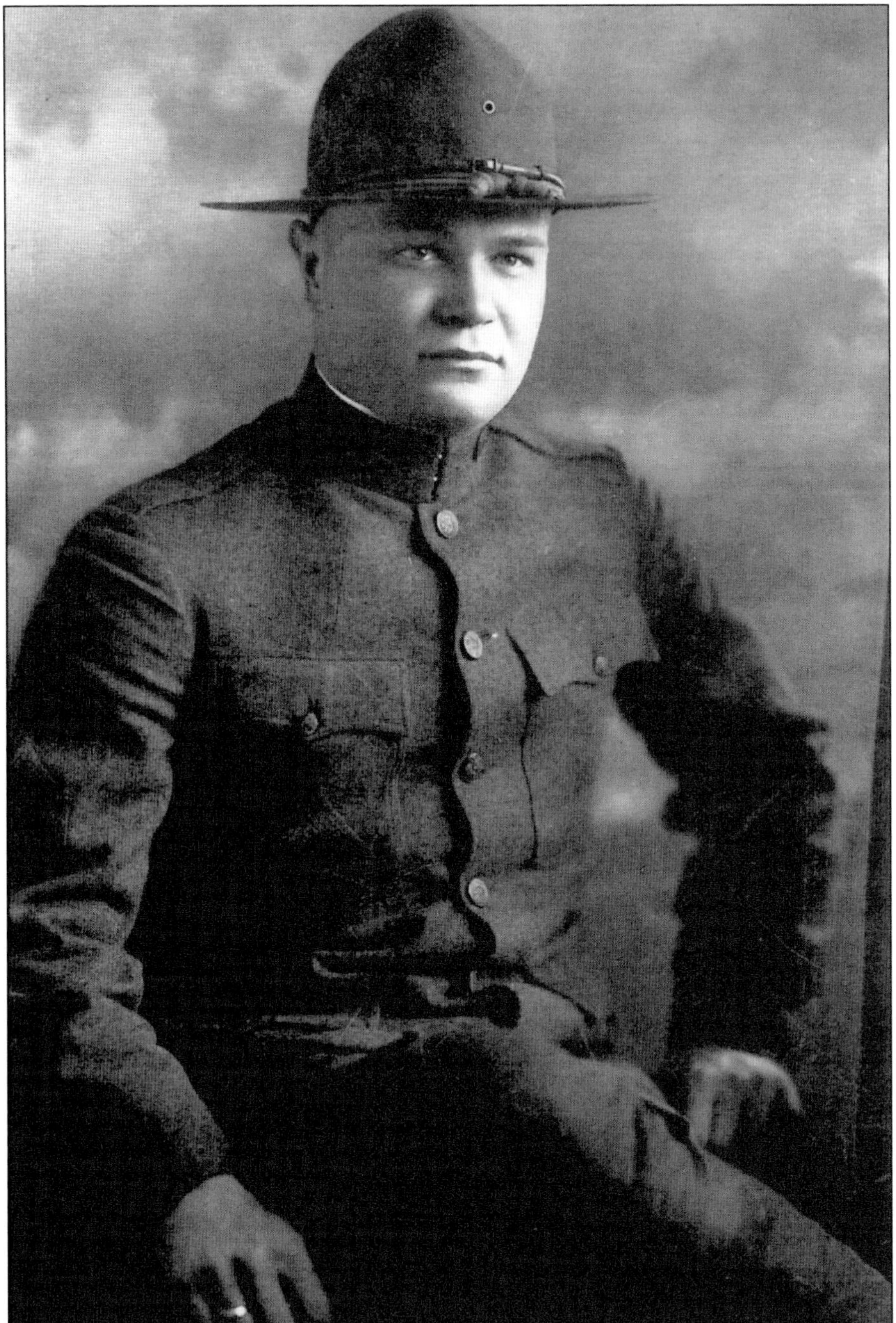

Frederick C. Peters, an heir to the Peters Shoe Company, was born in St. Louis, Missouri, on June 30, 1900. Peters played football at Washington University, served as a reserve officer in World War I, and was an avid tennis player. He married Berenice Todd in 1924, and his three sons, Frederick T., Lewis, and Ferguson, were all born in St. Louis. The Peters family traveled to Florida initially for the health of their son Lewis. They moved to Dade County permanently in 1931, where Peters developed his interest in agriculture, starting with potatoes. The Peters maintained a home in Miami Beach as well as their ranch in Plantation.

Two

THE 1940S

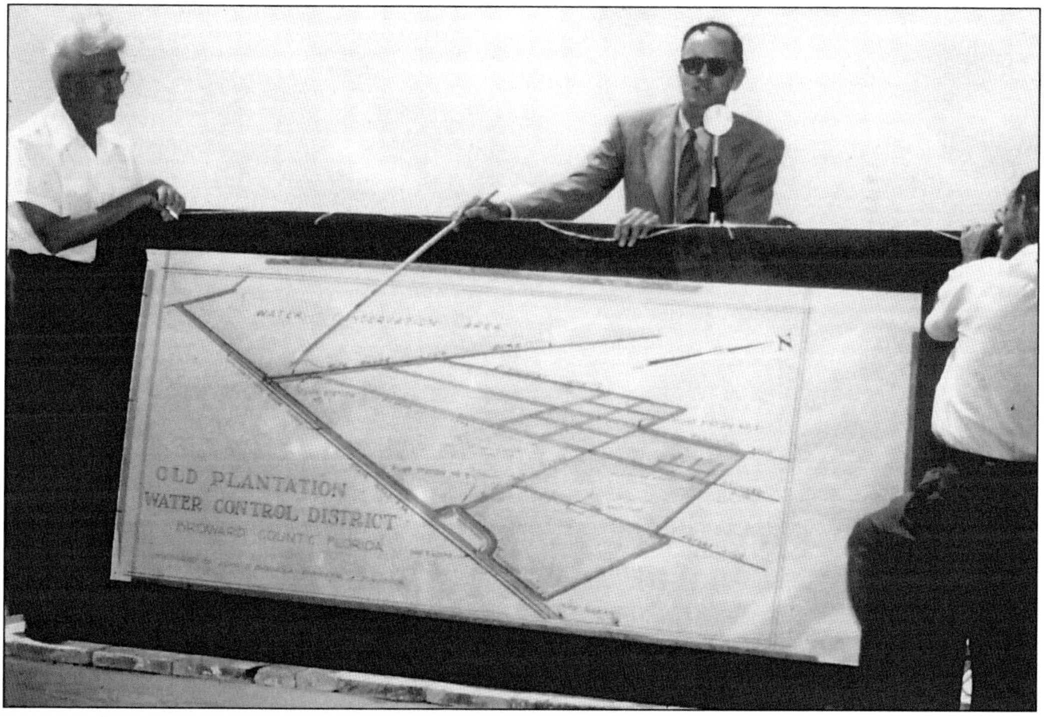

During the 1949 dedication of the newly completed water control system, Plantation engineer John O. Brendla points to a map of the Old Plantation Water Control District. The number-one priority in the comprehensive plan was to construct a large levee along the line dike recently completed by the Broward Drainage District, which bordered the 10,000-acre Plantation tract.

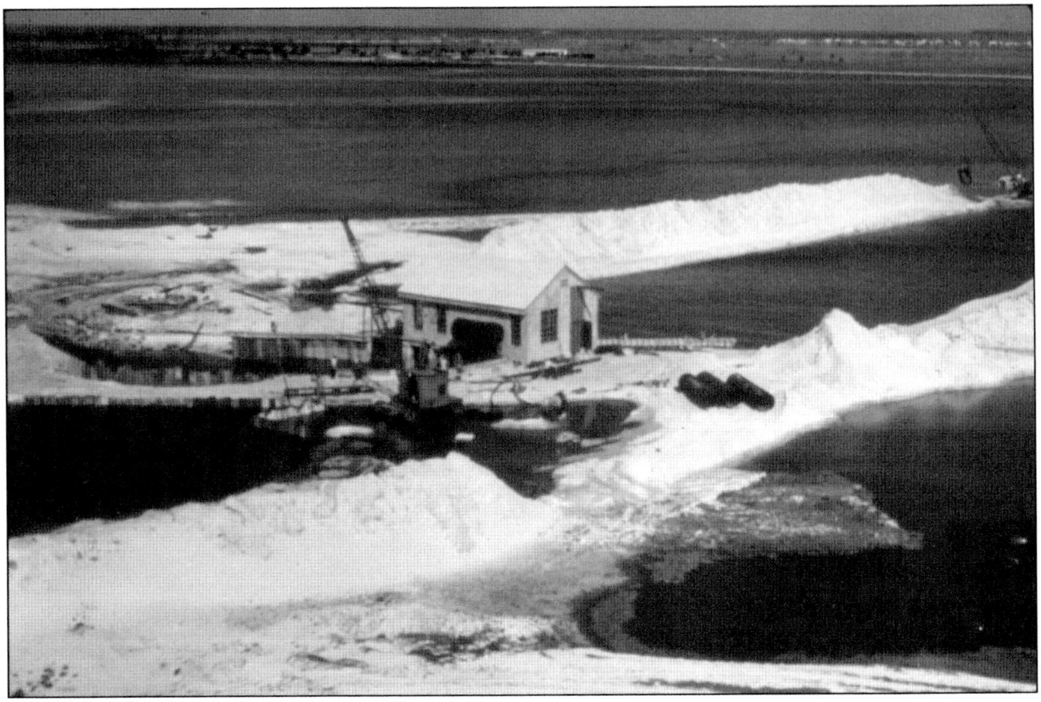

In 1944, Frederick C. Peters hired C. Kay Davis to design a water control system for his west Broward land. The pumping station and plant were positioned so that water would flow by gravity into the canals from the North New River and discharge into the North New River Canal. The station was dedicated on July 4, 1949, and could pump 126 million gallons of water per day. The photograph above shows the pump station under construction. Part of Peters's farm can be seen to the right of the station. The photograph below shows locals gathered at the pump house for the 1949 dedication.

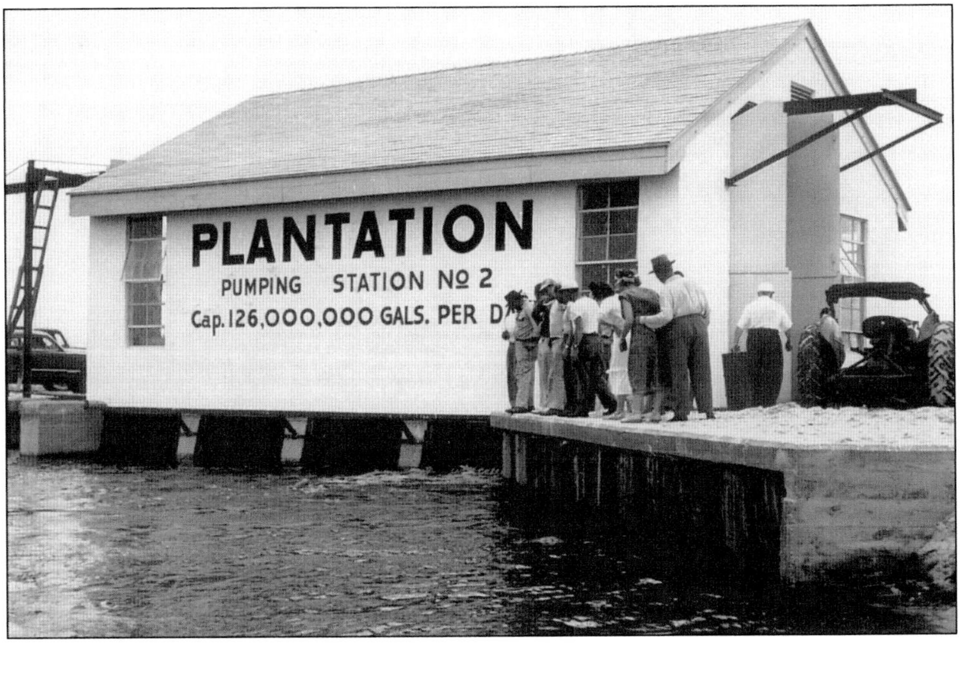

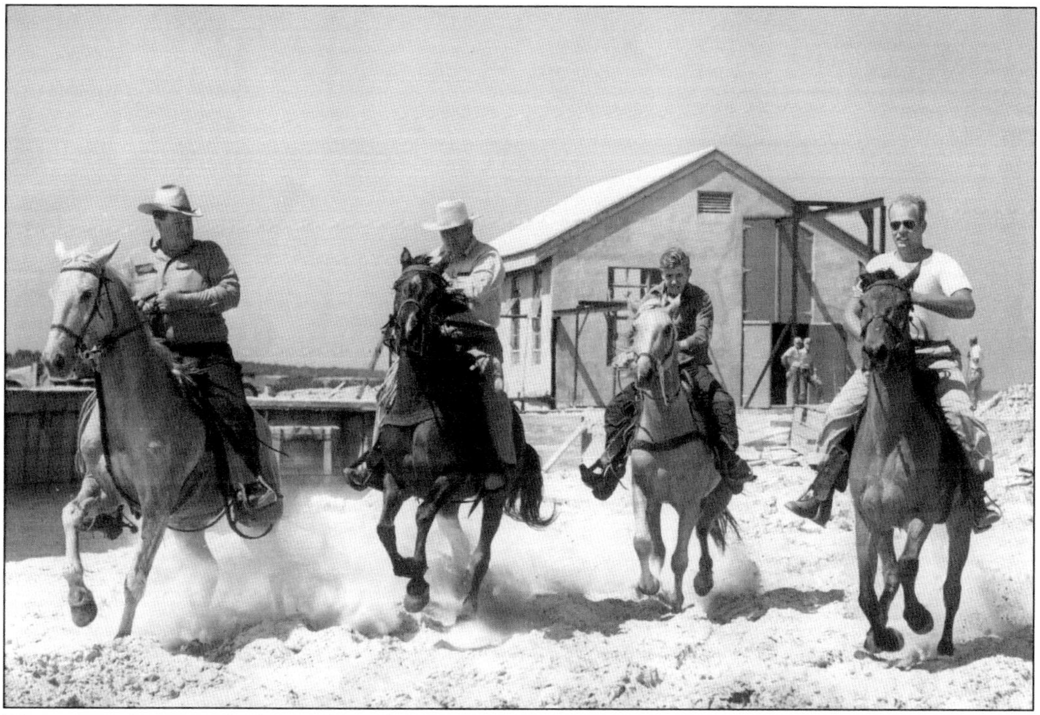

This 1949 photograph shows, from left to right, D.R. Daniels, Dewey Hawkins, Dewey's nephew Bernard, and Frederick C. Peters's son Fred T. Peters on horseback at the Peters ranch. The pump house pictured in the background is still used today and can be seen at Pop Travers Field at Seminole Park.

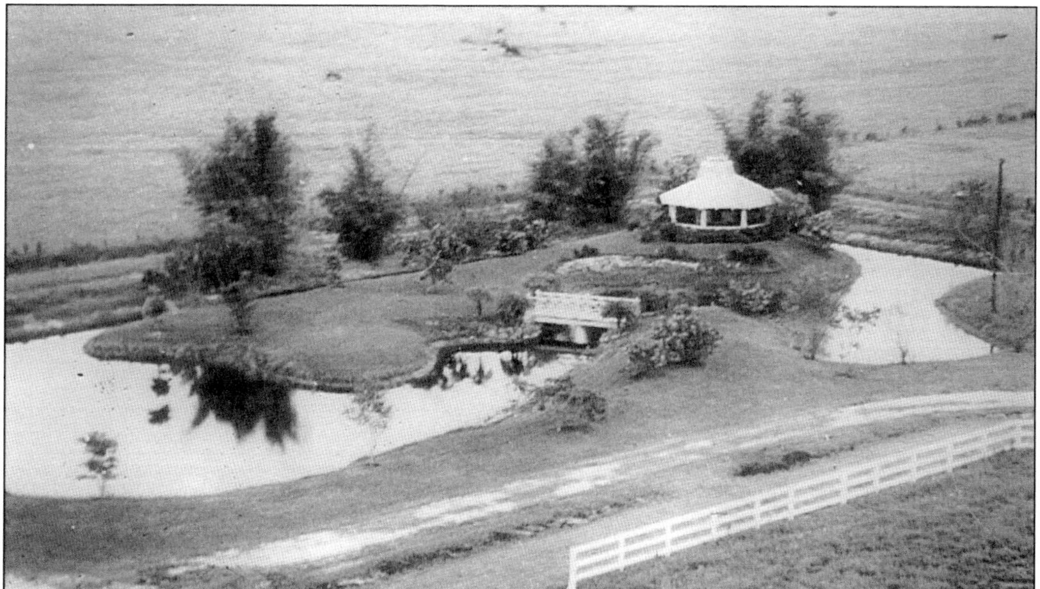

Frederick C. Peters constructed a summer home on the north side of what is now Peters Road. The "Duck Pond," shown above, on the south side of what is now Heritage Park, was part of the farm's original irrigation system. The gazebo was the site of the family's outdoor summer kitchen.

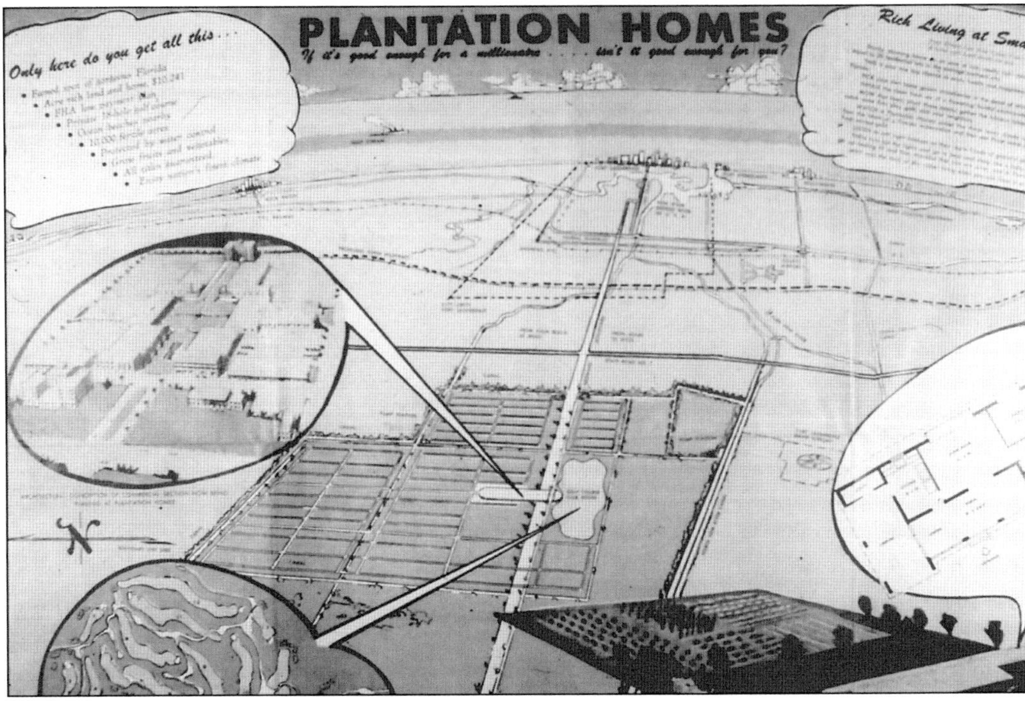

Pictured above is a late 1940s Plantation Homes Inc. brochure, advertising "Rich Living at Small Cost." Prospective buyers were offered two-bedroom homes on full-acre lots for $10,241 at an interest rate of 4.5 percent. A model home with a yard is shown below. Homes were built on one-acre lots and featured a landscaped front lawn with an area behind the house where homeowners could grow their own fruits and vegetables. Many residents joined a cooperative farmers' market.

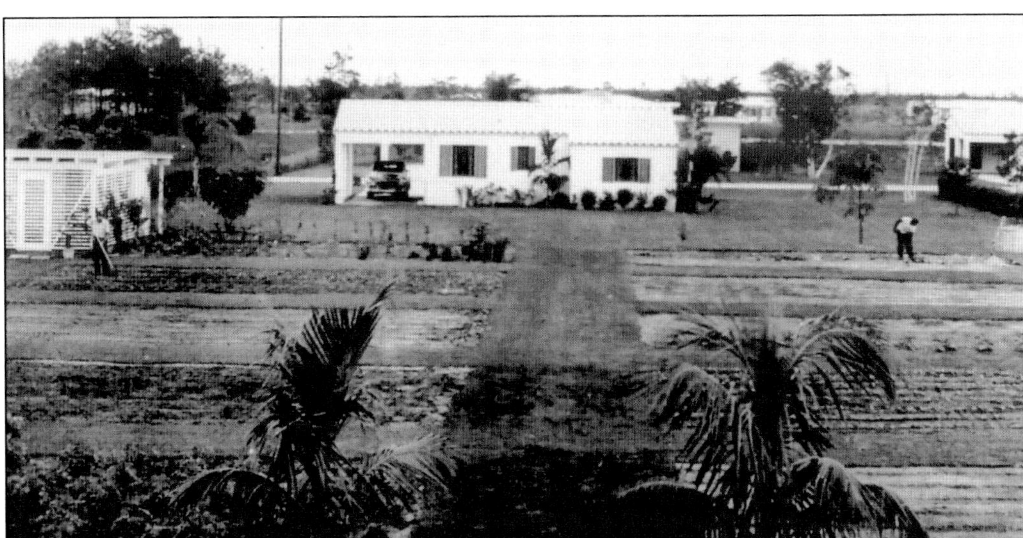

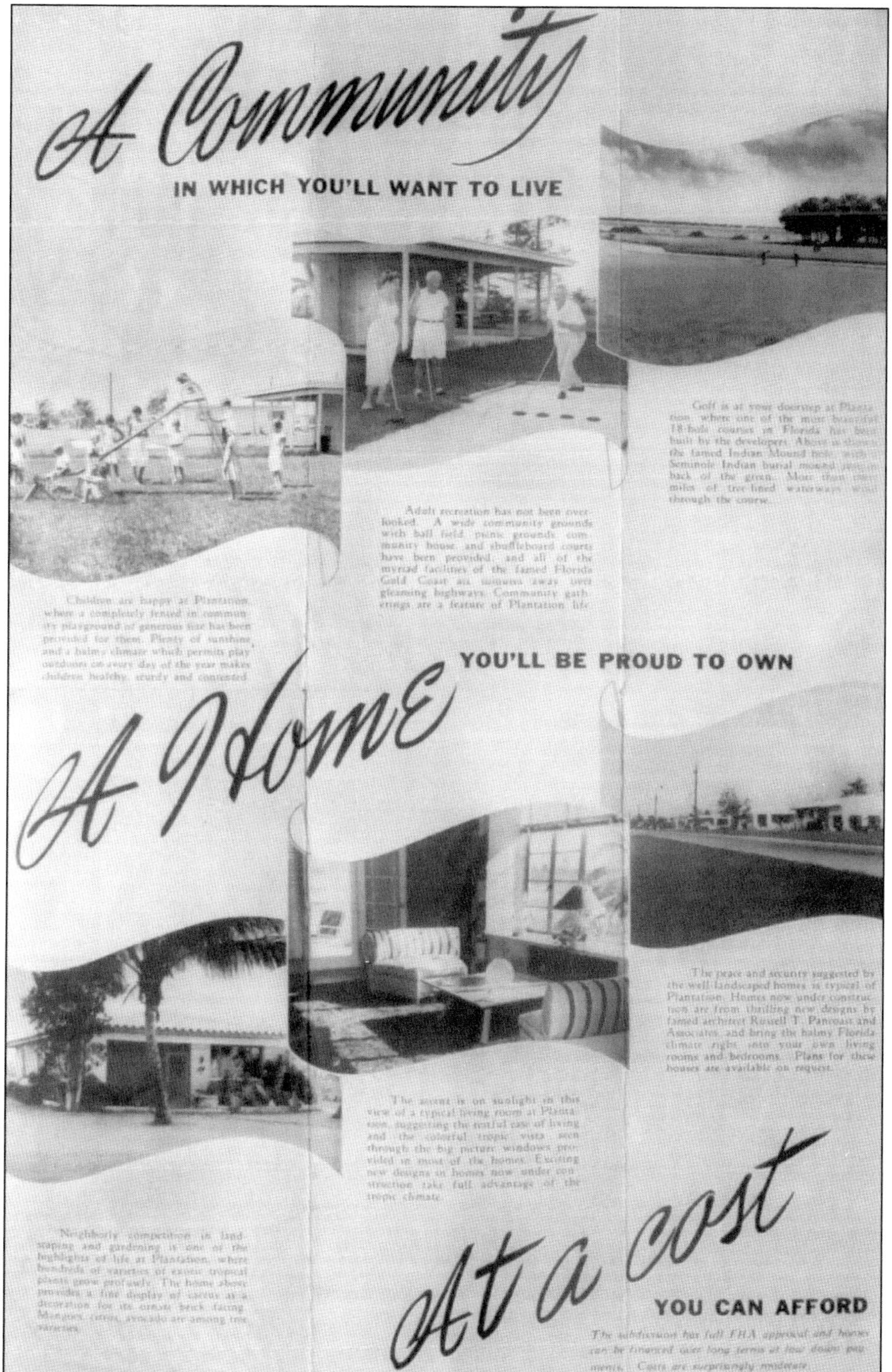

This late 1940s brochure promoted the newly planned development known as Plantation. Advertised as "the Place to Really Live," Plantation was just the spot for those "seeking a restful, spacious way of life under the famed Florida sun" in a "scientifically planned development." At the time, the development consisted of 280 one-acre tracts, 100 of which had occupied homes constructed on them.

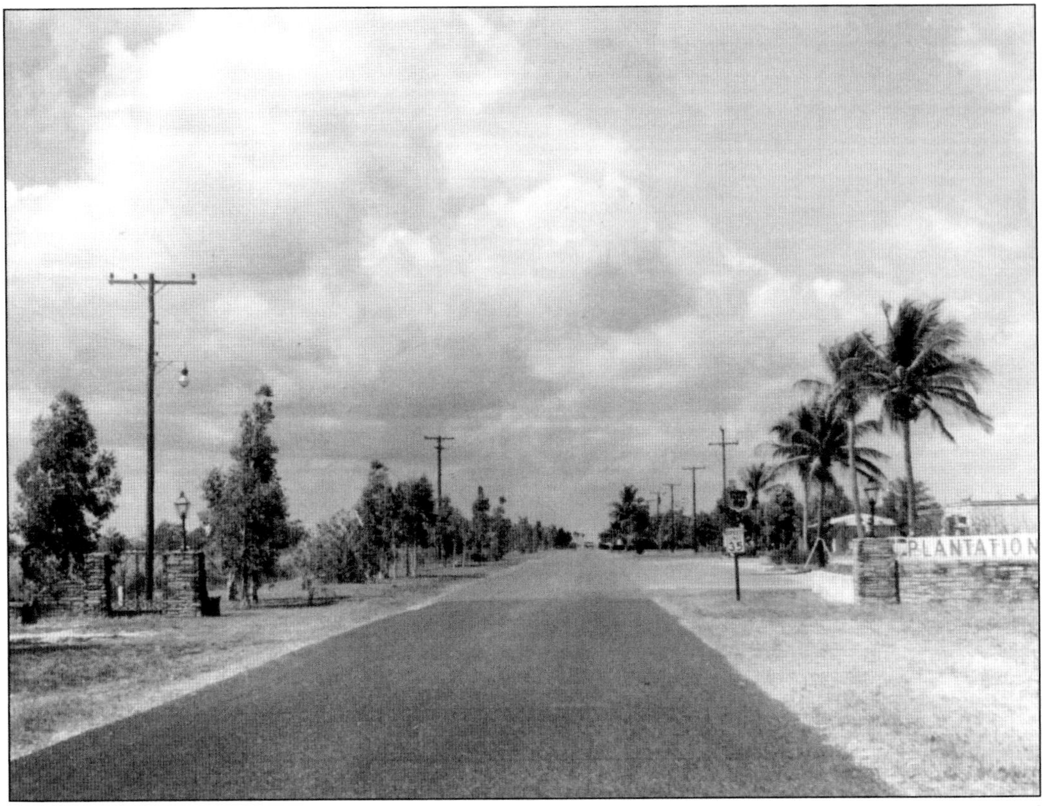

The original Plantation entrance sign, shown here in 1948, was constructed on Broward Boulevard just east of where the Florida Turnpike crosses Broward Boulevard. Today, it marks Plantation's eastern city limit. The young woman posing below on the entrance sign is believed to be Barbara Hoetzel, daughter of one of Plantation's original families. The lamp on the wall can be seen today at the Plantation Historical Museum.

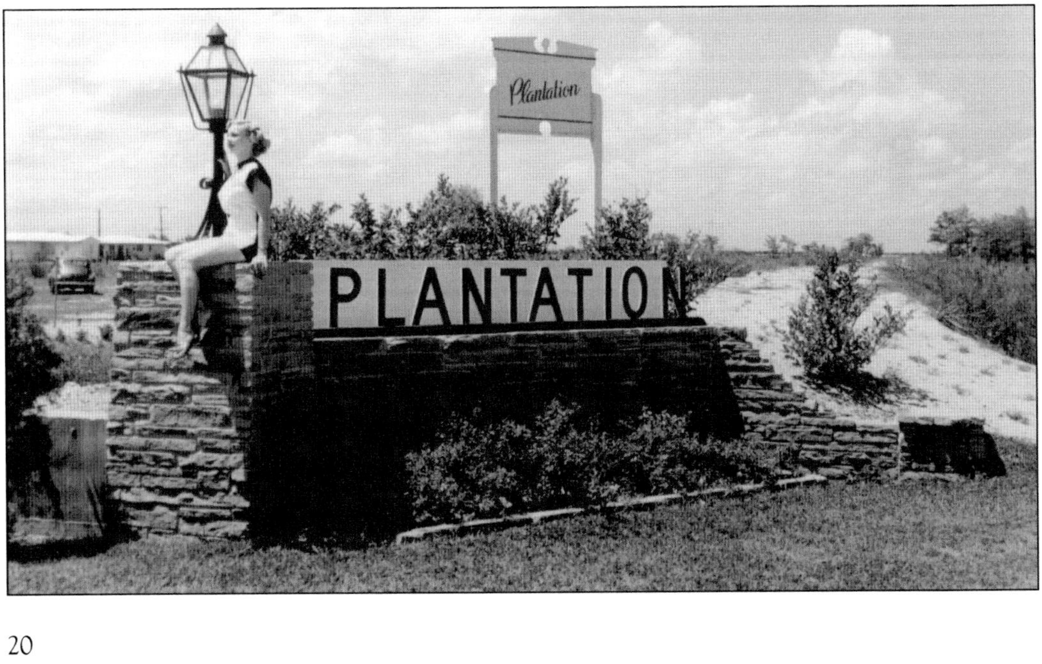

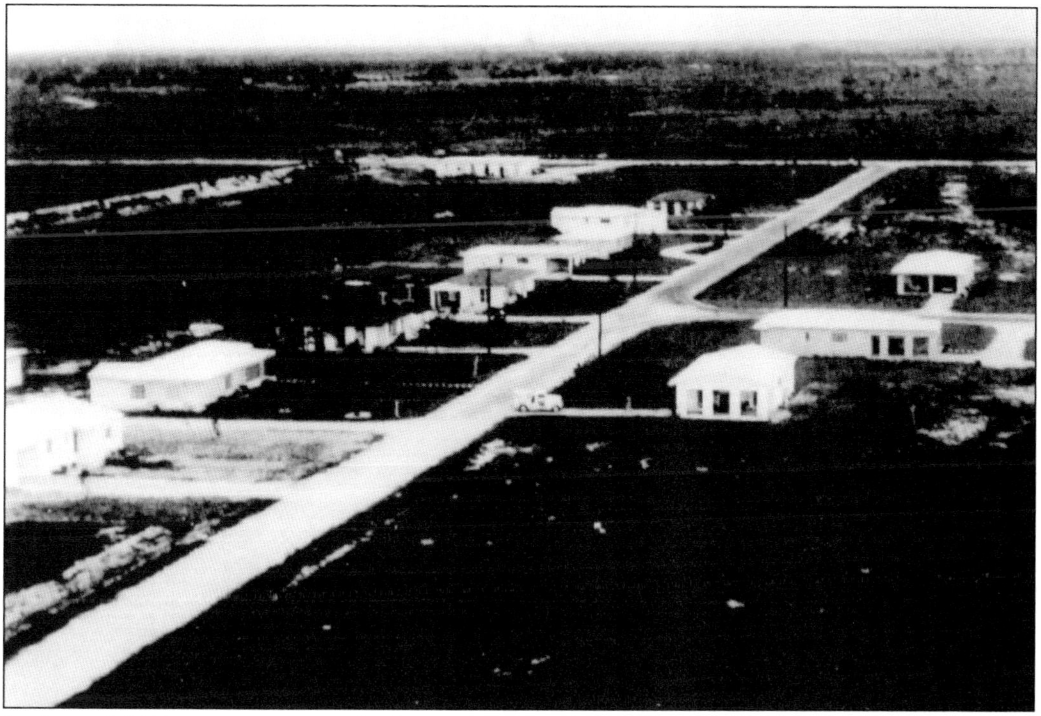

In the mid-1940s, property was valued at approximately $200 per acre. The first Plantation homes, seen in the photograph above, were built on East Acre Drive by Chauncey Clark, his brothers, and his son. Homes were on one-acre lots called "long acres," with the back two-thirds of the property designed for gardens and fruit trees. As Plantation grew, so did the number of families moving into the community. Pictured below is a late-1940s photograph of houses being constructed on the northern side of Broward Boulevard just west of East Acre Drive.

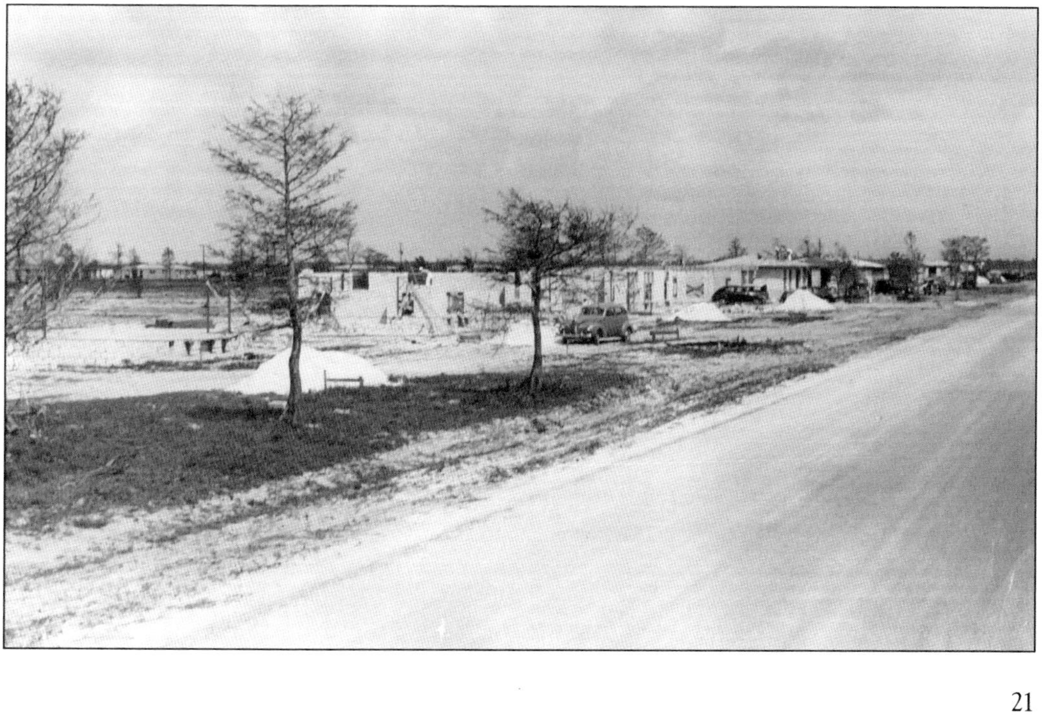

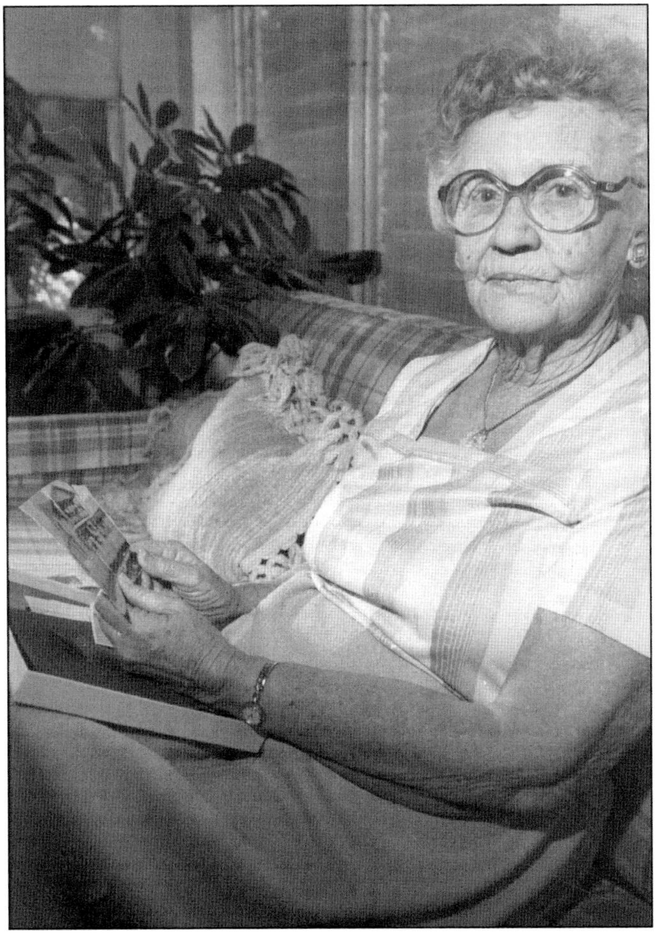

Mrs. Branch, seen in a 1980 photograph, along with her husband Price owned and operated the little country store on Broward Boulevard and East Acre Drive known as Branch's. This was the first store in Plantation where residents could buy basic supplies as well as catch up on the latest news. The photograph below shows Price Branch, left, with resident Claude Carter inspecting watermelons at Branch's that Claude had grown in his backyard to sell at the store. Claude is the father of the first child to be born in Plantation.

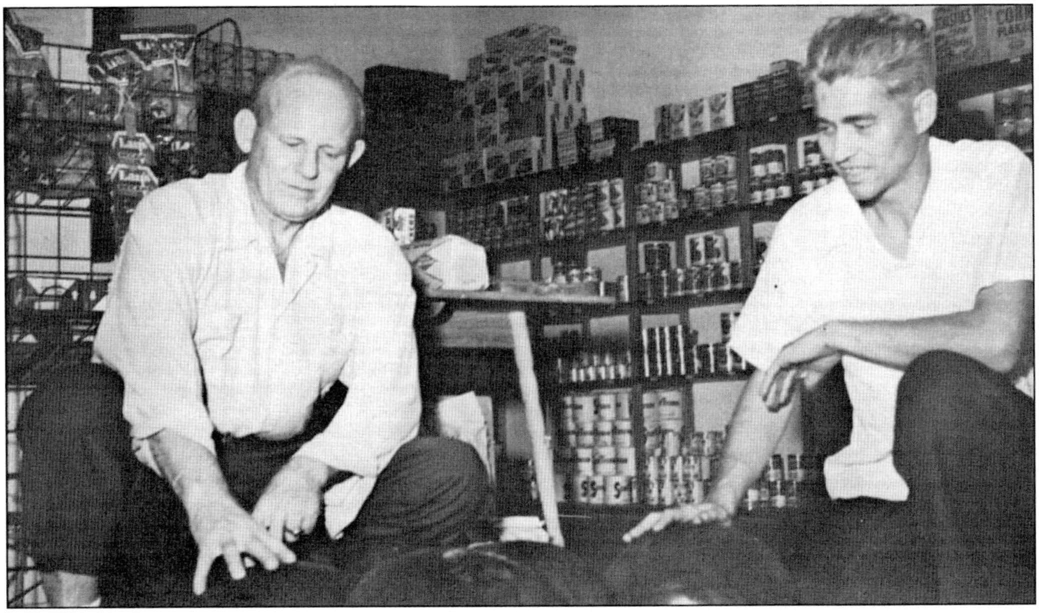

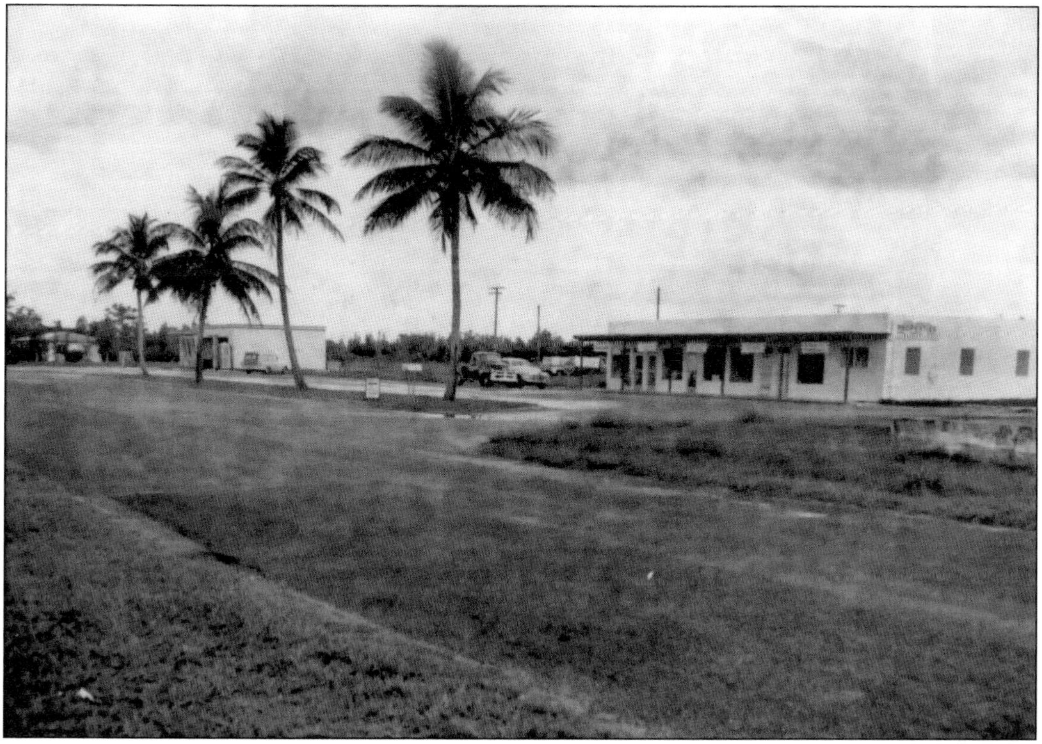

The late 1940s photograph above was taken looking northwest on Broward Boulevard from where the Florida Turnpike crosses today. The building to the far left is Branch's store, and a building containing Fred C. Peters's business office (second window from the right) is on the right. When space was needed for a city hall and police department, Peters offered his office. Maxine Grantham and her husband shot wild bobcats outside their store (pictured below) located on the southwest corner of US 441/SR 7. One could purchase everything from rolled ribs of beef, 72 kinds of snuff, and Sloan's liniment at Grantham's General Store, which also functioned as a post office.

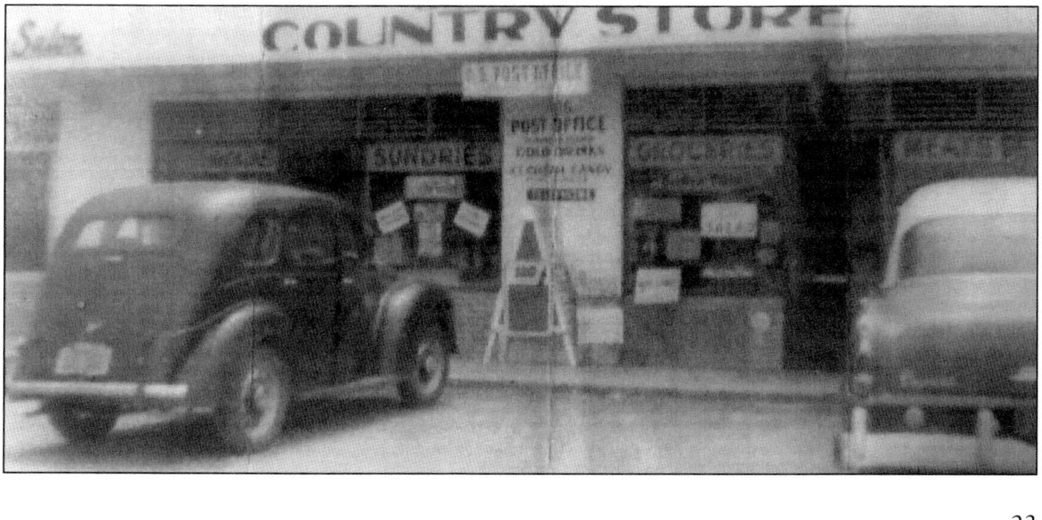

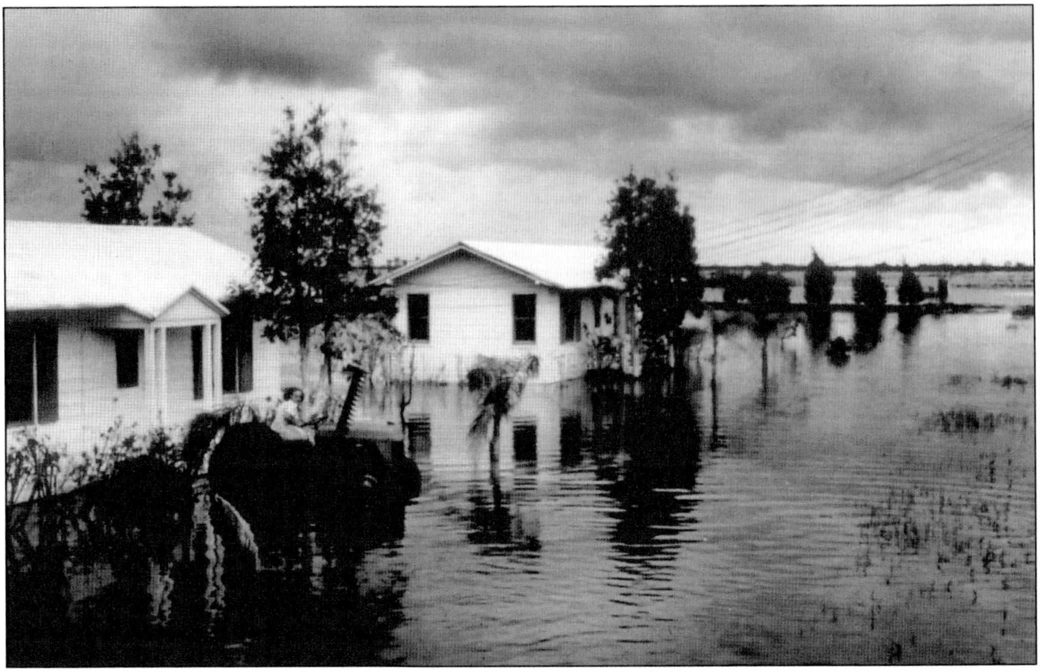

With the canal system incomplete, two hurricanes and flooding nearly ended Peters and Clark's dream. The first storm hit September 17, 1947, and it rained continuously until the second storm on October 12. The entire Plantation community was under two feet of water. Developer Chauncey Clark risked financial ruin but insisted on repairing all the homes he had built. These 1947 photographs record the damage done by the two storms. Pictured above are houses constructed by Chauncey Clark on East Acre Drive, and below, on Broward Boulevard, a car approaches what is left of the Plantation entrance wall and sign.

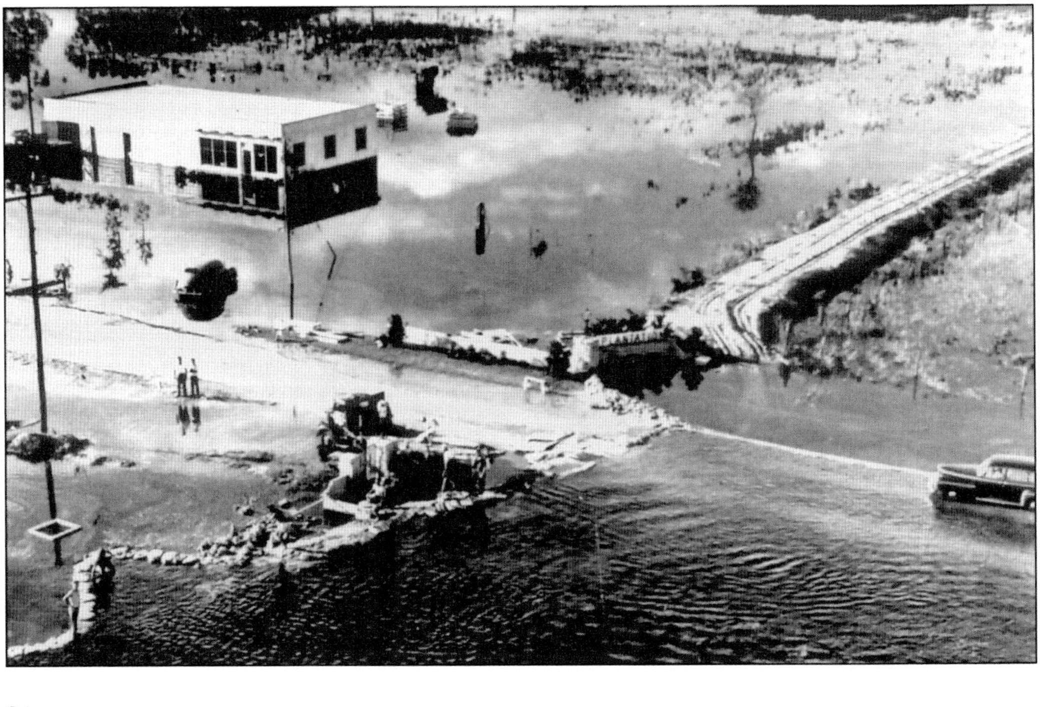

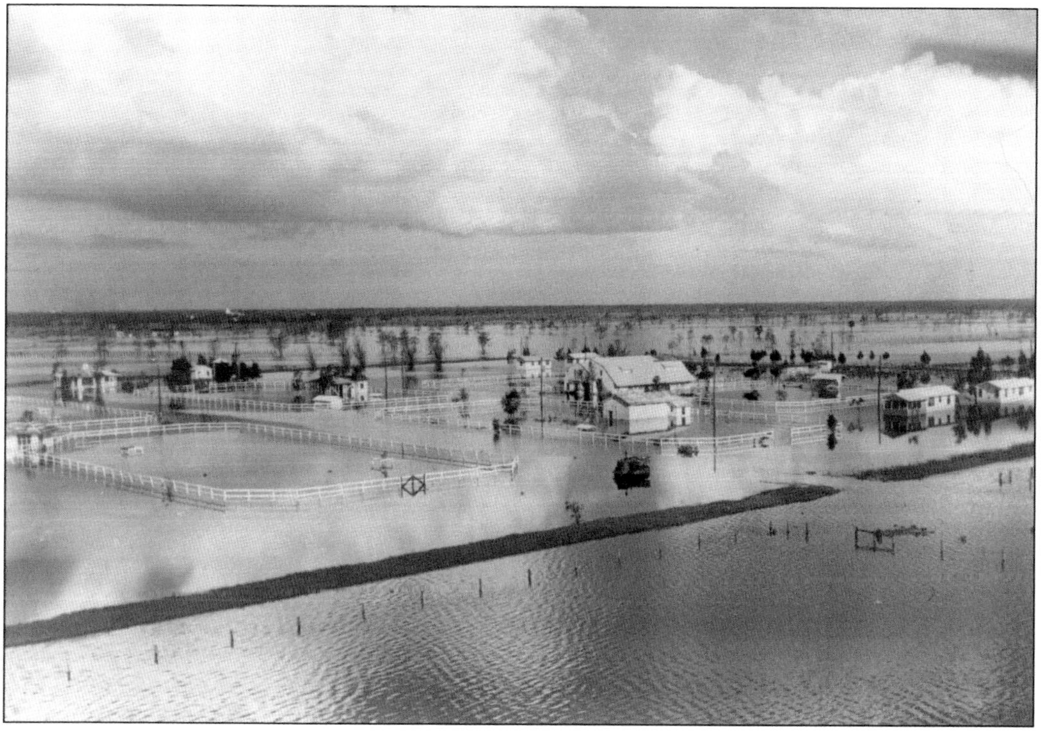

The flooded area south of Lake Okeechobee, including Broward County, was declared part of an 8-million-acre inland sea. The flooding was so extensive that Madge Walter, a resident and Red Cross member, related that she came out to the Plantation area during the Flood Relief Program on an "Army Duck," an amphibious vehicle. These photographs show the effects of the storm on Frederick C. Peters's farm, where Heritage Park is located today, and the original Fort Lauderdale Country Club and Golf Course.

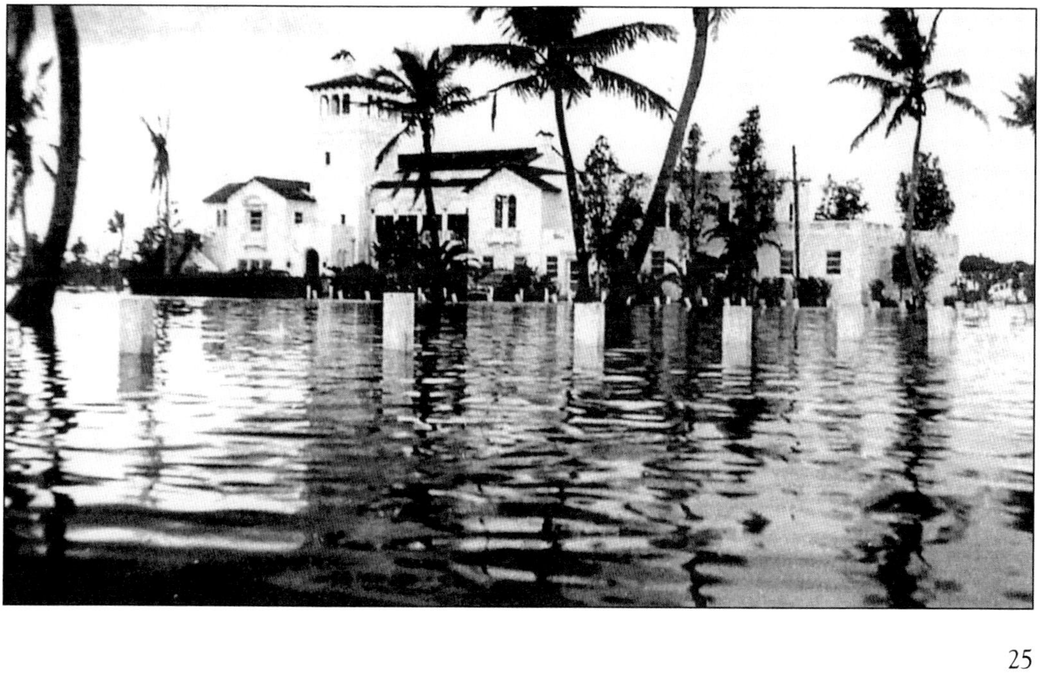

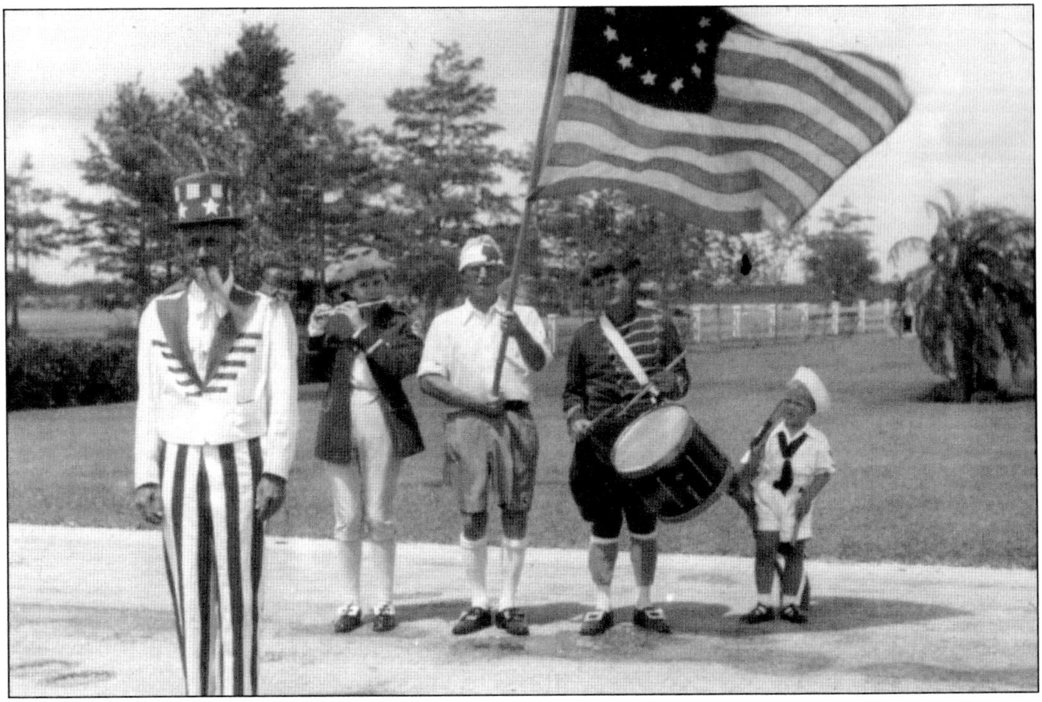

From the start, residents of the new community known as Plantation came together to celebrate Independence Day. The first Fourth of July parade was comprised of residents marching in patriotic attire and riding horses. It started at Branch's and made its way to Hoffman Park, where participants joined together for a picnic.

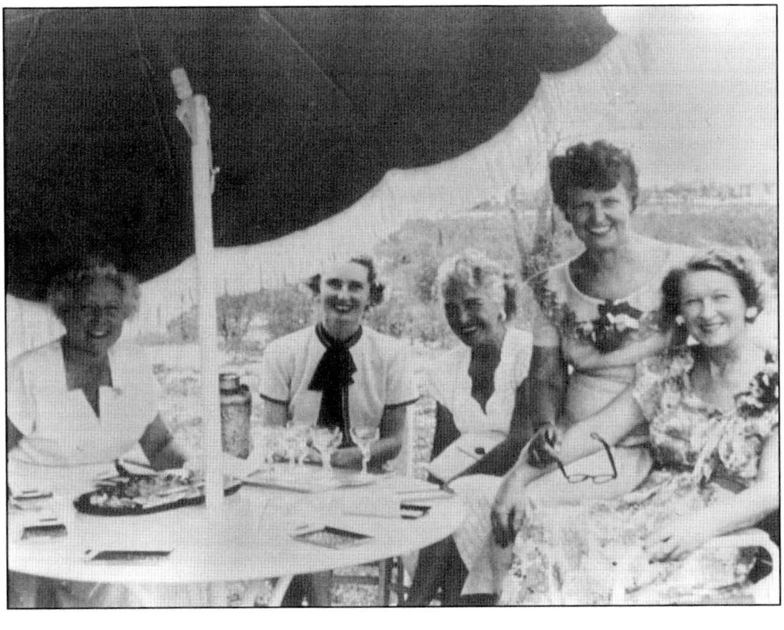

The Plantation Woman's Club was created on February 28, 1949, to share information and to welcome newcomers to the Plantation area. Pictured is a meeting of the first PWC board, taken on June 4, 1949, at the home of Dora Clark. Members are, from left to right, Pres. Dora Clark, Betty Clark, Lorette Seaney, Verna Clark, and Mary Burnham.

Claude Eugene Carter was the first child born at Plantation Homes, Florida. He is pictured with a certificate from friends and neighbors presented to his parents, Ann and Claude, commemorating his birth on June 21, 1948.

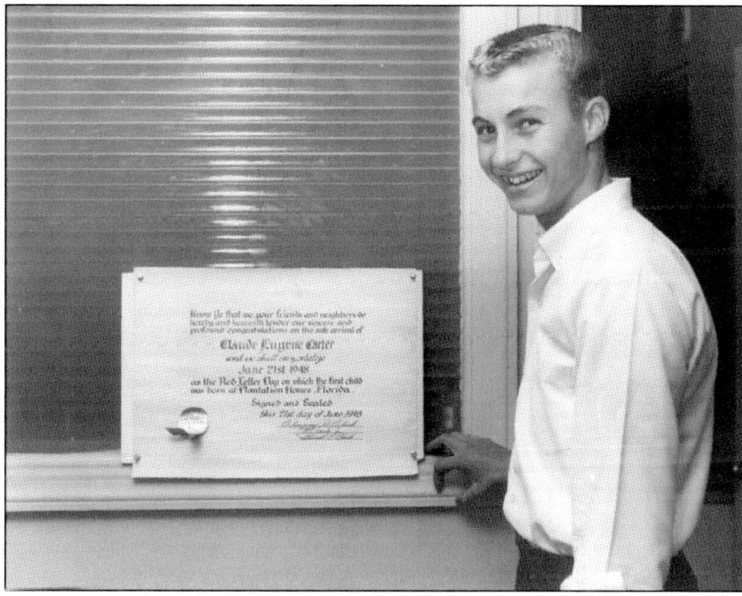

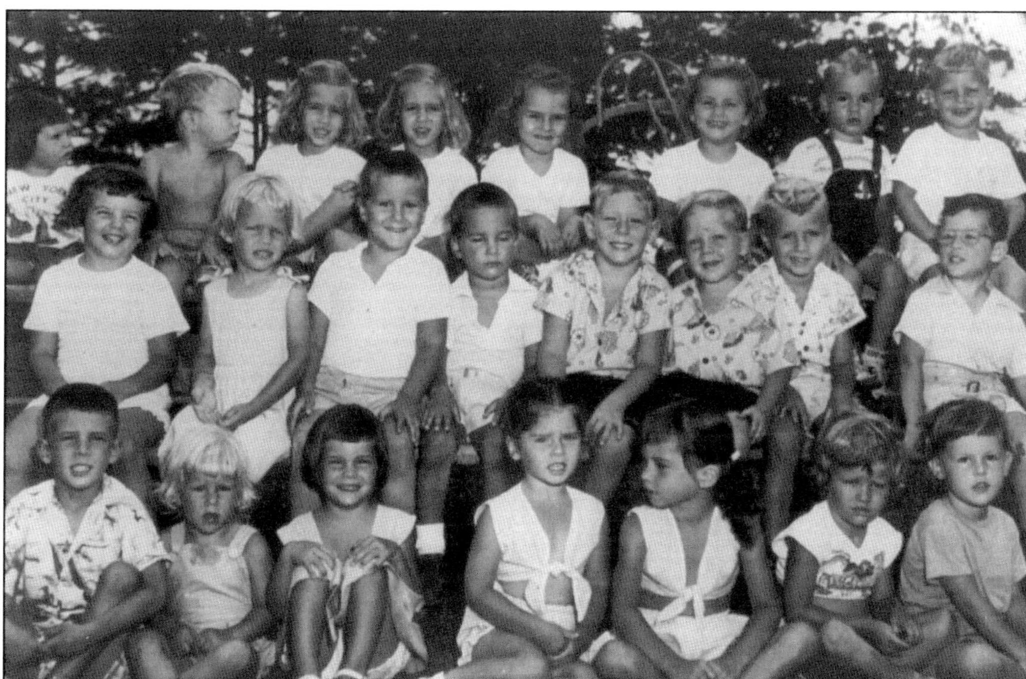

Mothers in the community formed a "play school" for local preschoolers. The activities were held in a building at Hoffman Park, which later became Deicke Auditorium. Known children pictured include, in no specific order, (first row) Candy Clark, Eve Bartlett, and Marilyn Dye; (second row) Pam Peters, the Horan boys, John and Jeff Standart, Gene Carter, and Warren Weber; (third row) James Standart, twins Pam and Barbara Desmond, and Keith Carter.

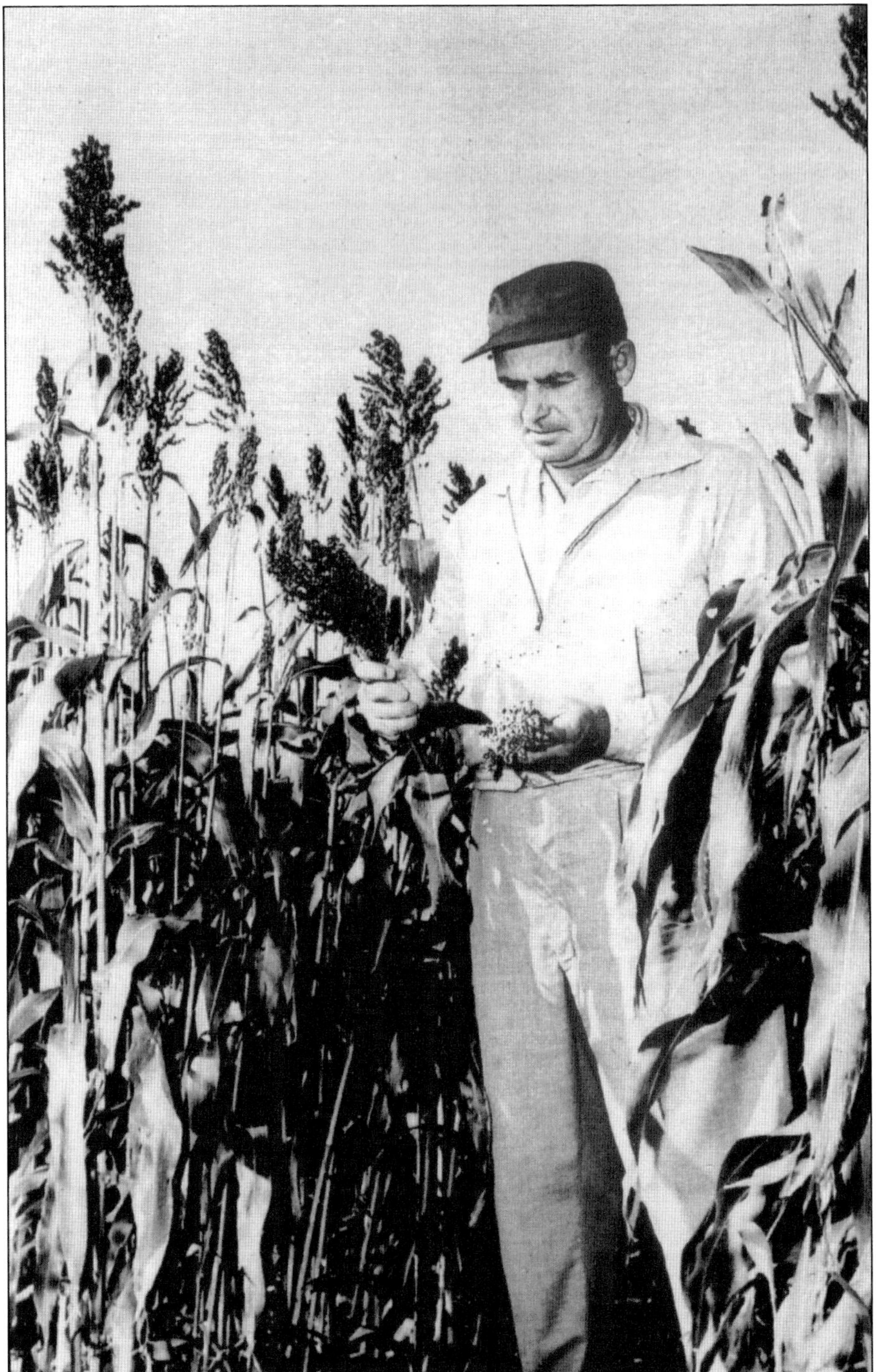

Dr. Frederick T. Boyd was in charge of the University of Florida Plantation Field Lab at the Peters ranch. Dr. Boyd is pictured examining "Plantation Pride," a variety of sorghum that was eventually used to feed livestock worldwide. Research on various fertilizers and agricultural disease control programs were also conducted at the lab.

Three

The 1950s

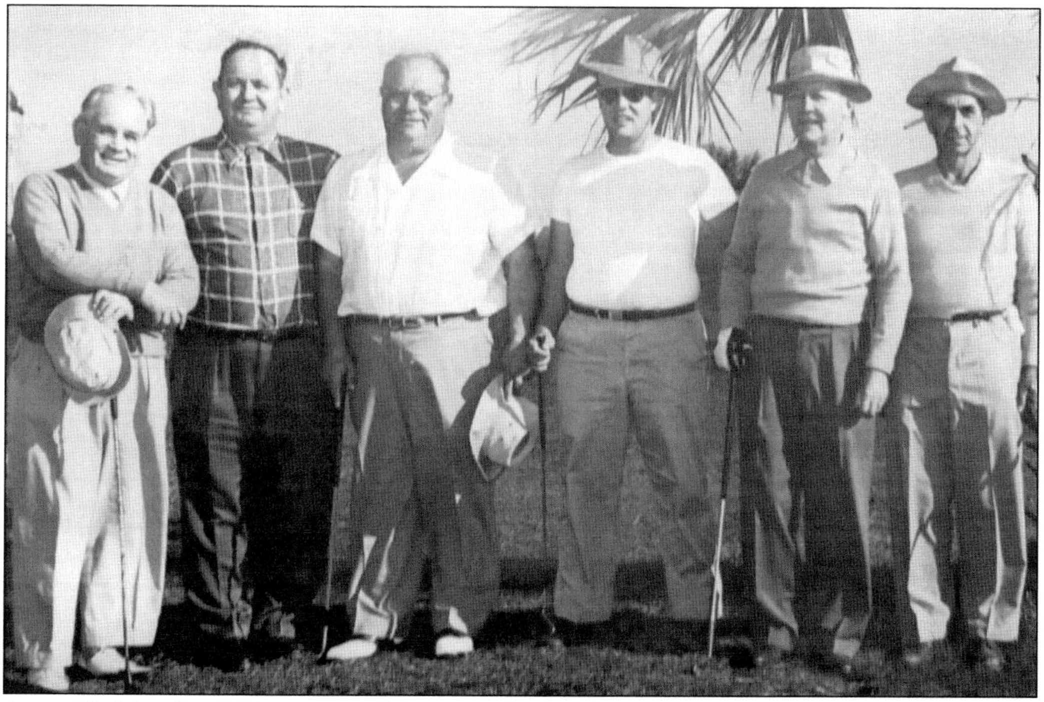

Assembled for the 1950 opening of the Peters-built golf course are, from left to right, Raymond and Edgar Peters (St. Louis brothers of Frederick C. Peters), Frederick C. Peters, F.T. Peters, Dick Waltke, and Col. Albert Allen.

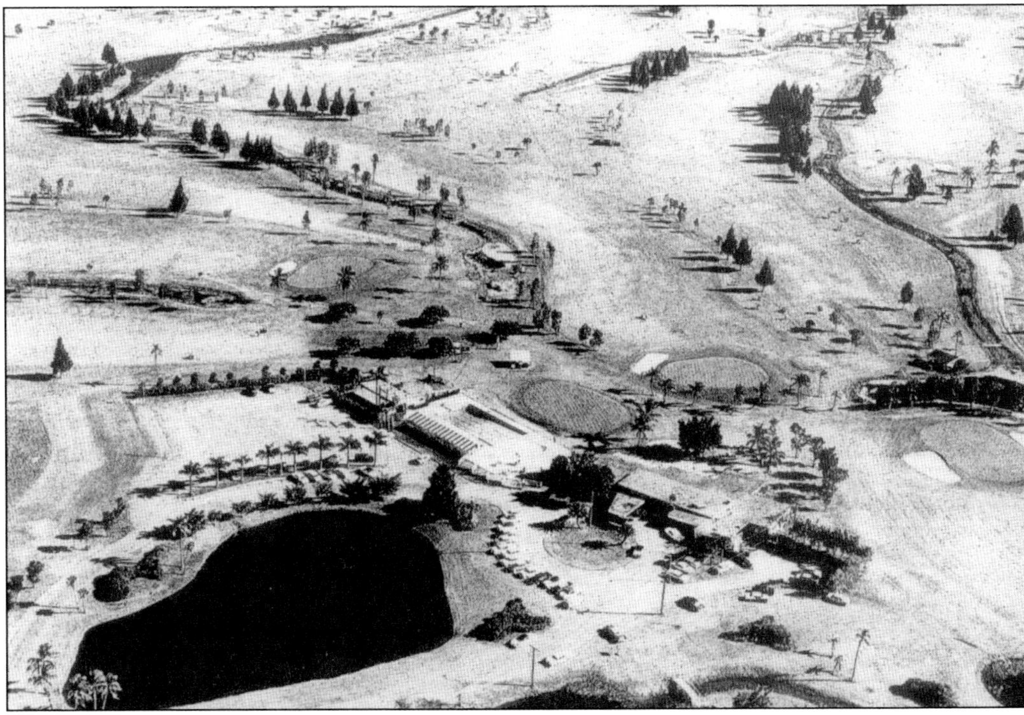

The Plantation Golf Course, designed by Robert F. "Red" Lawrence, opened in December 1950. During construction, a native burial mound was found on the site of the 14th hole. Each hole on the course was given a Native American name to honor early Tequesta and Seminole inhabitants. Designed by Russell T. Pancoast, the golf club, featuring a swimming pool, tennis courts, and clubhouse, became the center of Plantation social activity. Pictured above is an early aerial view of the golf course; below is a 1950s scorecard.

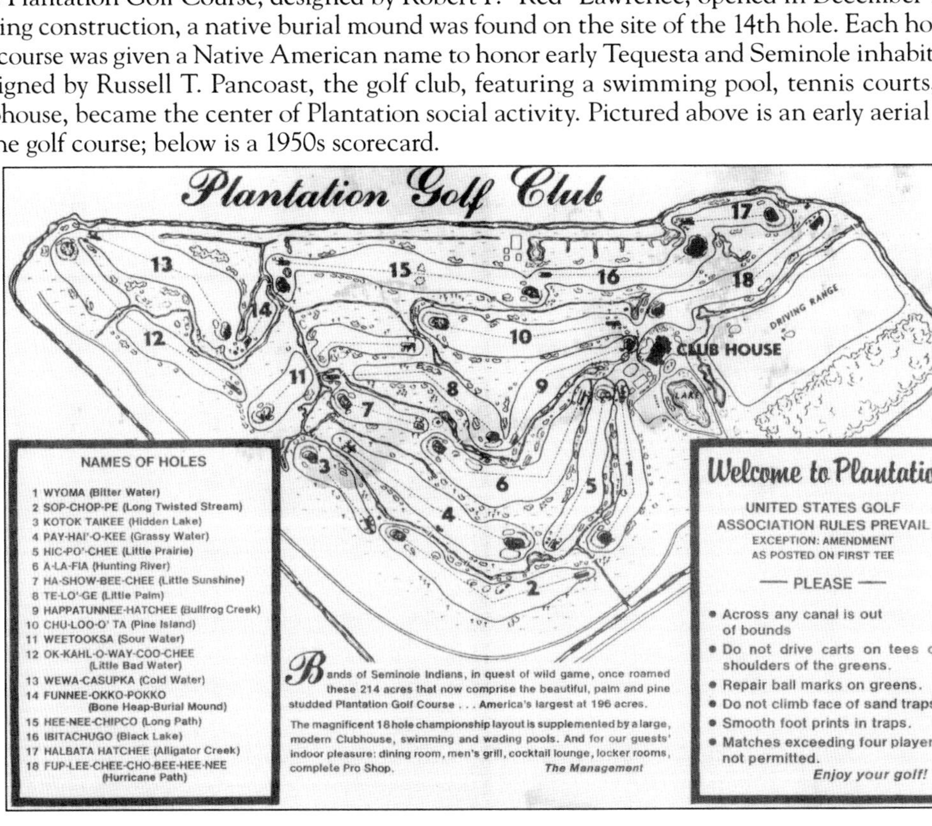

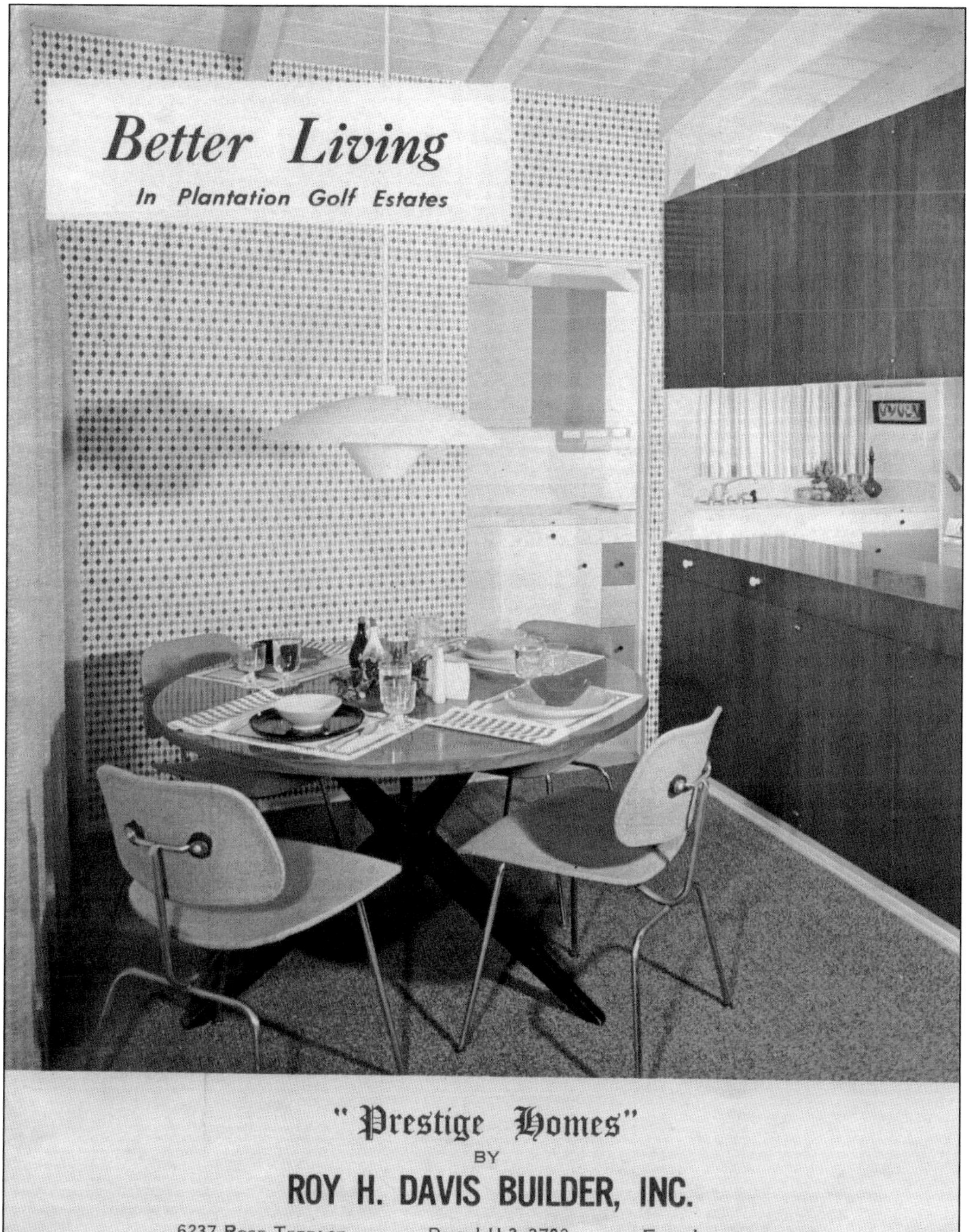

This 1950s brochure designed to promote the sale of homes surrounding the Plantation Golf Course by Roy H. Davis Builder Inc. extols Plantation Golf Estates as the "exclusive address of executives, business and professional men who prefer a finer way of life in an established community of quality homes."

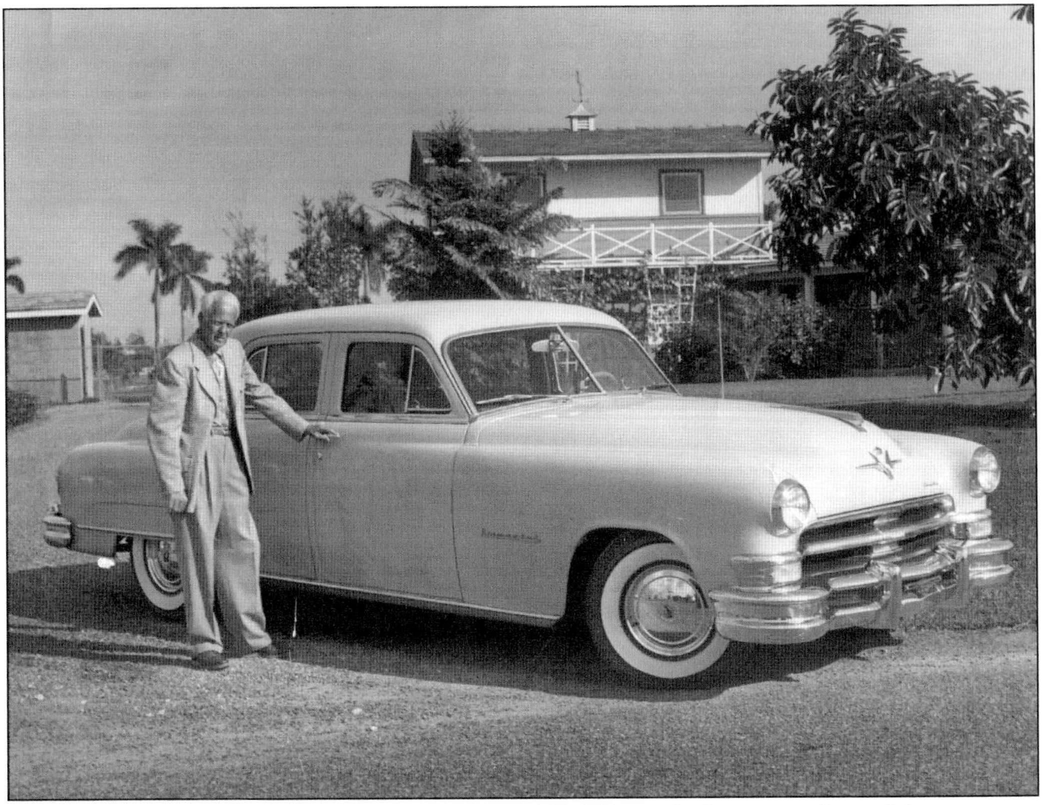

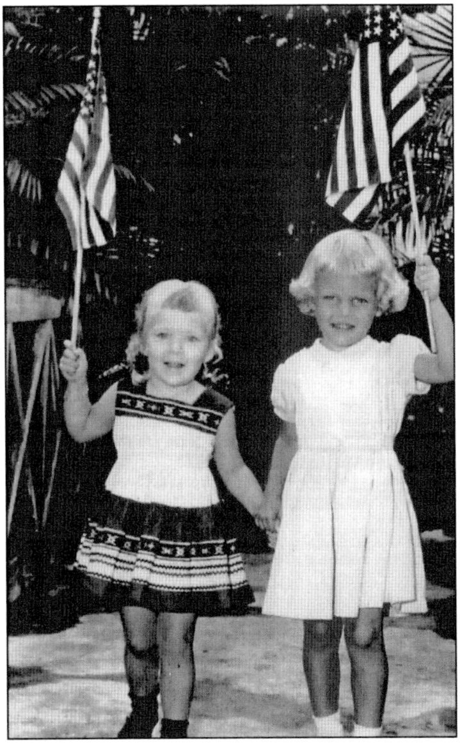

In 1953, Ellsworth Gage, president of the Plantation Homeowners' Association, was appointed mayor of Plantation according to the new city charter. He served until 1955. Mayor Gage is seen standing next to his Chrysler Imperial in front of his Plantation home.

Pictured are Frederick C. Peters's granddaughter Pam Peters (right) and friend on the bridge over Duck Pond to the summer kitchen on Peters Road.

In 1955, Plantation residents welcomed S. Robinson Estey as their first elected mayor. Prior to serving a four-year term as mayor, he had been the city's deputy sheriff.

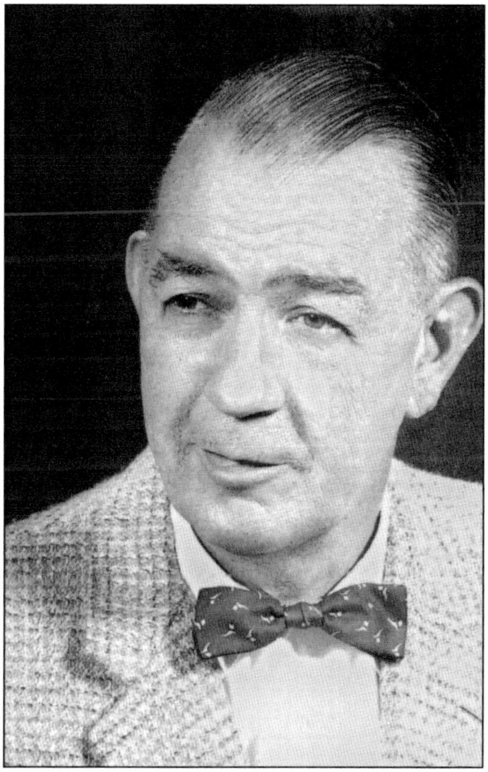

Chauncey Clark, developer of Plantation's first single-family homes, is pictured with his family in 1955. From left to right are Chauncey Robert Clark Jr., Chauncey Robert Clark III, Pamela Ann (Penny) Clark, Elizabeth Beene (Candy) Clark (back), and Betty Barnhill Clark.

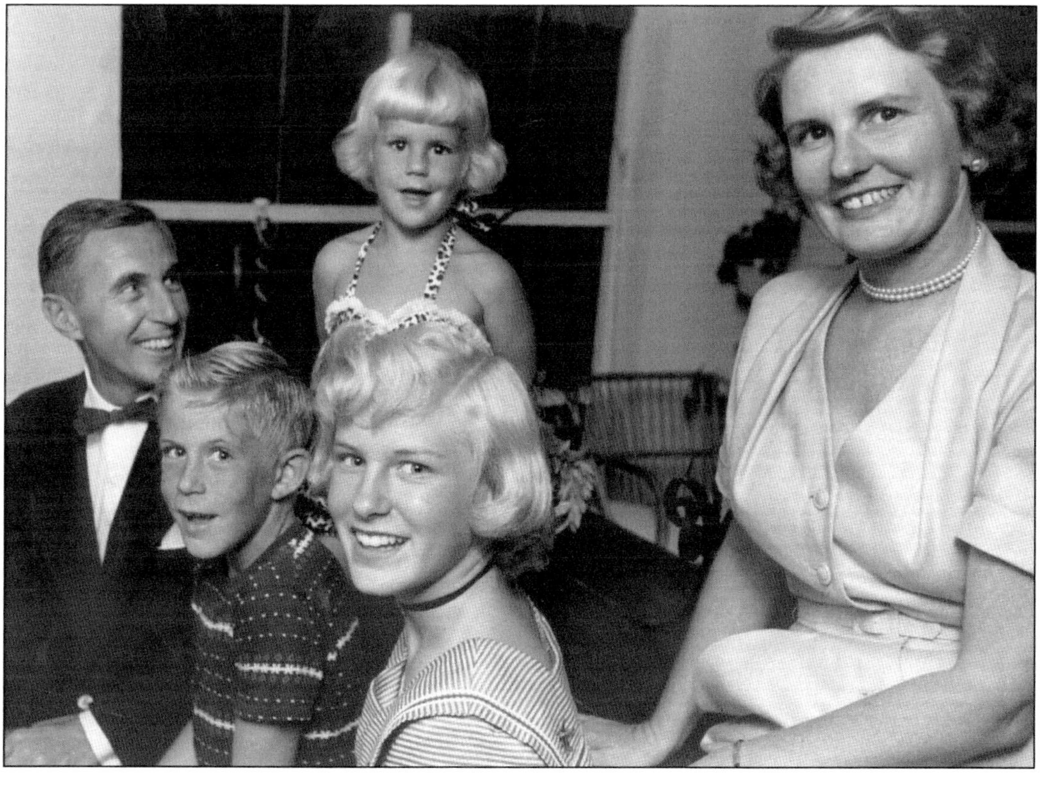

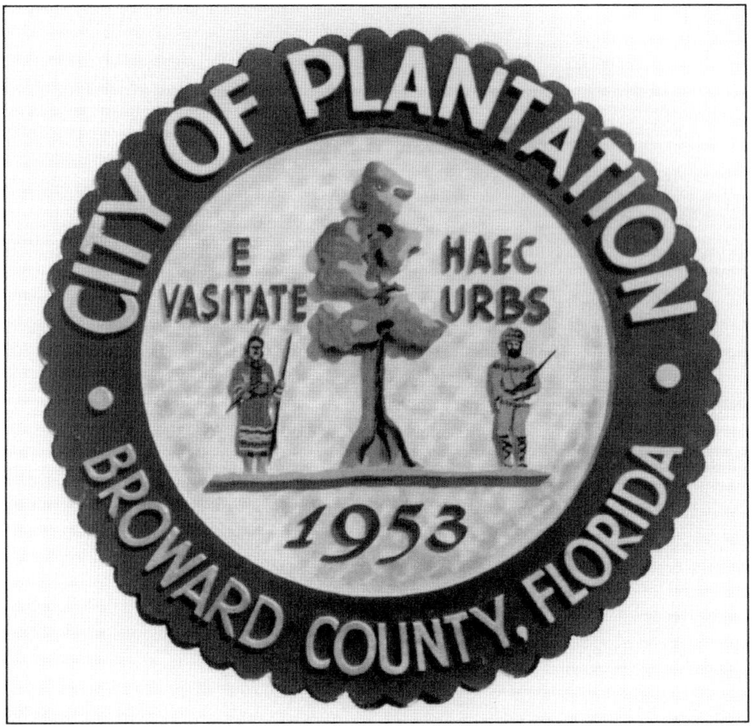

In 1953, the city motto "From the Wilderness, This City" was made official, and a city seal was adopted. This seal was designed by A.T. Hardel, a frequent guest in the home of Mayor Robinson Estey. The seal features a Native American and a pioneer standing on either side of a cypress tree. It is interesting to note the second word in the city's Latin motto is misspelled.

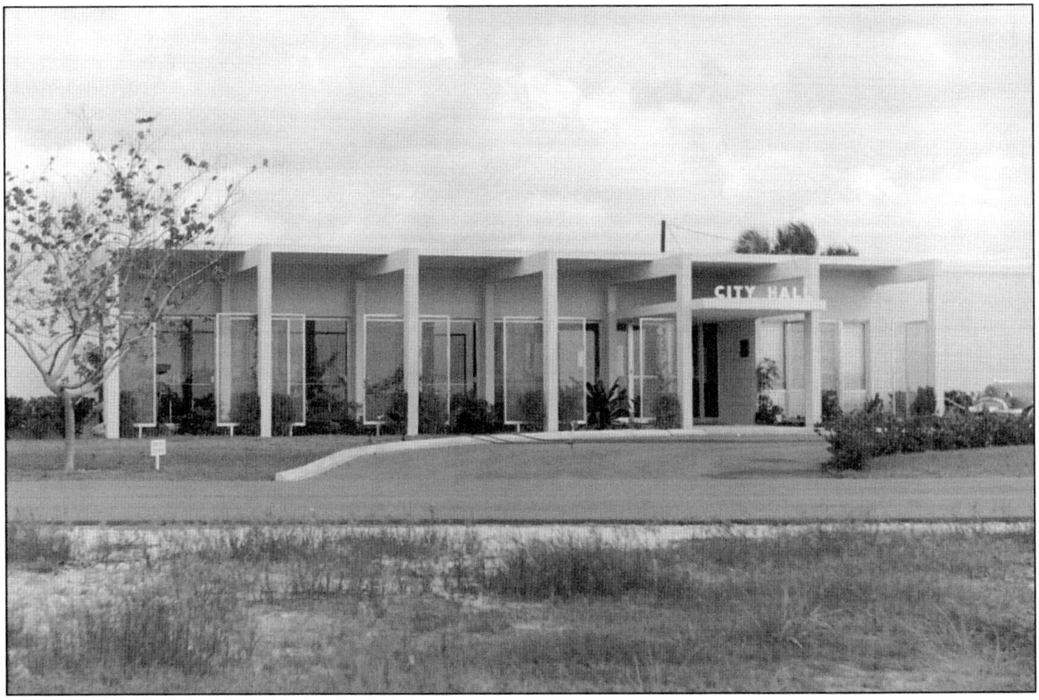

Plantation's very first "city hall" consisted of a desk in the real estate office of City Councilman Wilfred J. Perry. It was staffed by one part-time employee, Agnes Desmond, the first city clerk. In 1958, a new city hall facility (pictured) was built on Fifth Street for city offices and the police department.

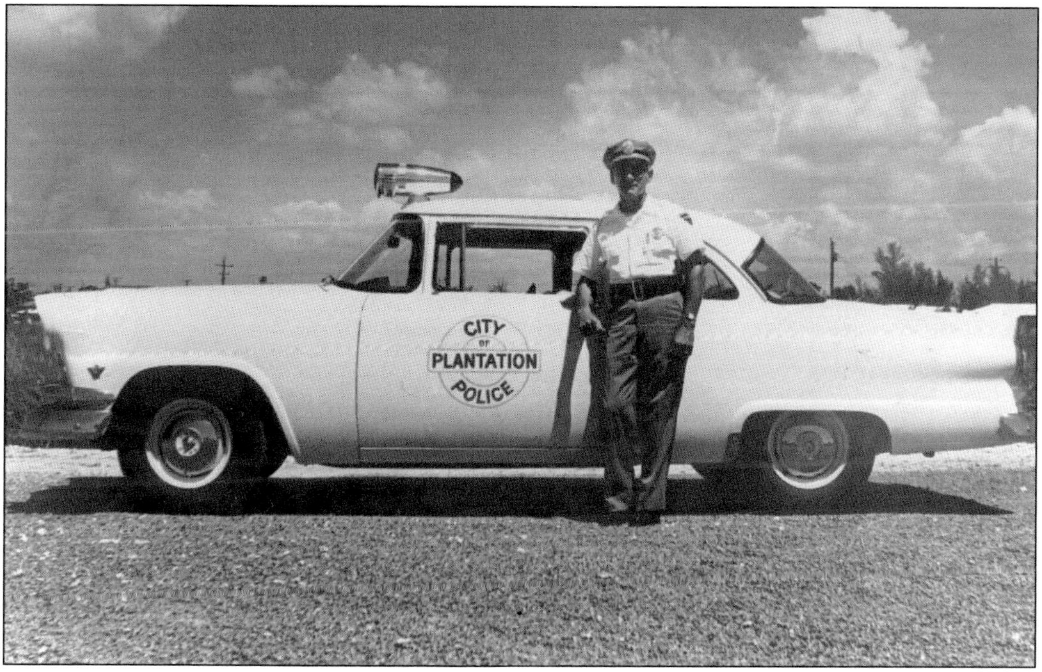

In 1955, city council gave approval to a plan for professional police protection. A police squad car was purchased, and a search was started for an experienced lawman. Henry C. "Hank" Donath was hired to work eight hours a day, but to be on call 24 hours, at a salary of $4,200 per year.

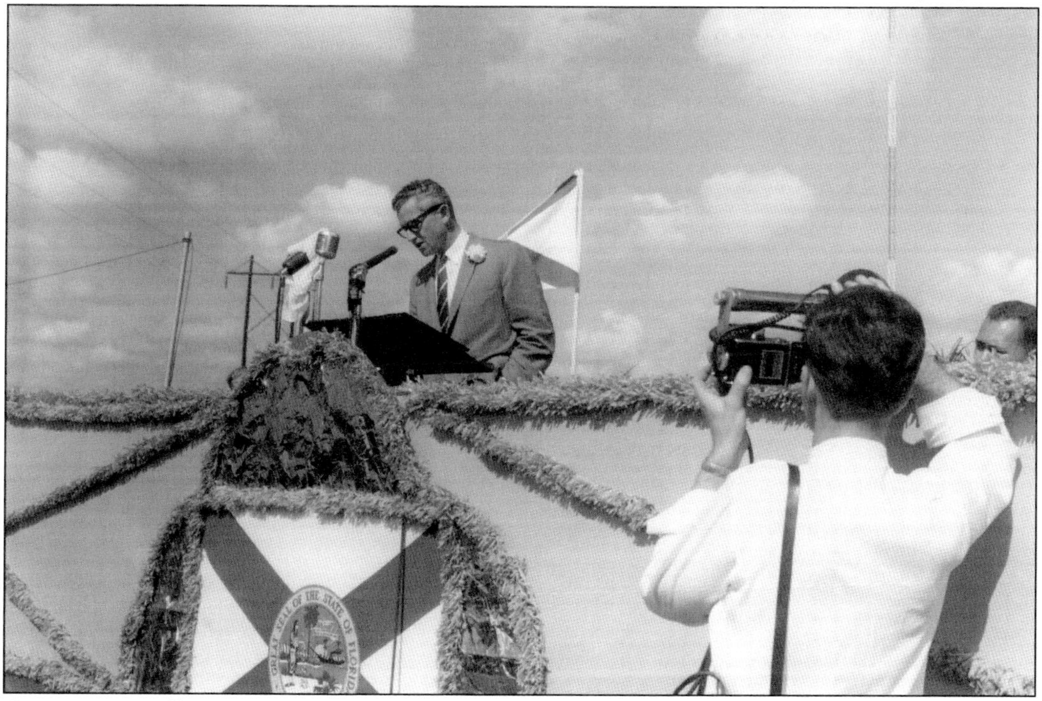

Gov. Leroy Collins speaks at the Sunshine State Parkway (the Florida Turnpike) dedication ceremony at the opening of the original 110-mile segment between Miami and Fort Pierce on January 25, 1957. (Courtesy of Florida Memory Project.)

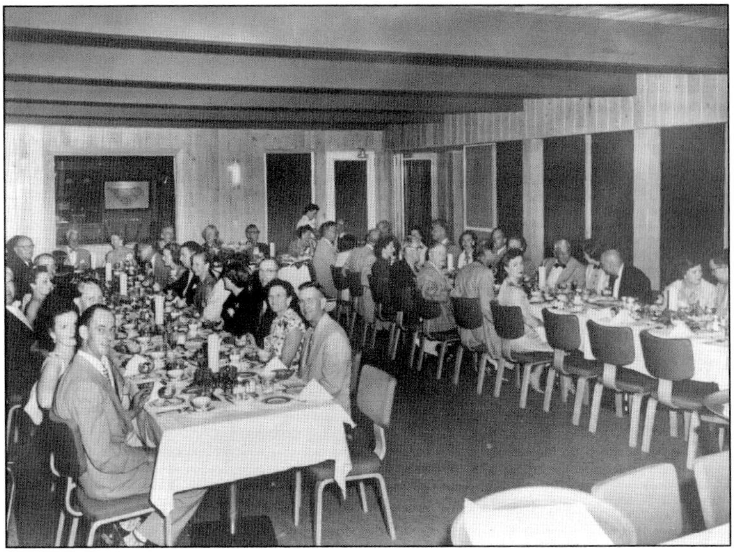

The Plantation Golf and Country Club was opened with great fanfare. The country club was the principal, if not the only, place for important community events throughout the 1950s. At left, Plantation Homeowners' Association members dine at the new country club.

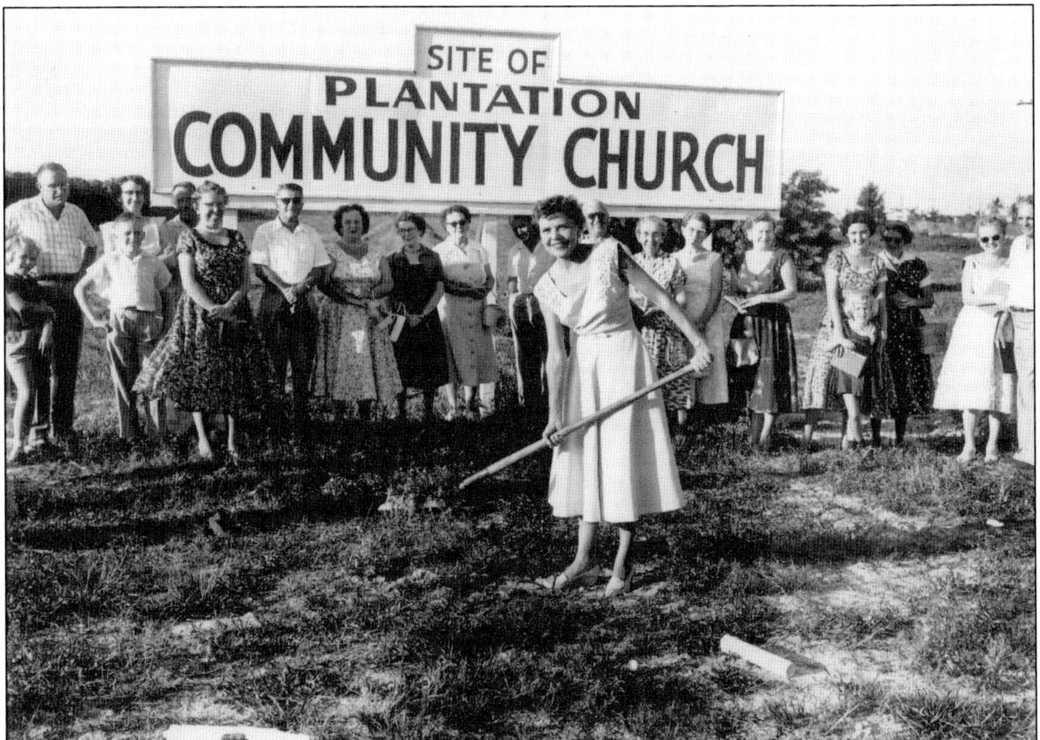

Plantation Community Church's first worship services were held in 1948 in a construction trailer. Two years later, in 1950, the church was incorporated. The Peters and Deicke families were generously instrumental in the early years of the church's growth. In 1957, the church erected its first sanctuary (now the Missions Prayer Chapel and music room). In 2008, the current sanctuary was consecrated. Dorcas Ward wields the shovel as Plantation Community Church members break ground for their own building on October 31, 1955. (Courtesy of Plantation Community Church.)

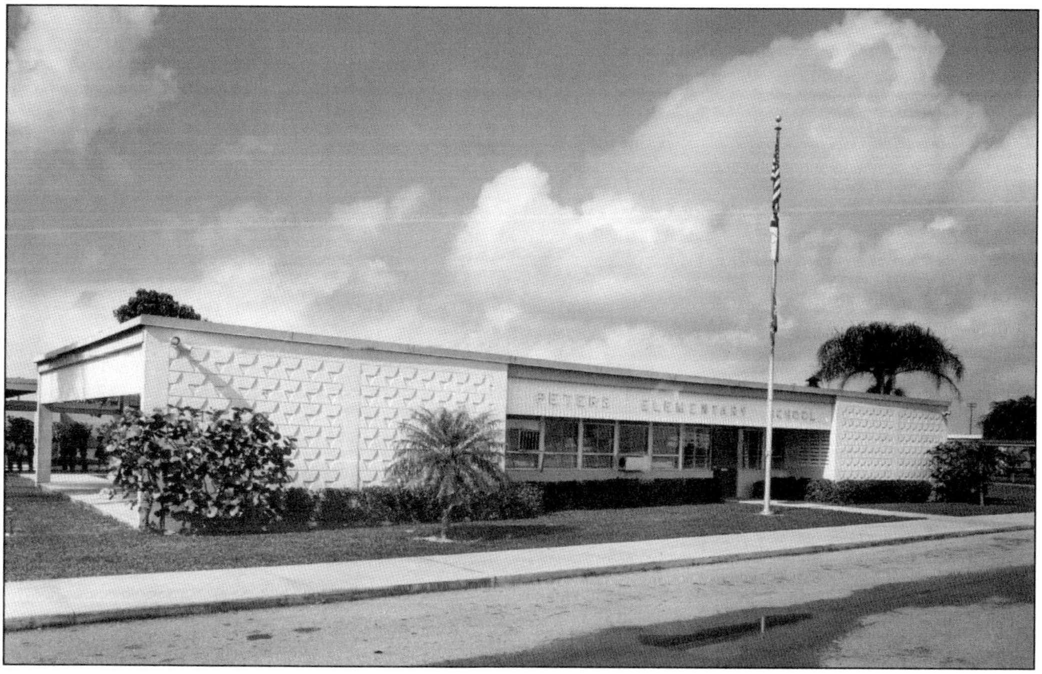

The Berenice T. Peters Elementary School at 851 Northwest 65th Avenue was formally dedicated December 6, 1959. It was Plantation's first public school and contained 24 classrooms, a library, an administration building, and cafetorium, and could accommodate 725 children. Below, Peters Elementary first-grade teacher Geraldine Farley poses in her classroom with students from the 1959–1960 school year.

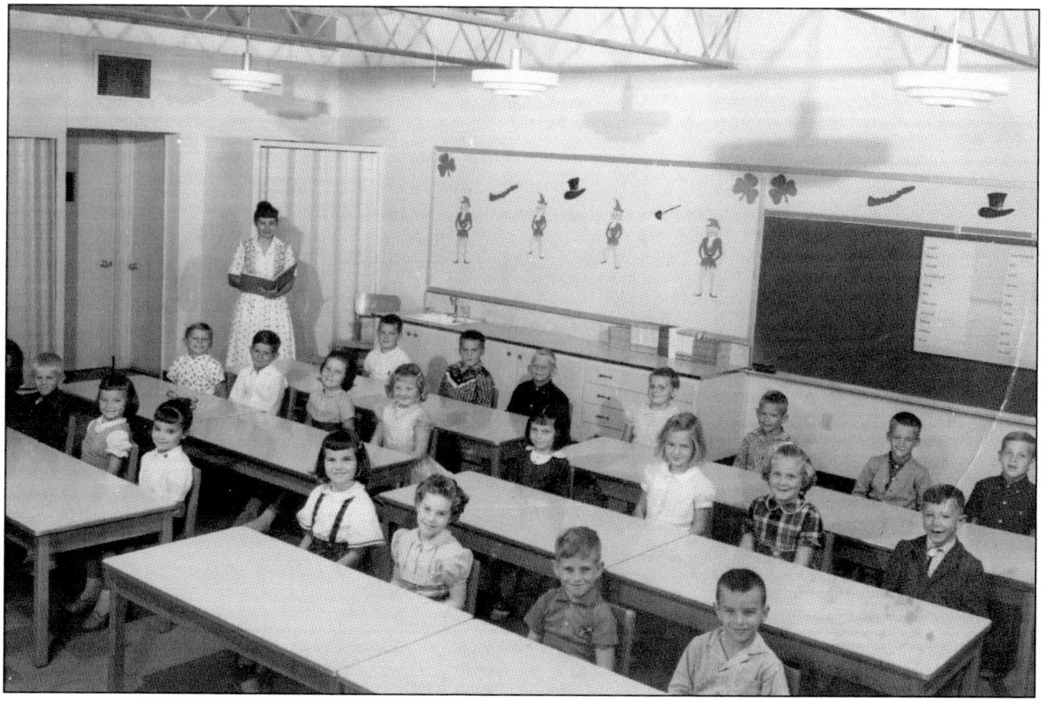

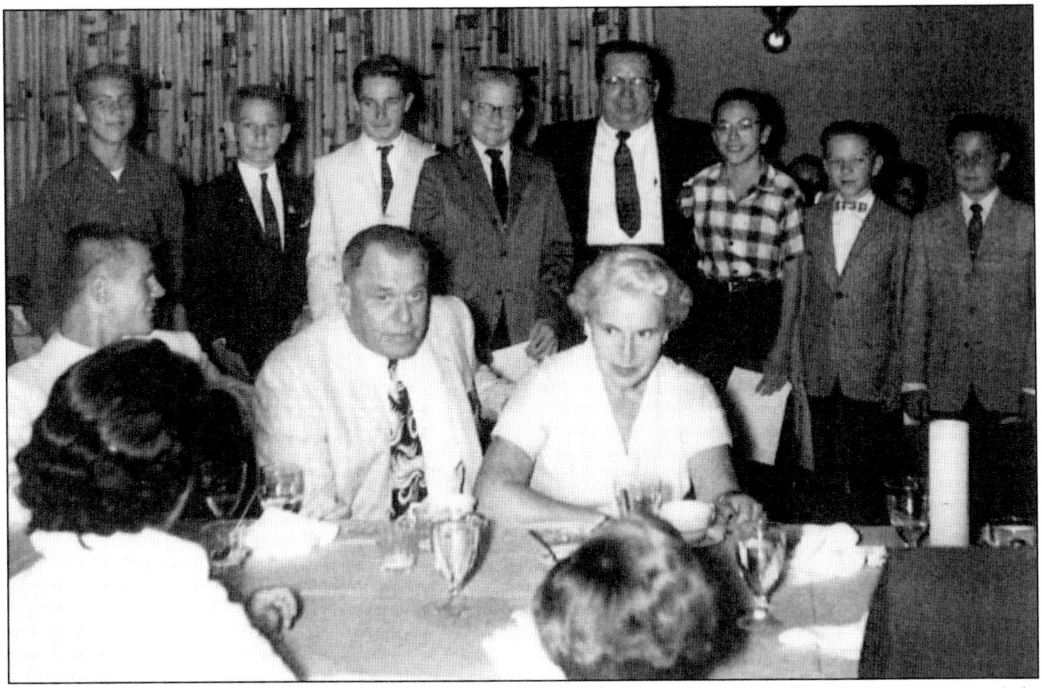

Plantation resident B.J. Carons (standing, third from left) receives an award at the Fort Lauderdale Optimist Club's 1958 Boy of the Year Awards.

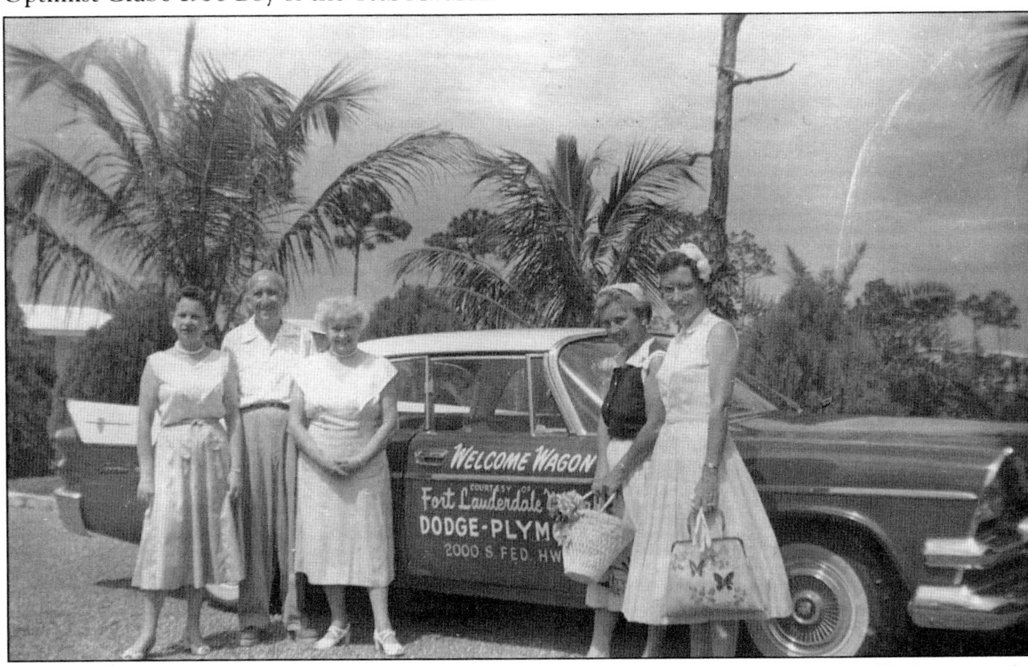

The Fort Lauderdale Westside Welcome Wagon Club of the late 1950s eventually became the Plantation Newcomers Club. Eligibility for club membership was limited to recipients of a Welcome Wagon Call. It was common for auto agencies to provide cars for local Welcome Wagon Clubs to use in their "calls." 1957 Welcome Wagon members pictured are, from left to right, Grace Harmon, Lorraine Abrahart, Lillian Williams, and Helen Ditzler.

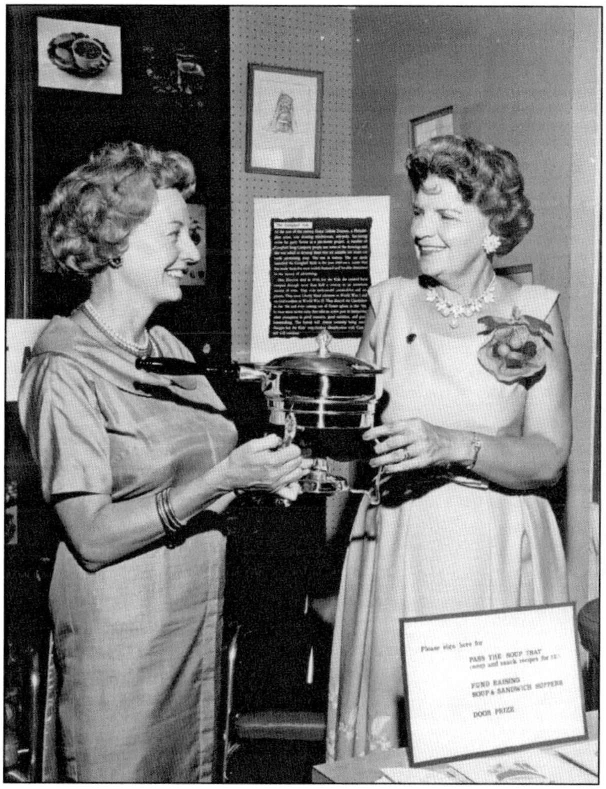

A silver chafing dish is presented to Mrs. William F. Coulter, right, president of the Plantation Woman's Club, by Marie Roberson, author of *The Chafing Dish Cookbook*, at the General Federation of Women's Clubs convention in the Fontainebleau Hotel in Miami Beach. Pictured below, Plantation Woman's Club members are gathered for a group photograph taken at the Florida Federation Women's Clubs Convention at the Fontainebleau.

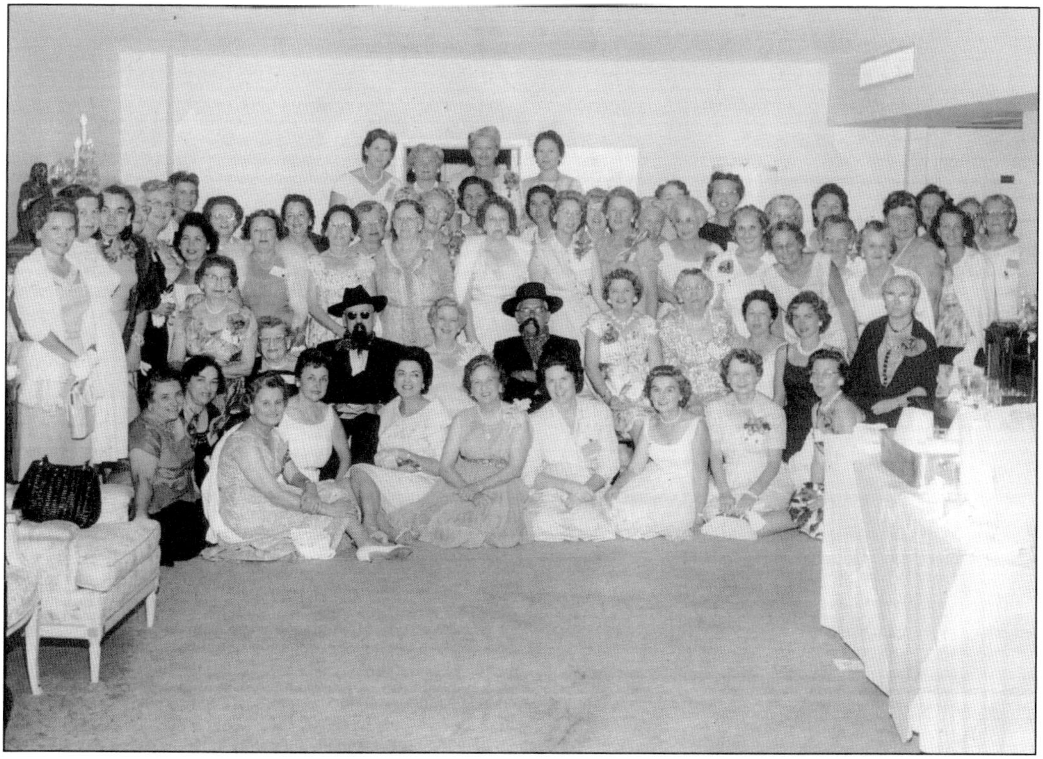

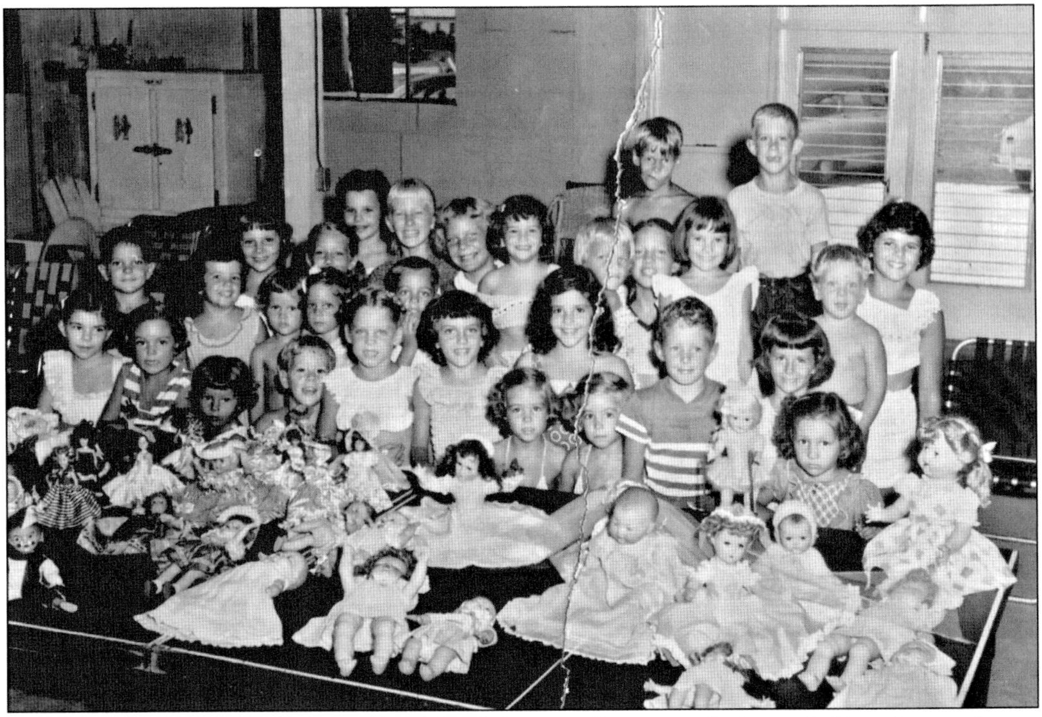

Plantation children attending the Play School Summer Program, which was held in the warehouse that became the first Community Center, now part of Deicke Auditorium, enjoy a doll show.

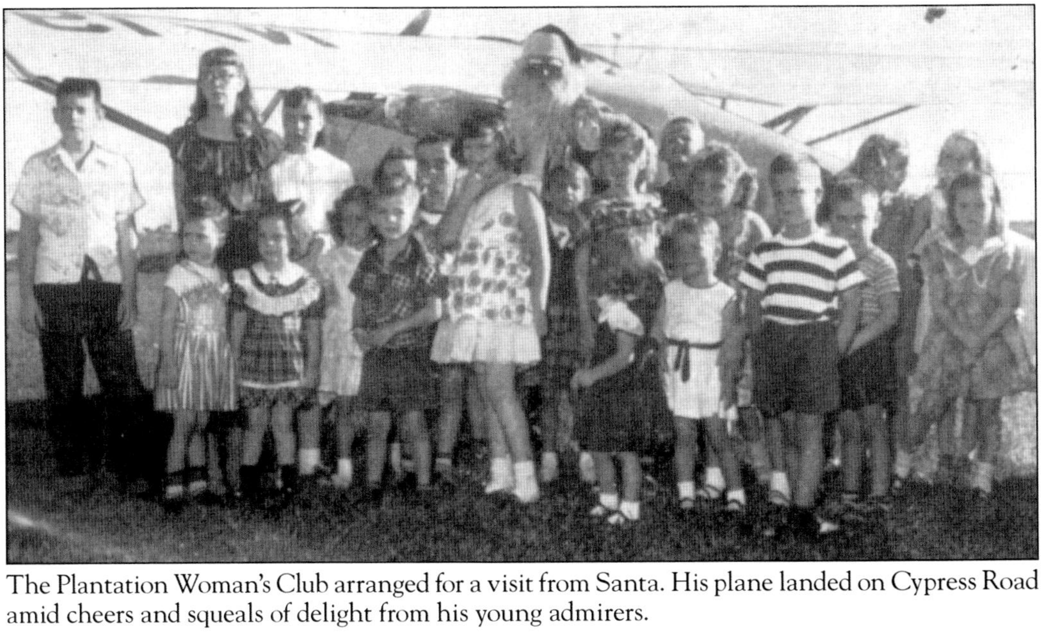

The Plantation Woman's Club arranged for a visit from Santa. His plane landed on Cypress Road amid cheers and squeals of delight from his young admirers.

Tom Dean is pictured on Plantation Road in 1953. The Dean family lived on Holly Lane and owned and operated Dean's Glass & Mirror Shop. It was one of Plantation's earliest businesses and was located on US 441/SR 7.

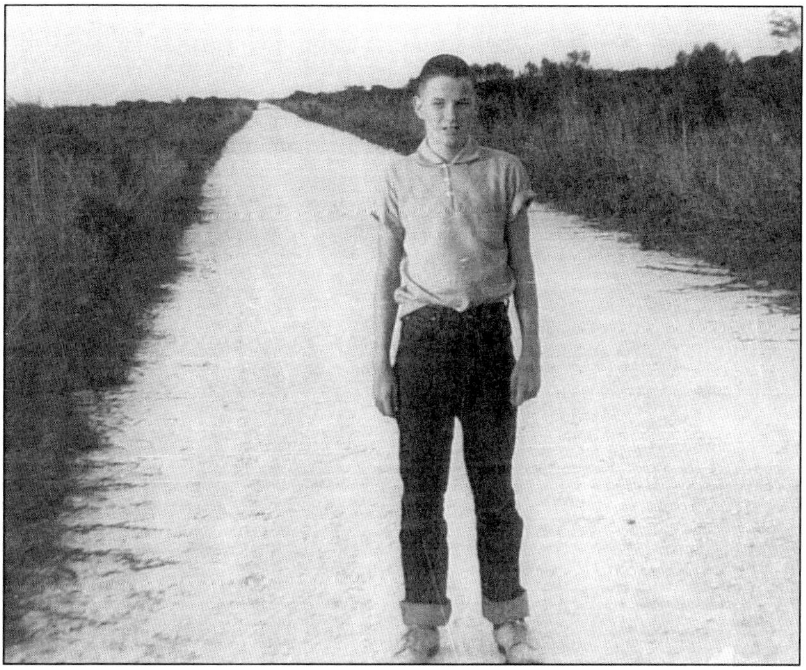

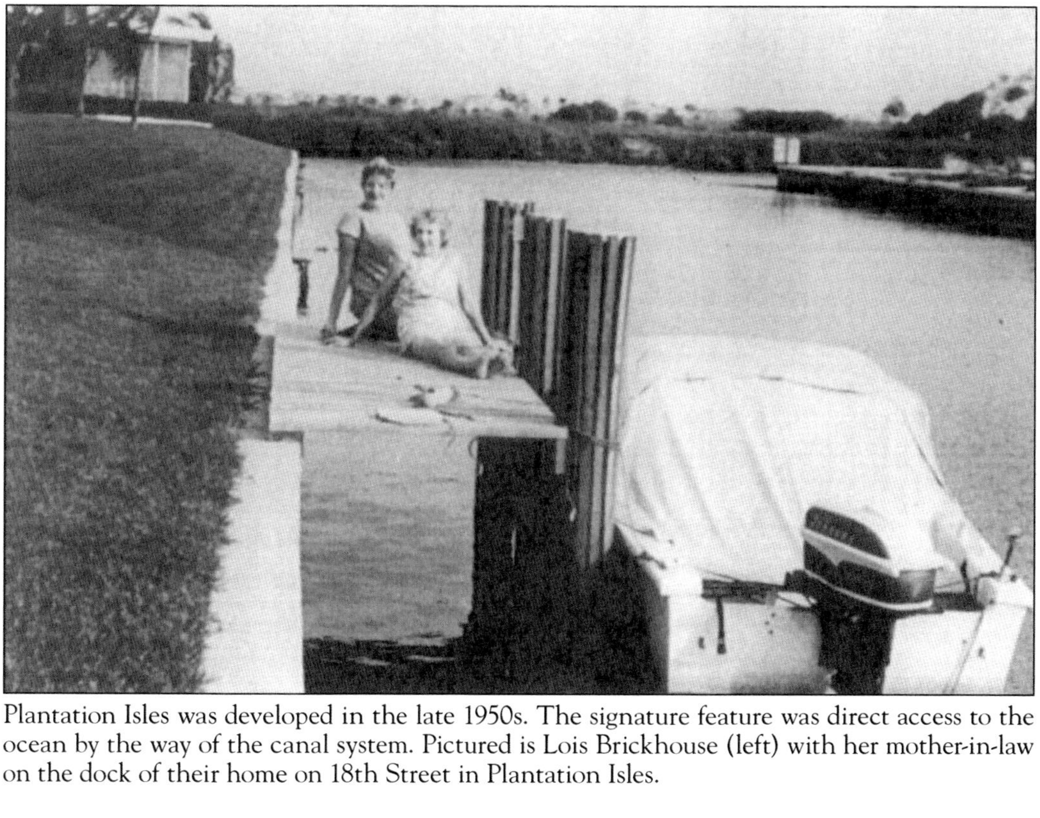

Plantation Isles was developed in the late 1950s. The signature feature was direct access to the ocean by the way of the canal system. Pictured is Lois Brickhouse (left) with her mother-in-law on the dock of their home on 18th Street in Plantation Isles.

Plantation Patter

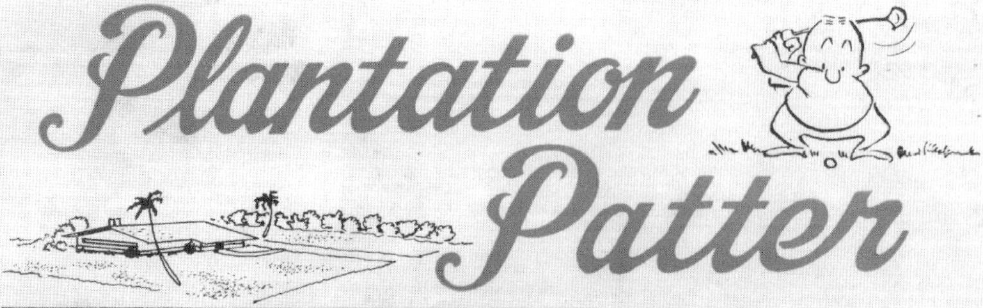

Vol. I, No. 2 PLANTATION, WEST BROWARD BLVD., FORT LAUDERDALE, FLORIDA September, 1951

Stork Gets Help From Plantation

Anyone expecting a visit from the stork? Then get set to hear the Plantation Patter of little feet, because you'll find that before the blessed little event is more than a few days old, someone from Plantation is helping out.

The writer had occasion to discover this recently when his wife presented him with a bouncing baby girl at Broward General Hospital.

While pacing the hospital corridor in my semi-spastic condition awaiting the inevitable, who came to soothe my pangs of approaching parenthood? None other than Miss E. M. Bunnell, the supervisor of the productive obstetrical department and enthusiastic Plantation resident.

Calming newfledged fathers is only a sideline in Miss Bunnell's busy

(Continued on Page Four)

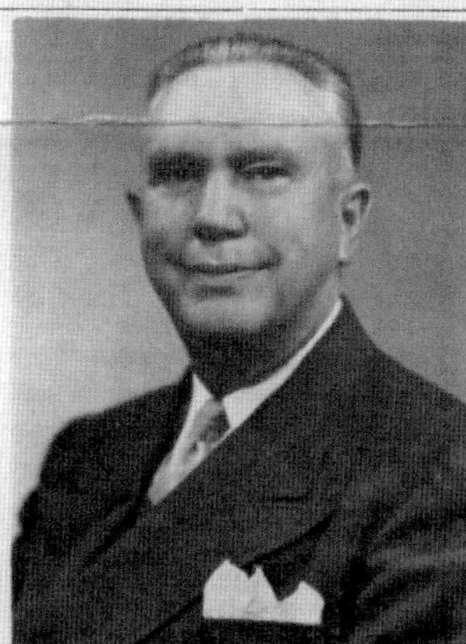

Mr. Edwin F. Deicke

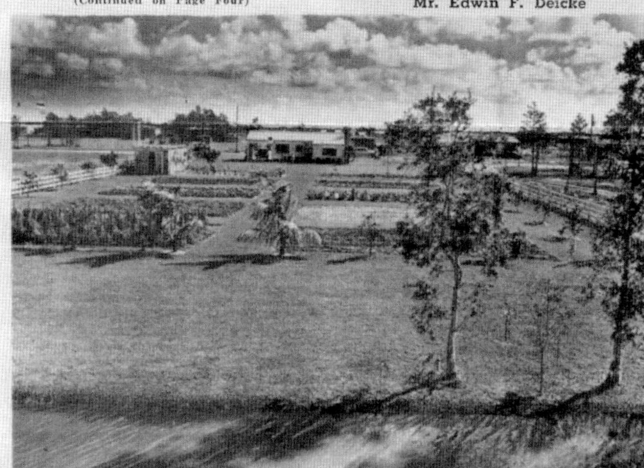

Spacious is the word for the beautiful, well-planned tropical garden in Mr. Deicke's back yard. Here, he raises the fruits and vegetables which he is such an expert at preparing.

Versatile Mr. Deicke Plantation Personality

Our Plantation Personality this month is Edwin F. Deicke who divides his time between his home in Lombard, Ill., and his residence here. He is one of the most active supporters of our community which he calls "the garden spot of the world."

Plays George Washington

When Plantation was planning its Fourth of July celebration, he was asked to participate as George Washington. Without hesitation, Mr. Deicke, who was at that time in his Illinois home, dropped his many business affairs, rented a Colonial uniform and caught the first plane south. Needless to say, he gave a top-notch performance on horseback in the parade as the Father of our Country.

Mr. Deicke is famed as a cook as those lucky ones can attest who have been invited to bite into those tasty steaks he prepares on his backyard grill. He can also perform culinary feats with the vegetables he raises that would make Duncan Hines do handsprings.

He is a charter member of Plantation Golf Club and he can be observed on the course most any time wielding his wicked driver. Among his other sport interests are farming, swimming, skeet shooting, horseback riding, hunting and fishing.

Smoked Fish?

His latest piscatorial feat was unorthodox and the fish got away but it deserves mention in "Believe It Or Not." It seems that Mr. Deicke was strolling along the waterway near his back yard and flipped a cigarette butt into the water. Before it hit, a five-pound bass leaped up and caught it in mid-air. Obviously, both Mr. Deicke and the fish smoke the same brand.

(Continued on Page Three)

The *Plantation Patter*, an early community publication, kept the residents up to date on local happenings, such as birth announcements, neighborhood events, elections, and more. It would be replaced in 1955 by the *Plantation Bugle*, a newsletter edited by resident Helen B. Hoffman.

Four

The 1960s

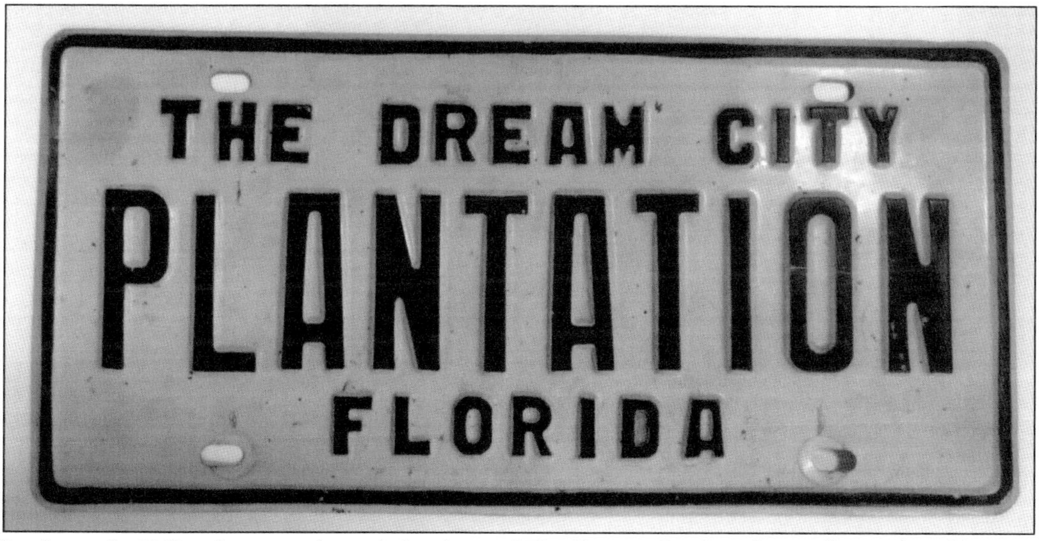

In the early 1960s, the city adopted the slogan "The Dream City" and proudly produced license plates touting the new moniker. The slogan was used to publicize Plantation as the perfect place to live and raise a family.

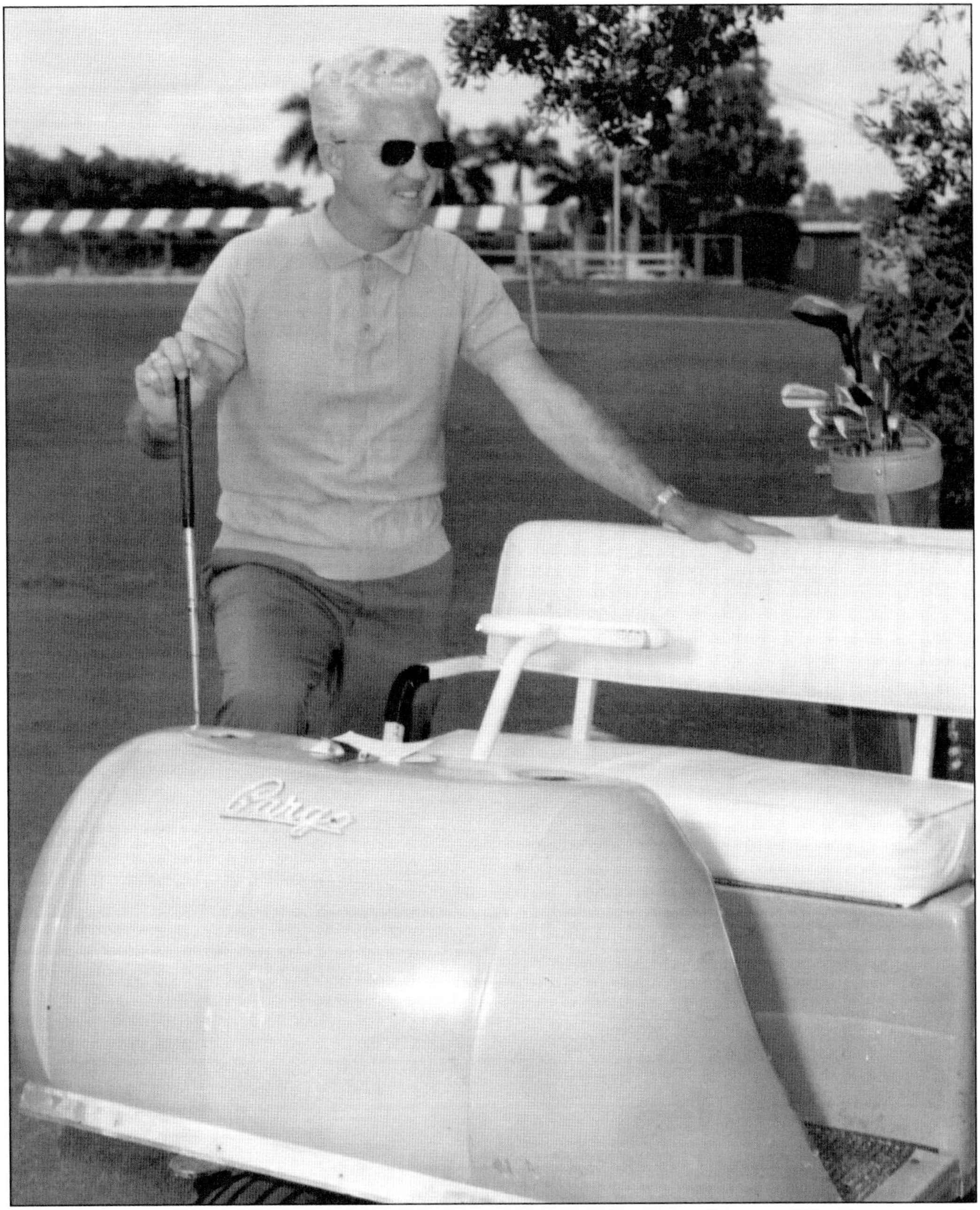

James J. Ward Jr. was elected mayor in 1959, serving until 1971. One of Mayor Ward's major goals was to expand the city's recreation facilities and programs. In this photograph, Mayor Ward gets ready for a round of golf at the Plantation Golf Course.

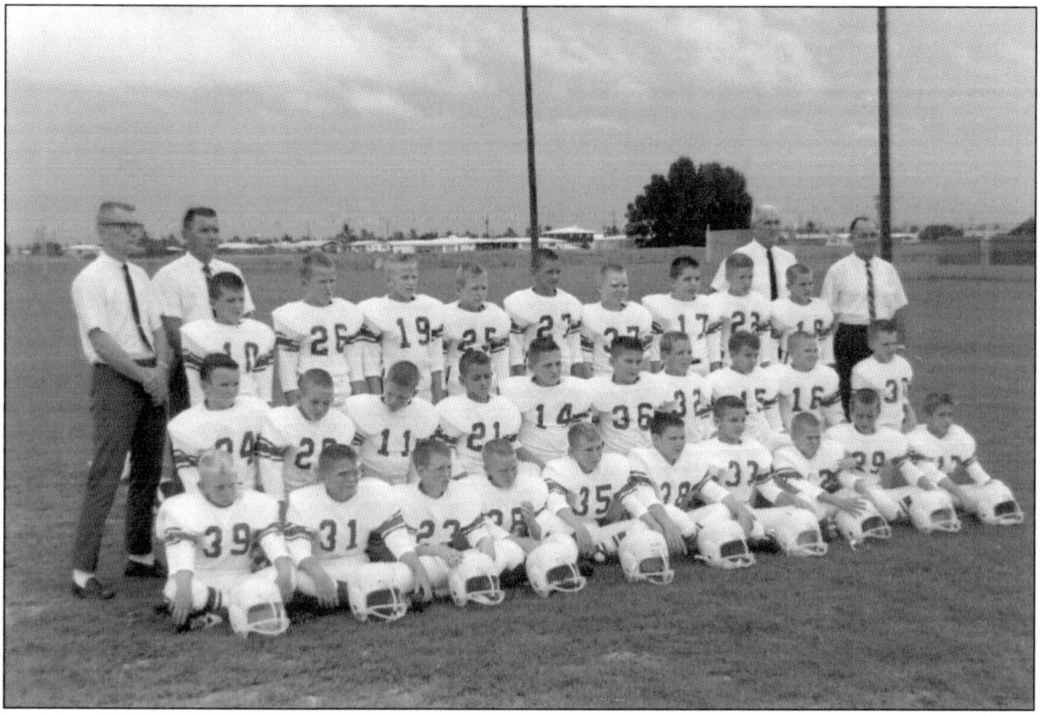

In February 1960, Roy Salmon, Dave Bishop, and Hank Donath created the Police Athletic League (PAL), and by March, 85 boys ages 8–12 years old were assigned to one of six spring baseball teams. As the program grew, other sports, such as football, were added, and in 1962, the first girls' softball team was organized and coached by Genevieve Veltri. These photographs show early 1960s PAL football and baseball teams.

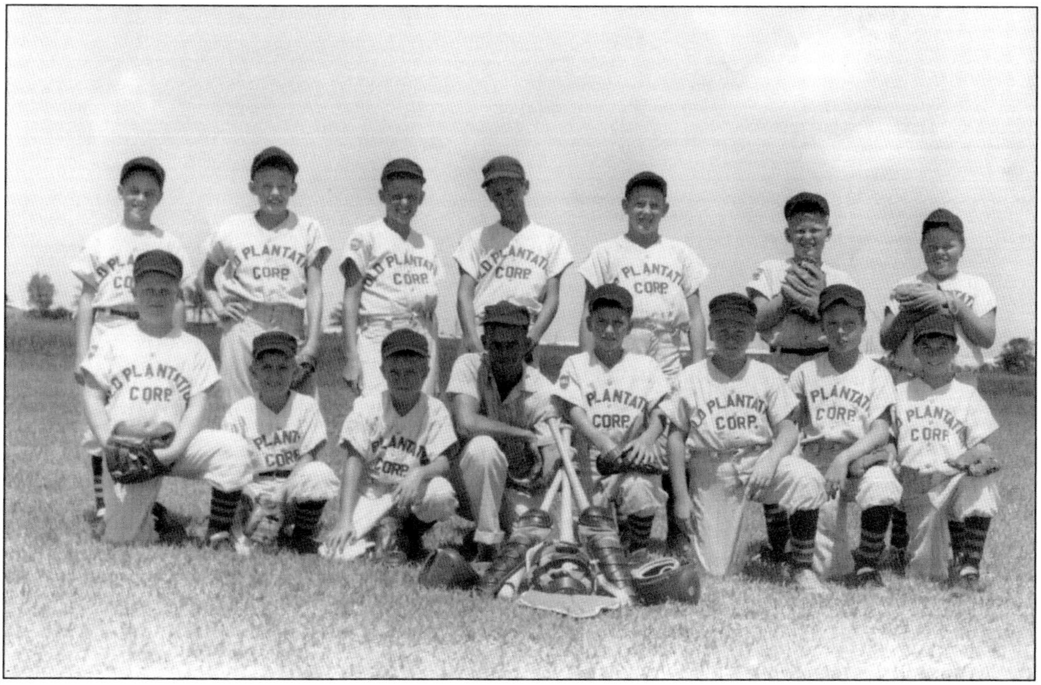

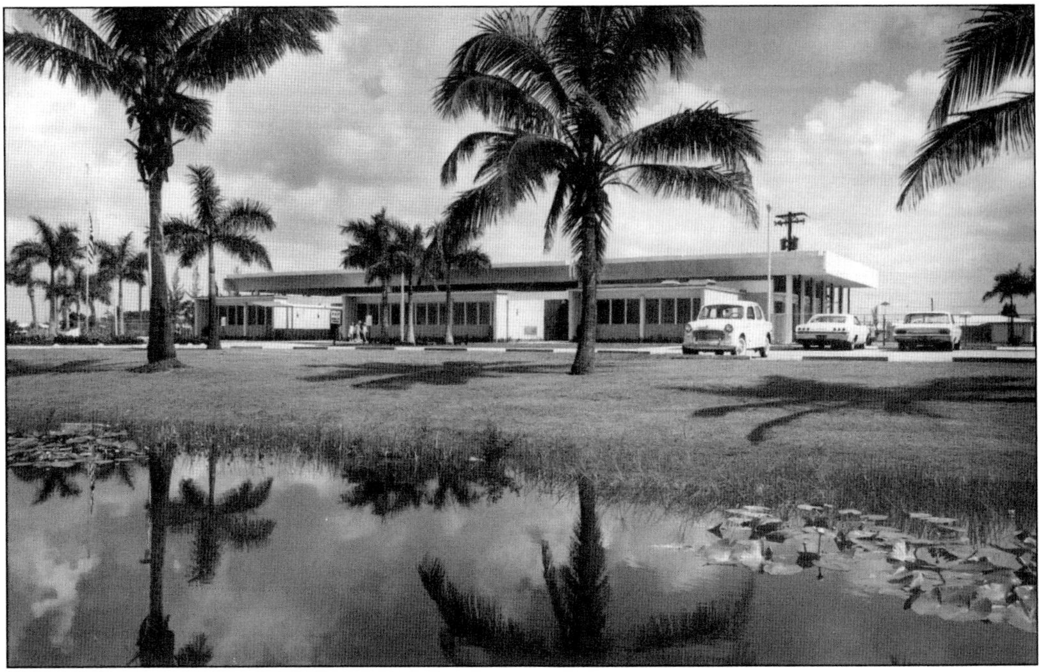

The Community Center, dedicated on May 1, 1963, was built by contractor William Vander Linde at a cost of $139,272.38. Architect Russell T. Pancoast was the designer. The Modernist style features several individual units around a central atrium, covered by a barrel-vaulted concrete canopy containing open square sections to allow sunlight and rain water to penetrate to the planted area below. The Plantation Library moved from its Peters Elementary location to the center. The facility's auditorium was used for recreational and social activities; the rooms were used for classes and meetings.

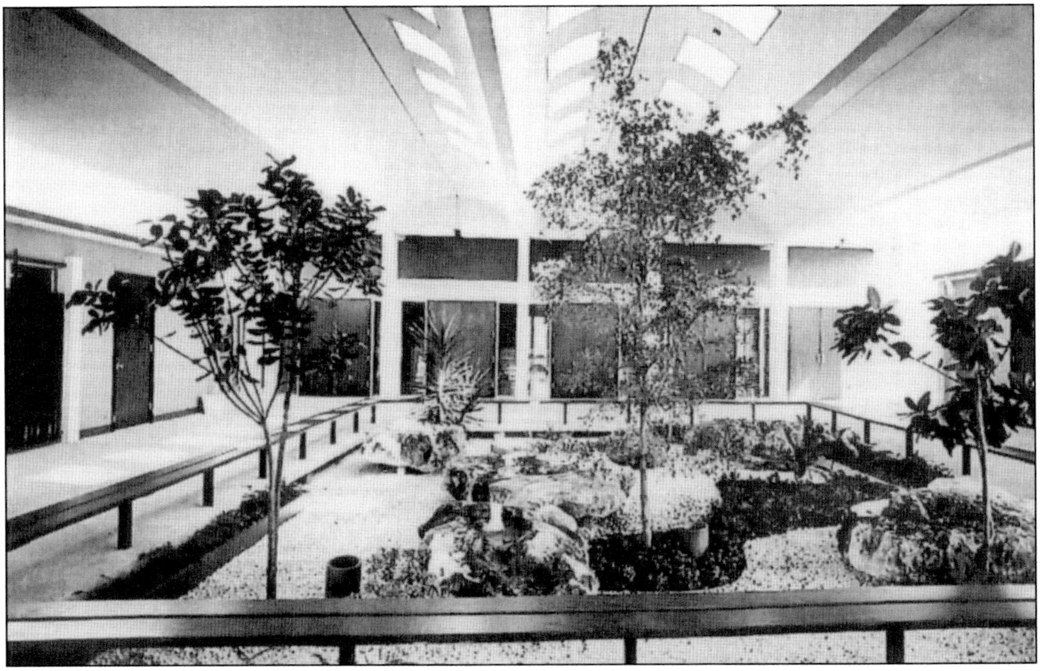

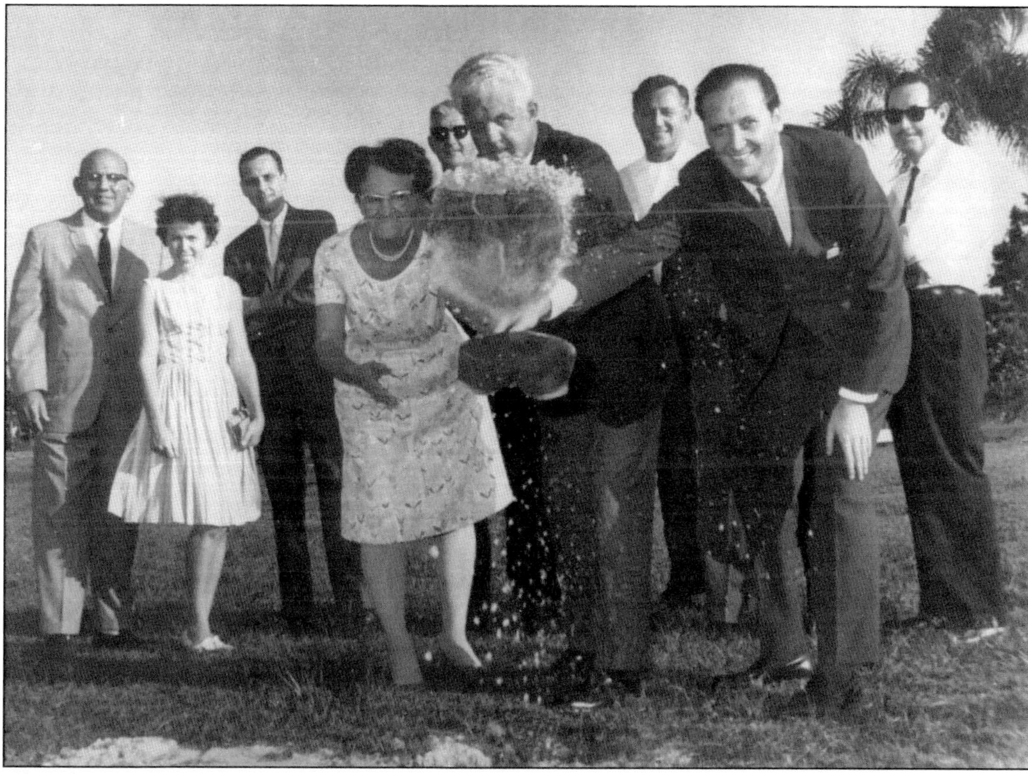

The Plantation Library was established in the late 1950s by Helen B. Hoffman and members of the Plantation Woman's Club as a volunteer library to help local children with their homework. In 1981, the library was renamed the Helen B. Hoffman Plantation Library in honor of Mrs. Abram Hoffman. The picture above is of the 1968 library ground breaking ceremony. Pictured are, from left to right, Councilman John Dye, library board member Linda Lee Infante, Franklin Lotz, library board member Betty Hoffman, Councilman Al Fairley, Mayor Jim Ward, contractor John H. Gossett, and architect Philip Pearlman. Pictured below in 1968 are Plantation officers in front of the police department and city office facility that was built between Fourth and Fifth Streets. The original building faced Fourth Street.

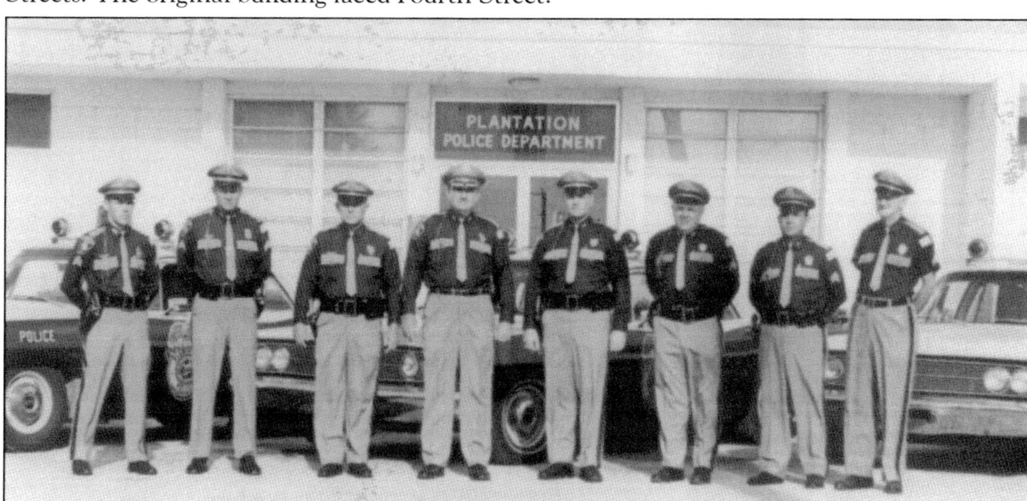

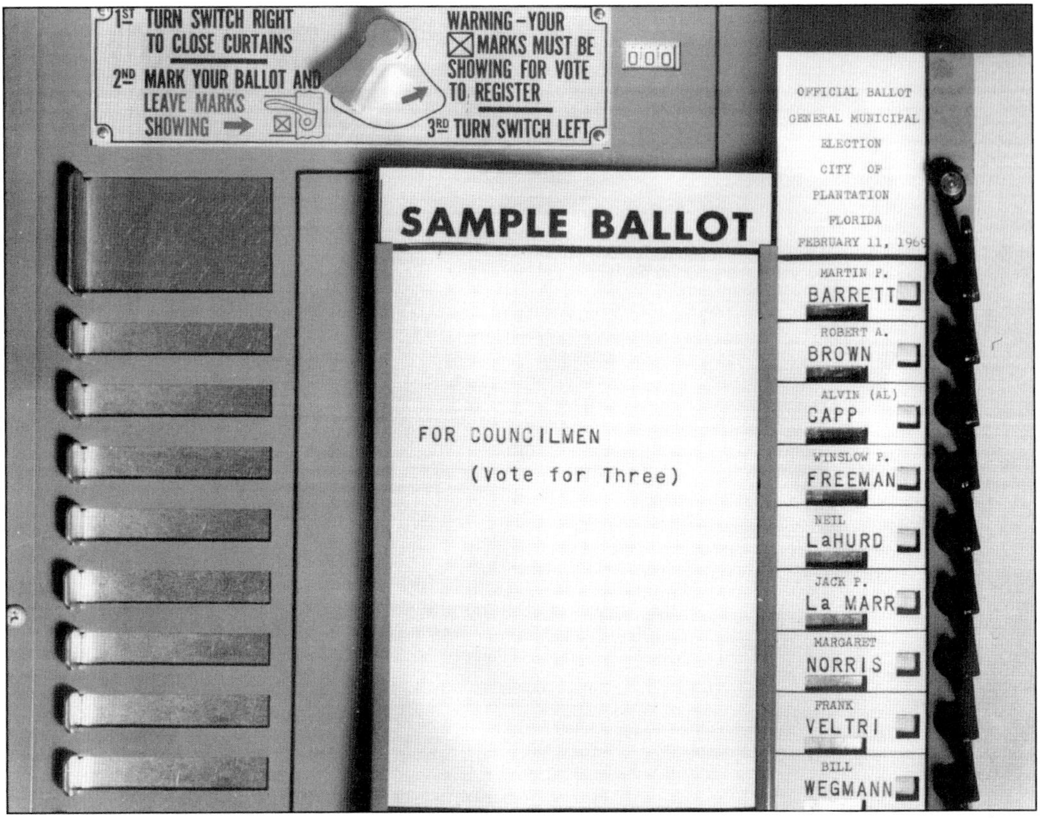

Above is a voting machine from 1969, featuring a sample municipal ballot for Plantation. Residents were to vote for three of the council member candidates listed. The 1969 election winners were Winslow Freeman, Neil LaHurd, and Frank Veltri. Pictured below is a city council meeting held in the "old" city hall in 1970. Pictured are, from left to right, Councilman Frank Veltri, Mayor Jim Ward, council president Bryan Dye, Councilman Jack Spellacy, Councilman Winslow Freeman, and Councilman Neil LaHurd. In the foreground is City Clerk Beatrice Browning.

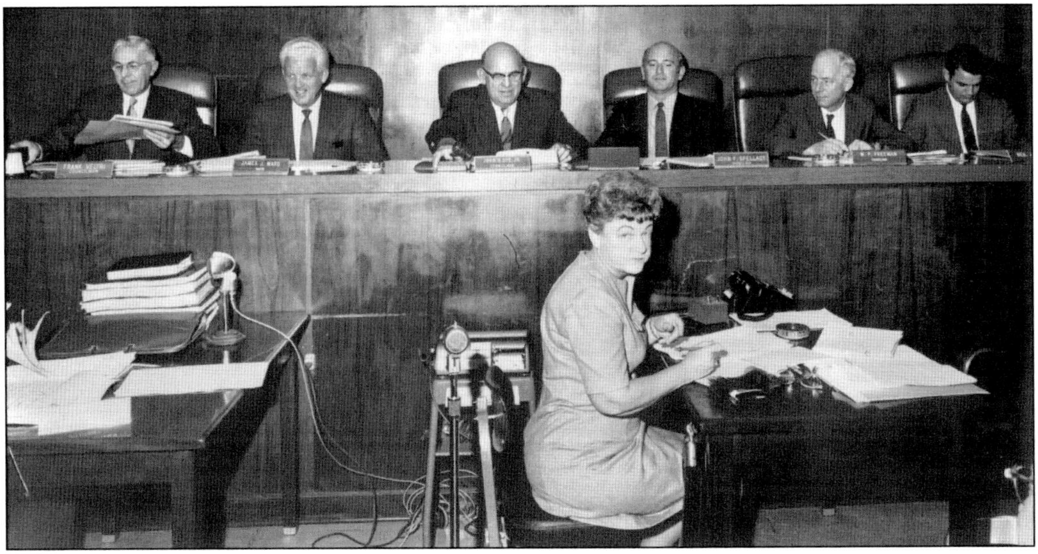

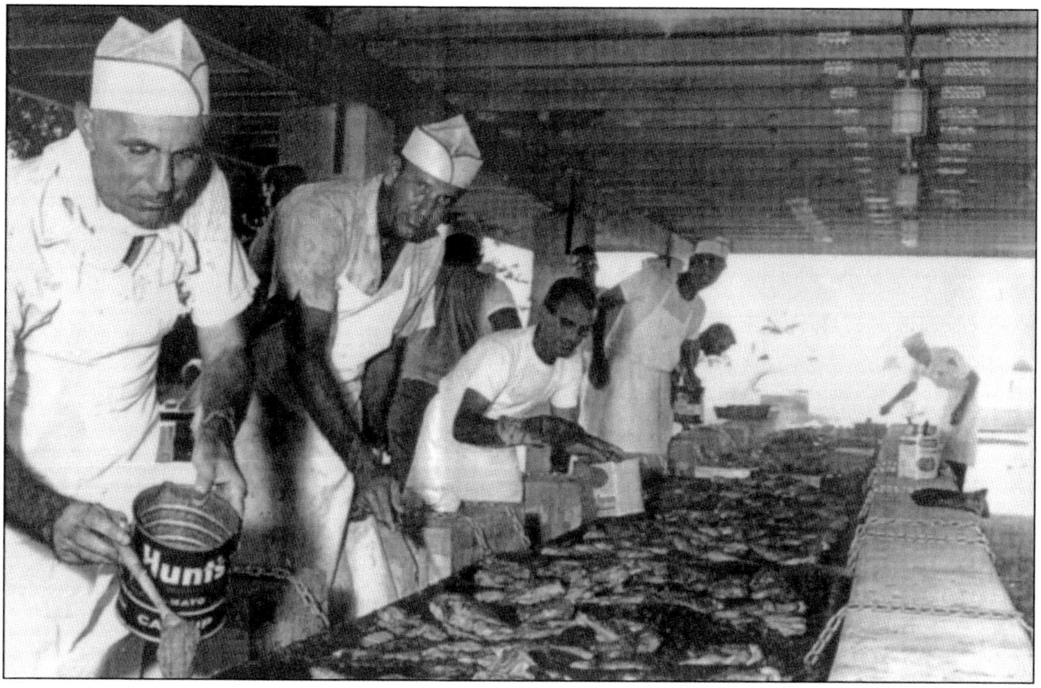

The fire department's barbecue originated in 1956, the year the fire department was formed, as a fundraiser. Pictured above in 1965 is fire chief Phil Amman, second from left, and former fire chief and "head chef" Frank Veltri, far left, applying his "secret sauce" to chicken and ribs. Veltri left his famous recipe with the fire department, and many residents continue to flock to this annual event to enjoy the outstanding food. Pictured below is a 1961 training operation using Engine No. 1, which today can be seen at the Plantation Historical Museum.

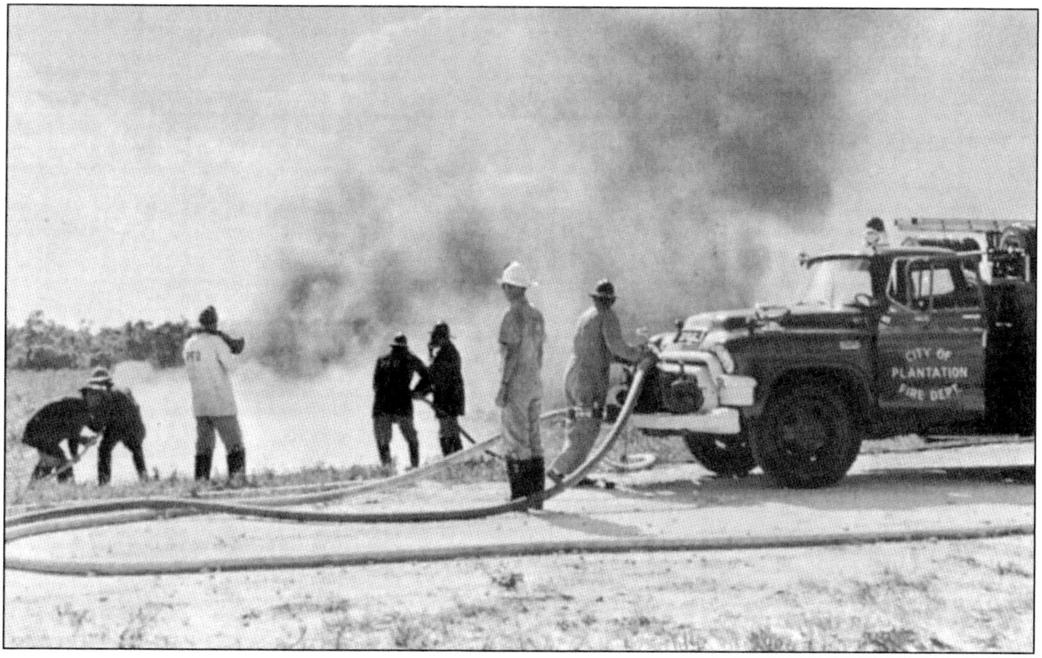

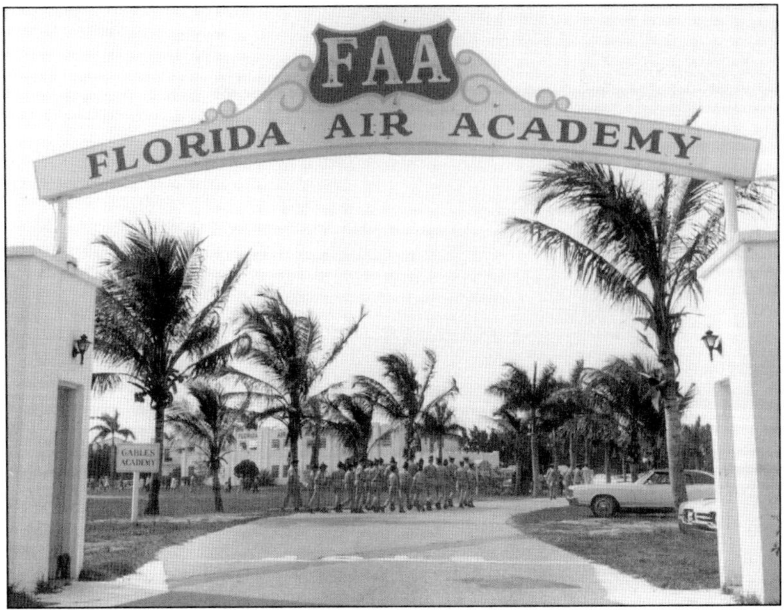

The Florida Air Academy opened on Sunrise Boulevard in 1965. For 14 years, this Plantation military-style preparatory school provided yearly housing and education for over 200 cadets. In 1979, the academy closed, and the property was sold to the Jewish Community Center.

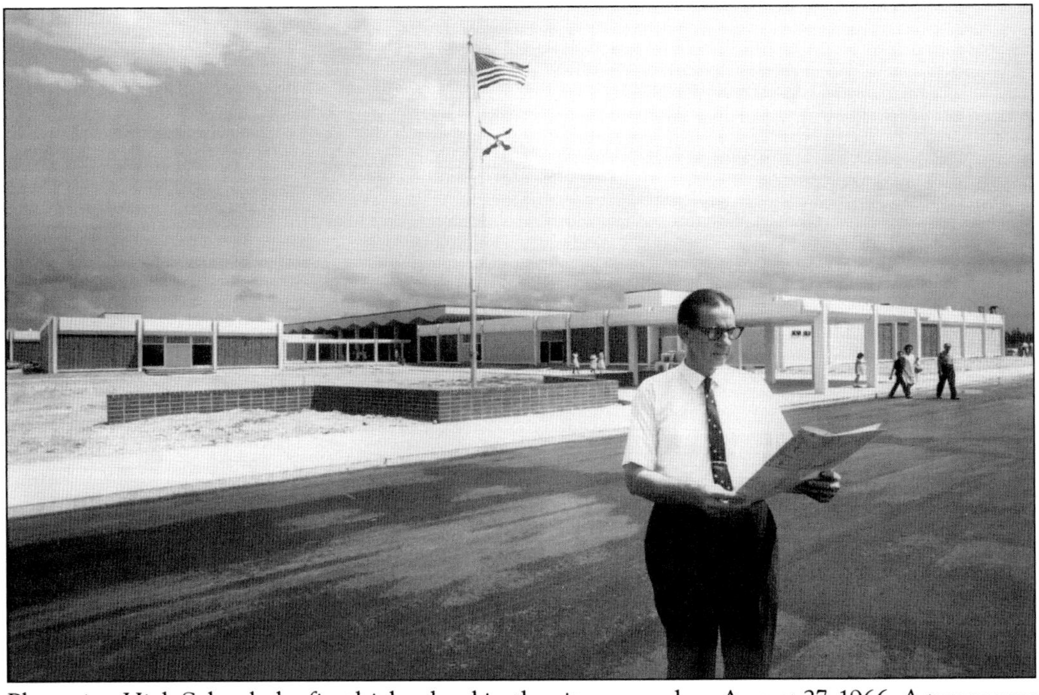

Plantation High School, the first high school in the city, opened on August 27, 1966. A temporary facility at the US Naval Air Station at the Fort Lauderdale airport was used until the new school was constructed. Pictured is the school's architect, William T. Vaughn, standing in front of the new high school.

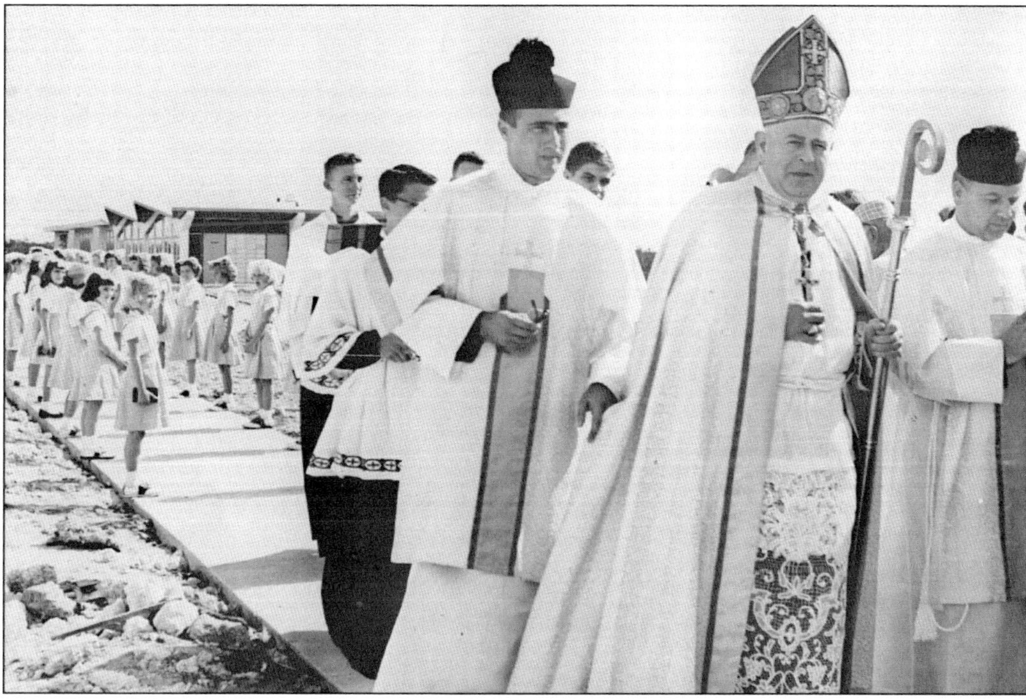

St. Gregory the Great parish was established on July 23, 1959, and the first parish Mass was celebrated in the cafetorium at Peters Elementary School. On September 6, 1960, prior to the completion of the church, St. Gregory's school opened, in portable classrooms, at its current location on University Drive. Rev. Mother Mary Romuald was the first principal, overseeing an enrollment of 143 students. Pictured here is Coleman F. Carroll, the bishop of Miami, at the January 8, 1961, dedication of St. Gregory's Church.

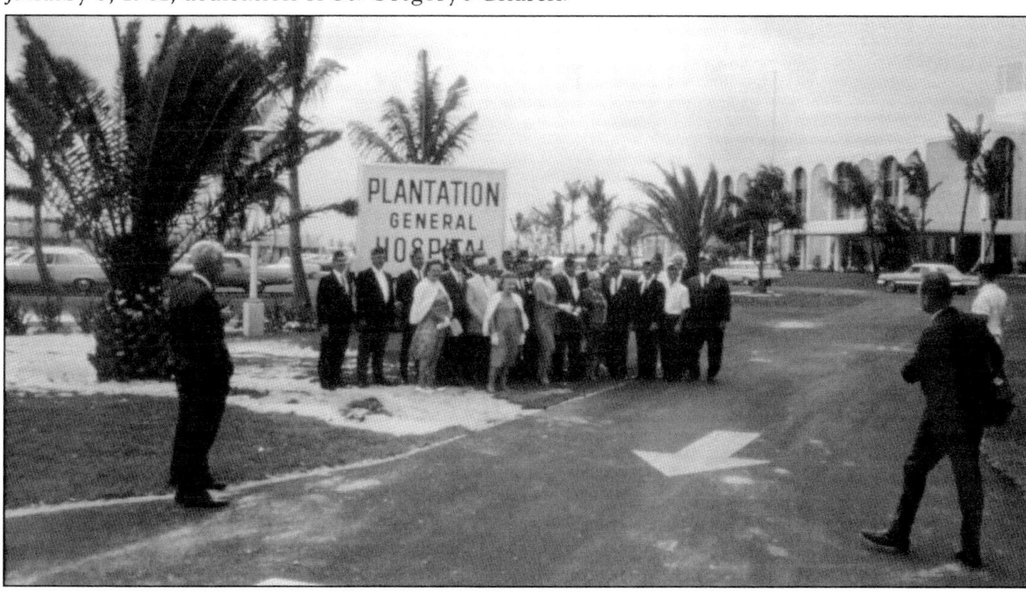

Dignitaries pose for a photograph at the grand opening of Plantation General Hospital in November 1966. Mayor Jim Ward is at the far left. This health care facility located on US 441/ SR 7 continues to provide quality medical services to the community.

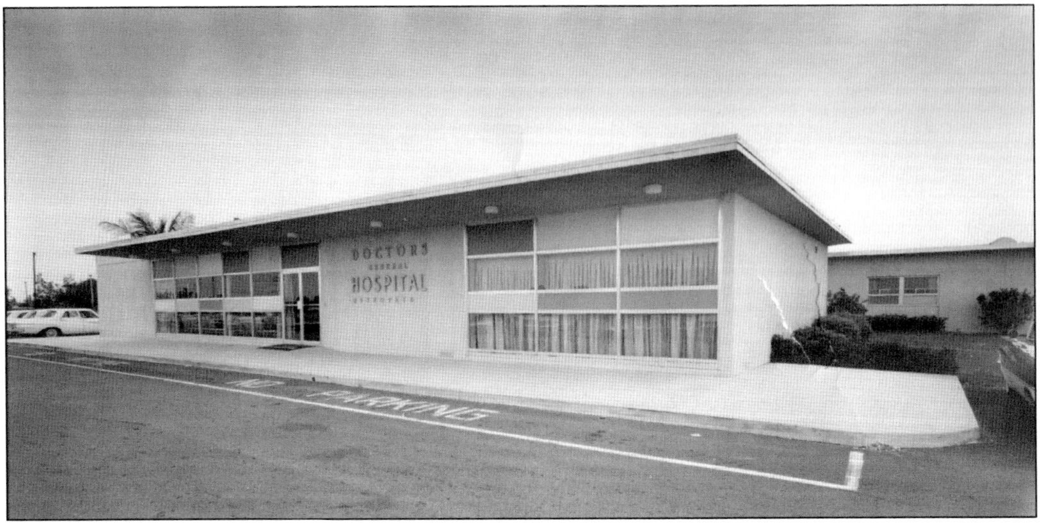

Plantation's first hospital, constructed for $1.4 million, opened on Sunrise Boulevard in July 1962. At the time, Doctors Hospital contained Broward County's first cobalt center for the treatment of cancer. Plantation teenagers could volunteer their time in the candy striper program at Doctors Hospital. As seen in the 1968 photograph below, a participant was awarded a cap on the successful completion of training and 50 service hours.

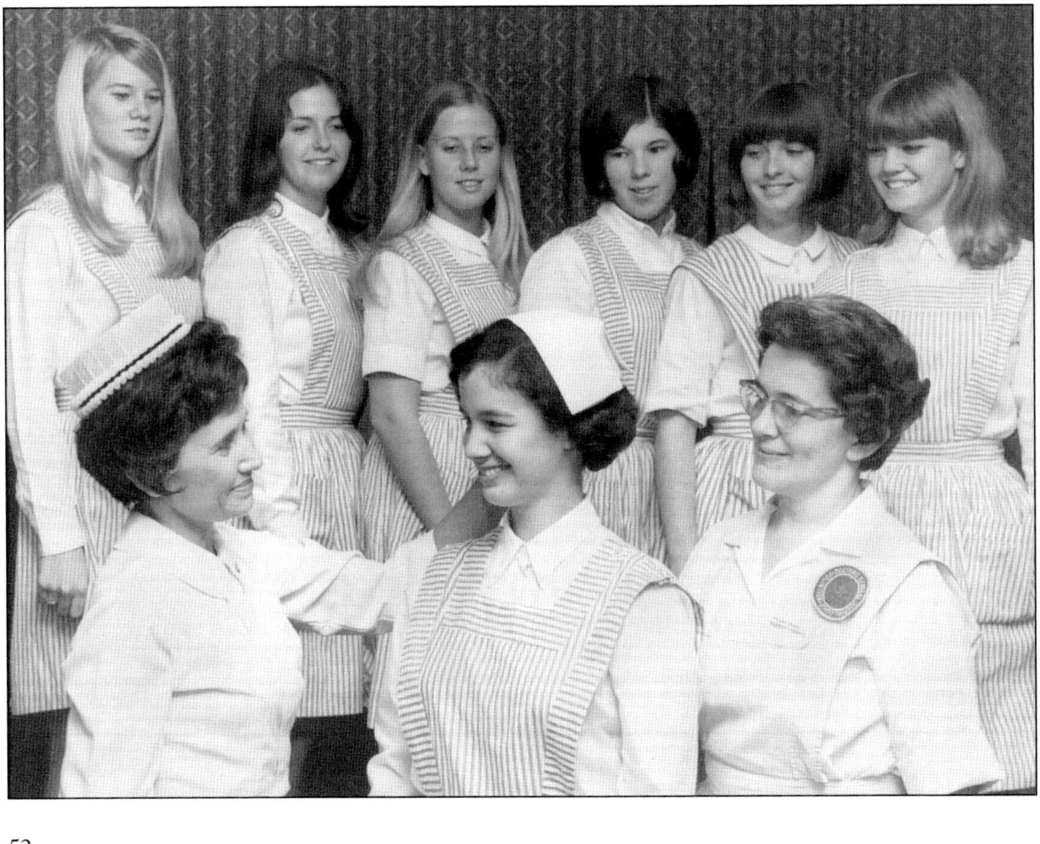

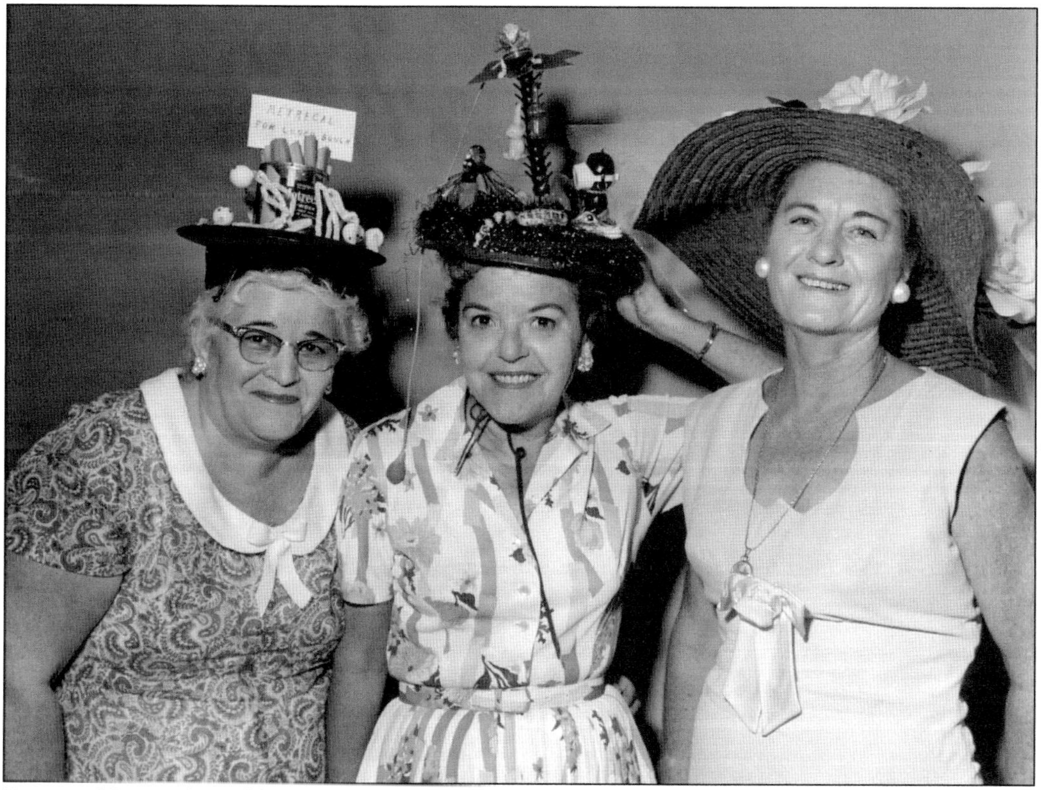

Doctors Hospital Guild, a service organization, raised funds to support the hospital through luncheons and other events. In 1964, the funniest hat award went to Mrs. James Wills, center, at a "Hats for Spring" luncheon.

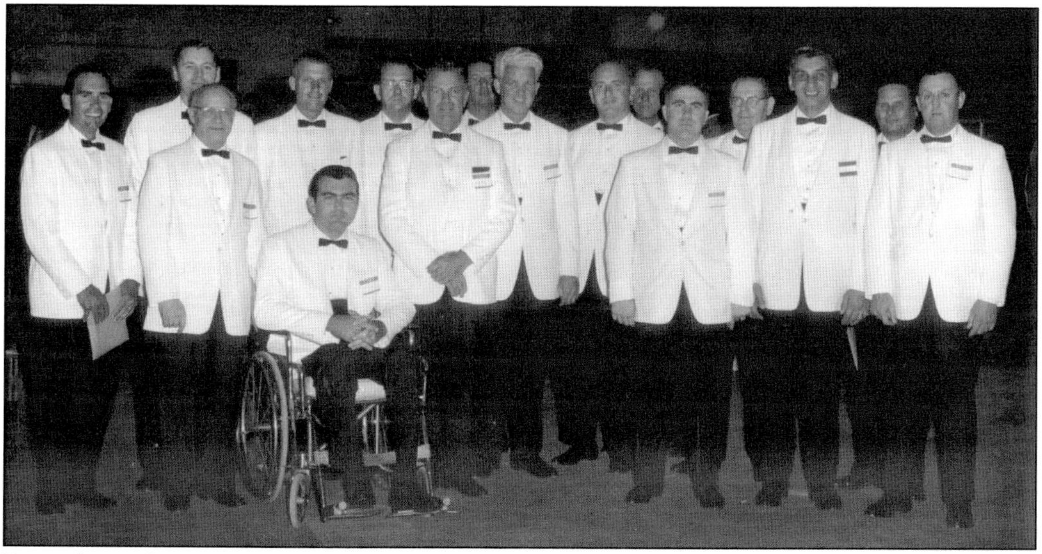

From the mid-1960s until the early 2000s, the Plantation Elks Club was located on Northwest Fifth Street. Many of Plantation's early leaders were part of the organization, including Jim Ward, standing at center in the second row, who in 1963 was elected the first exalted ruler of the Plantation lodge.

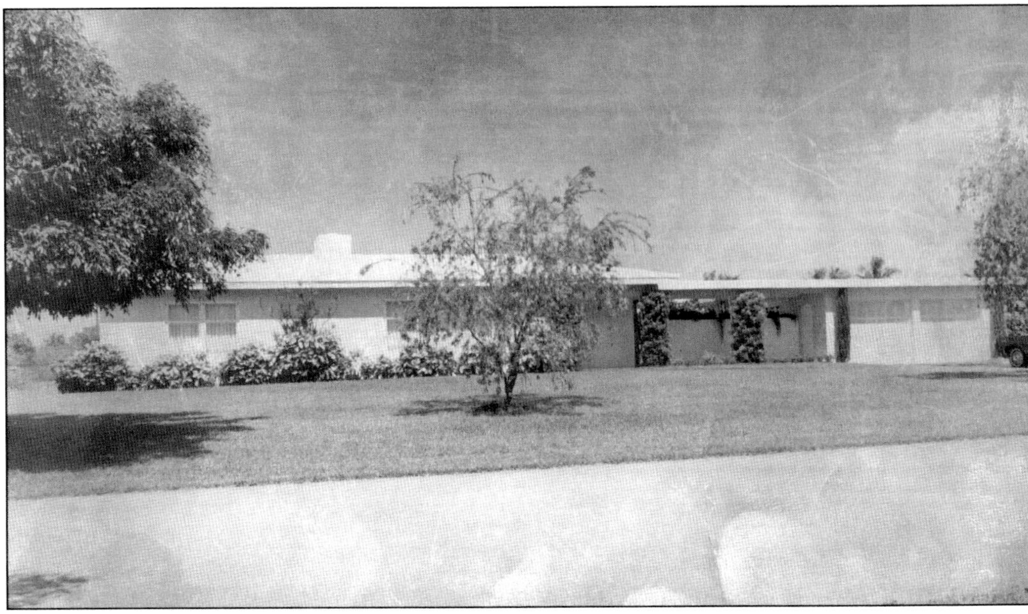

This home on Bel Air Drive was typical of Plantation properties in the 1960s. It was constructed on an oversized lot and contained three bedrooms, two bathrooms, terrazzo floors, and a garage for a price of $27,000. Real estate listings at this time were featured on large index cards with a photograph of the property on one side and specific details on the other. It was common to even list the reason for selling.

FORT LAUDERDALE
MU‸TIPLE LISTING SERVICE, INC.

MLS

List No.: R25, 099

$ | F
$ CTM | Down
Change | Date

File: 52368/4 | W.F. No | Seawall: | Dock: No | B.R.: 2 | Baths 2

Constr: CBS Zoning: R-1	Heat (type): Central	Community
Lot Size: 208 x 185	Air Cond: Yes Central: Yes Units:	Reason for selling: Transferred to N.J.
Sewers: Yes Connected: Yes Paid: Yes	Range: Gas: Elec: Yes Blt-In: Yes	Remarks, additional features, extras:
Year Blt: 1953 New:	Refrig: Yes Dishwr: Yes Disp: Yes	Beautifully landscaped oversized lot-
Roof: Tile	Patio Size: Open: Scr:	kitchen newly remodeled with all new
Floors: Terrazzo	Fences (type): 5' CL-entire rear yd	cabinets & fixtures including new
Windows: Awning	Pool Size: Scr:	refrig., washer & dryer.
Liv. R. Size: 17 x 15	Taxes Year: $247.21 H.E. Yes	Wood burning fireplace - Living room
Din. R. Size: 17x9 Din. Area Size:	1st Mtg. Hldr: 1st Fed-Ft. Laud.	and dining room newly panelled and
Kit. Size: 19 x 11	Balance $ 15,962	wall-papered.
Fla. R. Size: 19 x 9 Den:	Pay $ 151. per Mo. Inc:	
Fam. R. Size:	5.75 % for 17 Years to go	
B.R. and 13 x 11	2nd Mtg. Hldr:	
Sizes: 16 x 11	Balance $	
Baths: 2 Tub: 1 Shwr: 2	Pay $ per Inc:	
Porches Size: 20x8 Open: X Clsd:	@ % for Years to go	
Carport: Garage: 2 Car	Owner will take $	Trade: No
Util. Rm: In Garage	Commt: $ @ %	To show: Call owner or LO
Spr. Sys: No Well & Pump: Yes	By: Yrs:	Occupancy in immed. days: OK to adv: Yes
Shutrs (kind): Awning & Panels	Pay $ per Inc:	Key: Owner

Listing Realtor: M. R. McTigue & Co. Salesman: John Bury, Jr. Phone: 522-5416
Owner: Crawford M. & D. Address: 21 N. Bel Air Drive Phone: 587-4214

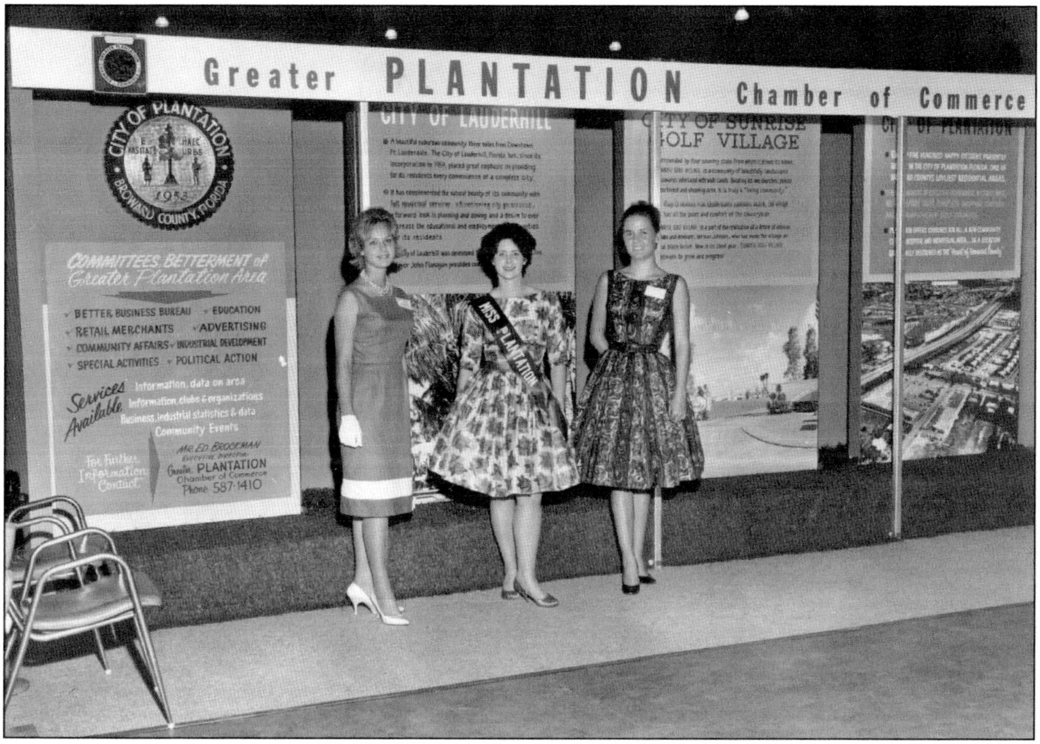

A group of business leaders formed the Greater Plantation Chamber of Commerce in 1962. As part of an ad campaign to attract new residents to the city, there was a contest to seek "Miss Plantation." The finals were held at the Plantation Country Club on February 23, 1963.

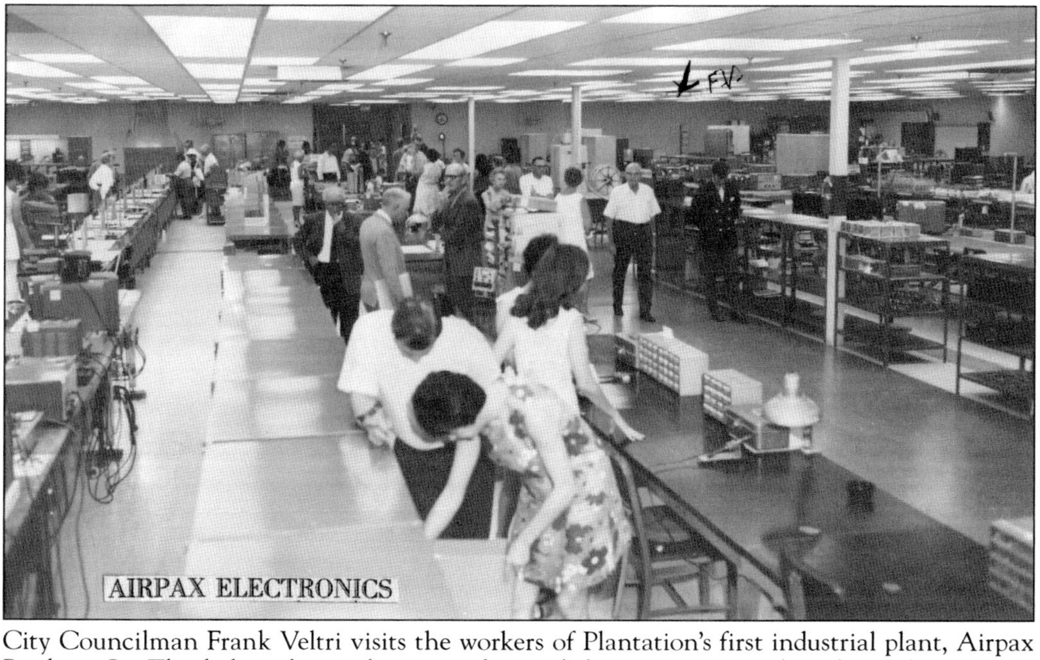

City Councilman Frank Veltri visits the workers of Plantation's first industrial plant, Airpax Products Co. This light-industry plant manufactured electronic parts and was located on Sunrise Boulevard in what is now the Plantation Technology Park.

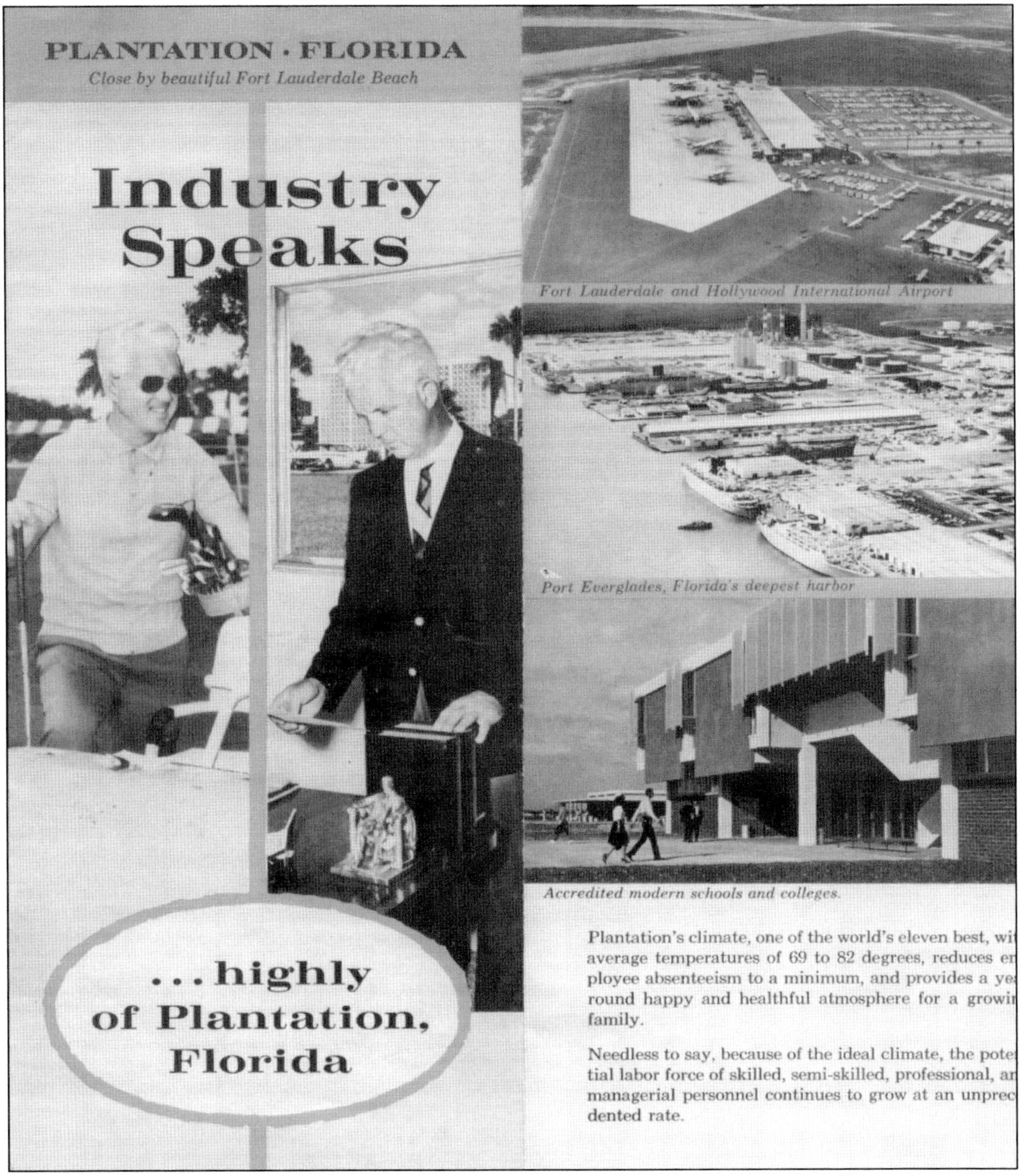

This brochure, created by the Greater Plantation Chamber of Commerce, extolling Plantation's climate, schools, recreational opportunities, and its proximity to rail, road, water, and air transportation, was used to attract businesses to the city. Mayor James Ward is pictured.

Five

The 1970s

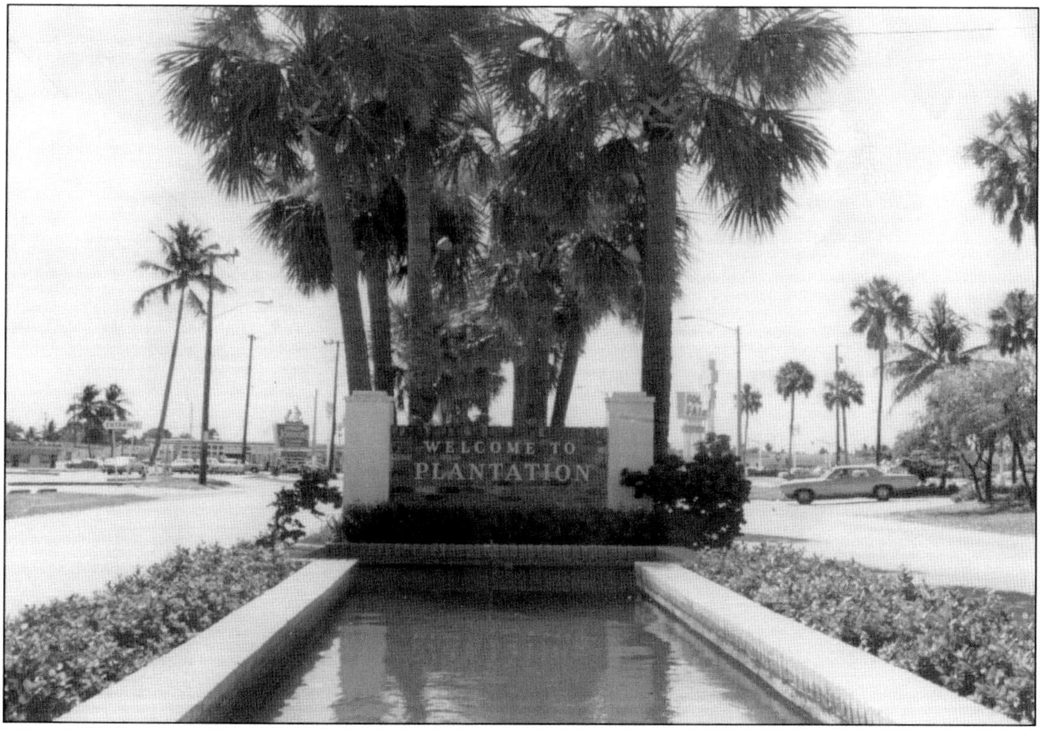

This entrance to the City of Plantation on Broward Boulevard and US 441/SR 7 featured a flagpole and fountain and was nicknamed "Gilligan's Island" by city officials. The structure was removed when the intersection and street were widened.

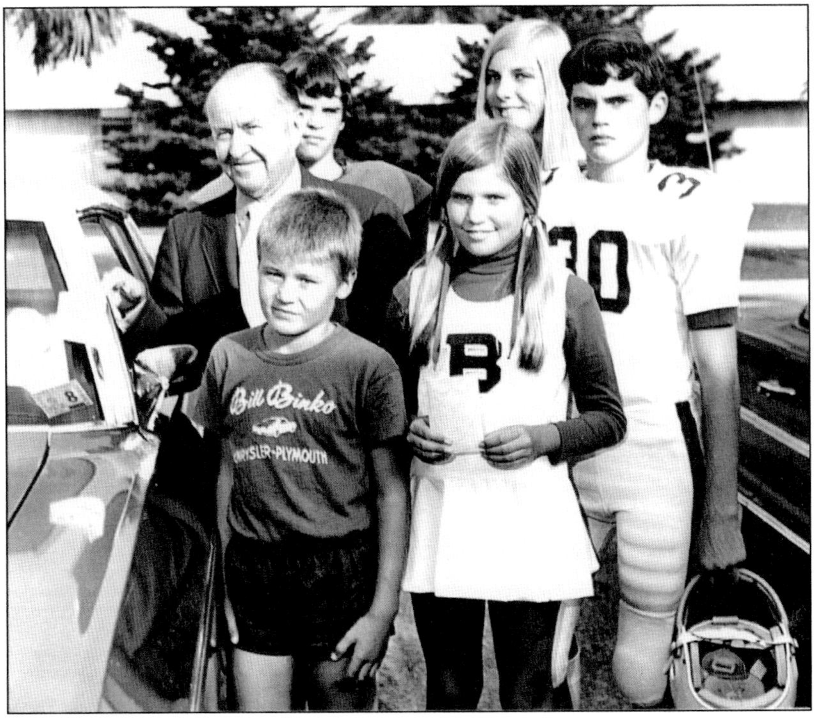

Jack Carter, mayor from 1971 to 1975, stands with children from the Plantation Athletic League, holding a car decal that was sold as a fundraiser for the football program. Pictured are, from left to right, (first row) Bill Radeka and Laura Radeka; (second row) Mayor Carter, Tim Kett, Amy Creekman, and Kevin Kett.

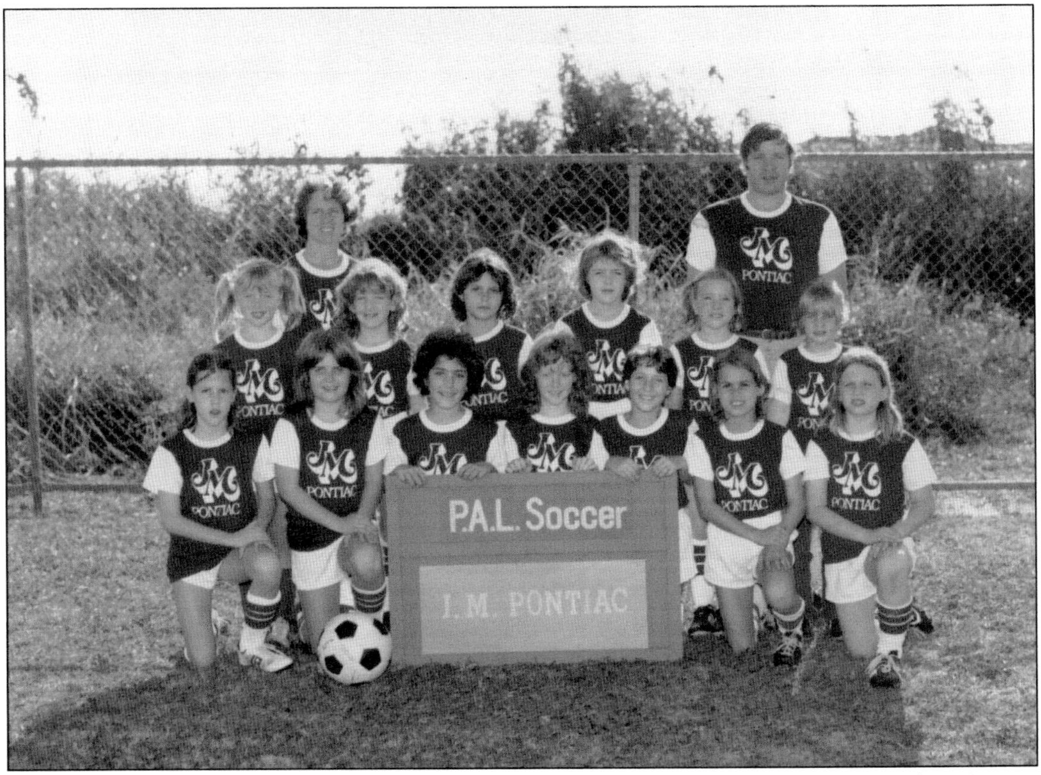

PAL added boys' and girls' recreational soccer to its list of sports in the 1970s. Coaches George and Susie Knapp are pictured with their daughter Sara's team.

The Plantation High School varsity football team shows its spirit in the fall of 1978. The PHS Colonels' original school logo was a cartoon of a traditional "Southern colonel." In the 1990s, the logo was changed to a large red letter "C."

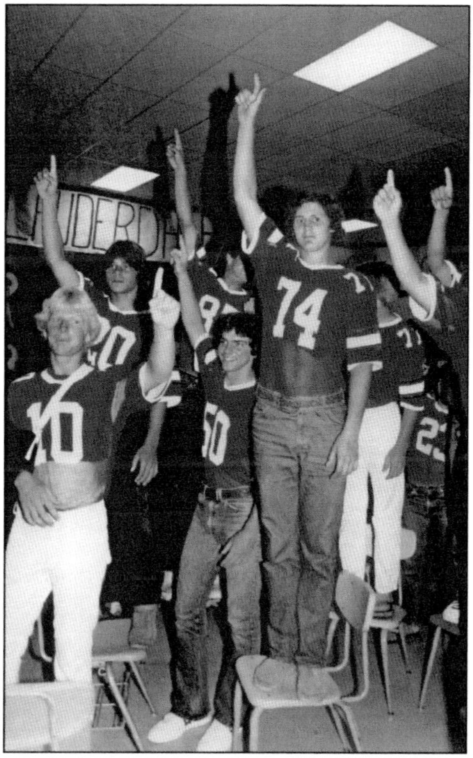

The original PAL cheerleaders were called the Palettes. This squad photograph was taken at the PAL Field on Northwest 70th Avenue, which is now called Roy Salmon Stadium. Roy Salmon served as a detective in the police department and director of the City of Plantation Parks and Recreation Department from 1963 to 1979 and was one of the founders of PAL.

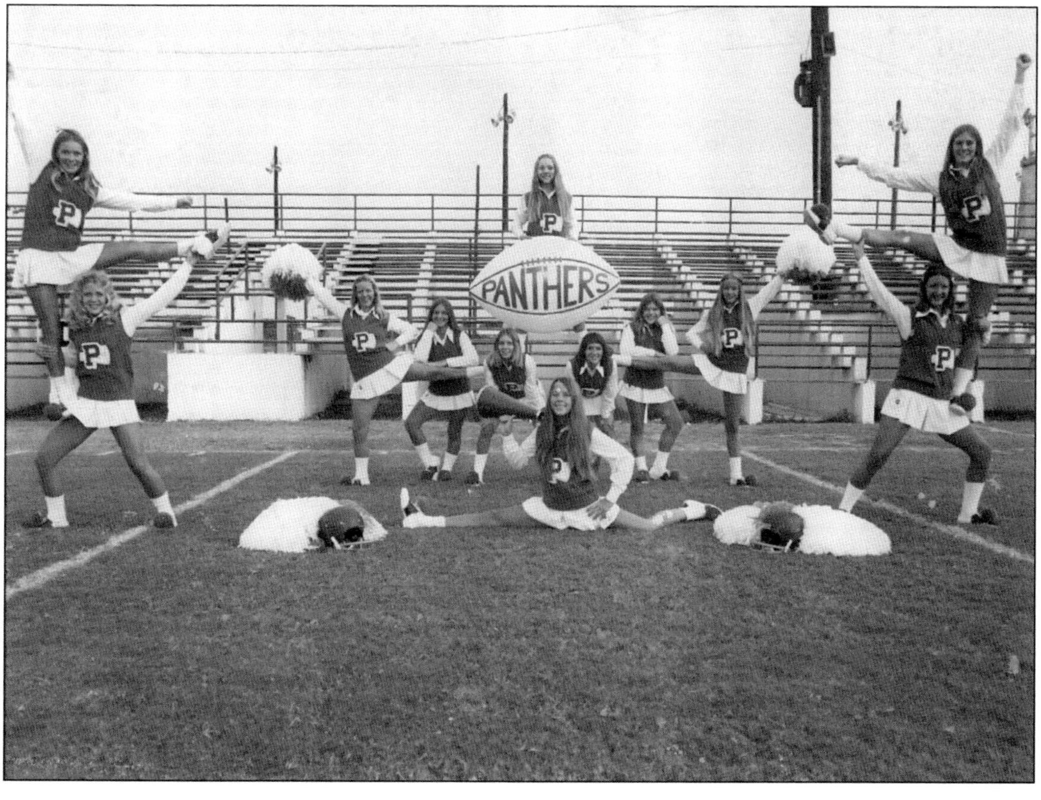

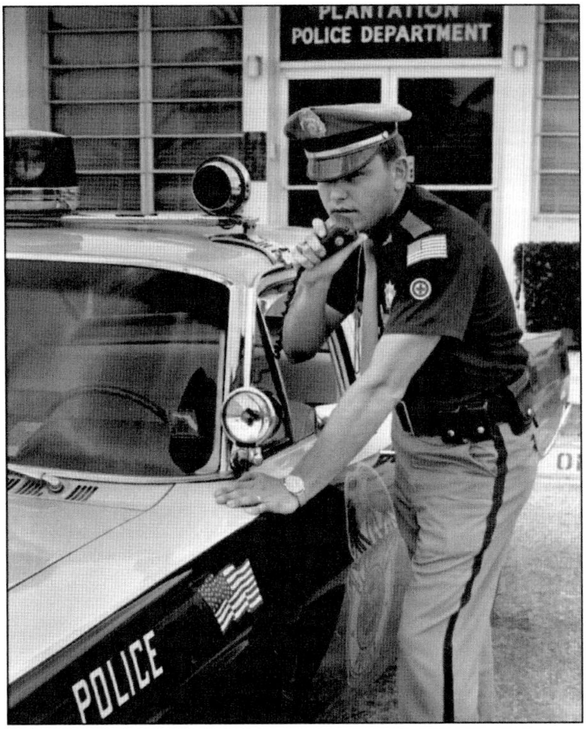

Patrolman Rogers demonstrates the new patrol car radio in his brown and beige cruiser in 1969. Pictured below are three officers of Plantation Police Department's early 1970s motorcycle unit, from left to right, Don Caridad, Howard Harrison, and Chuck Taylor.

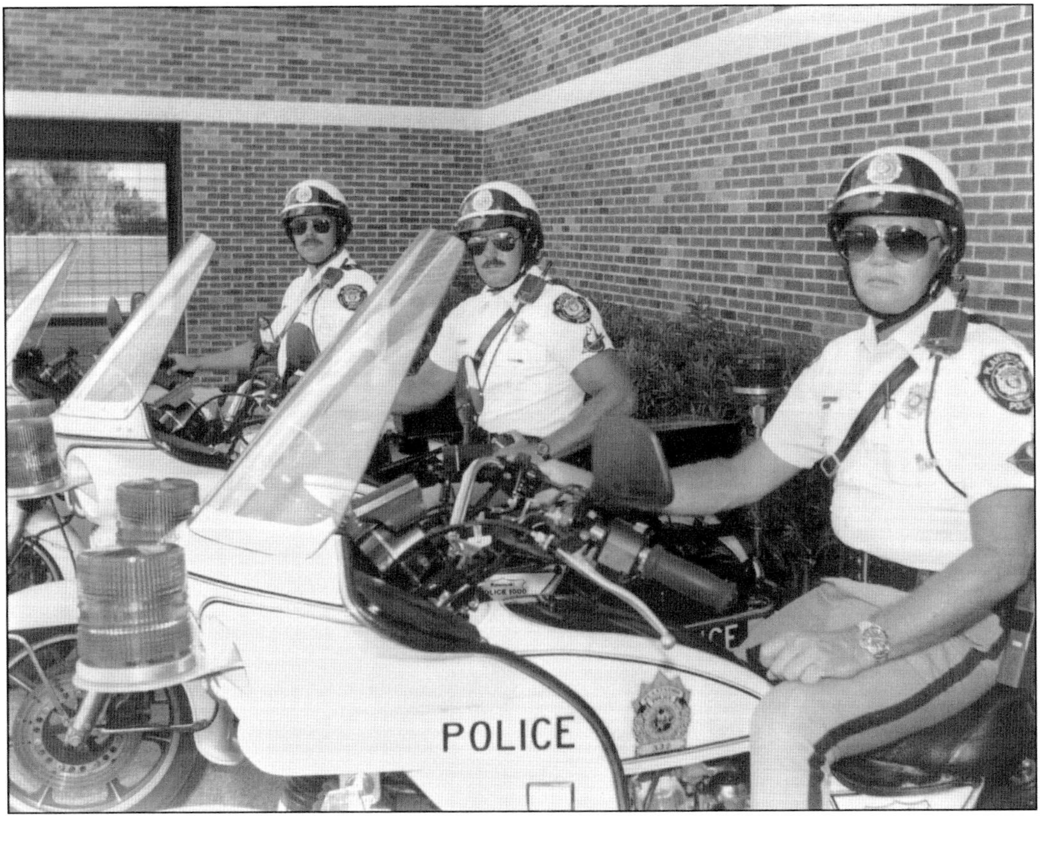

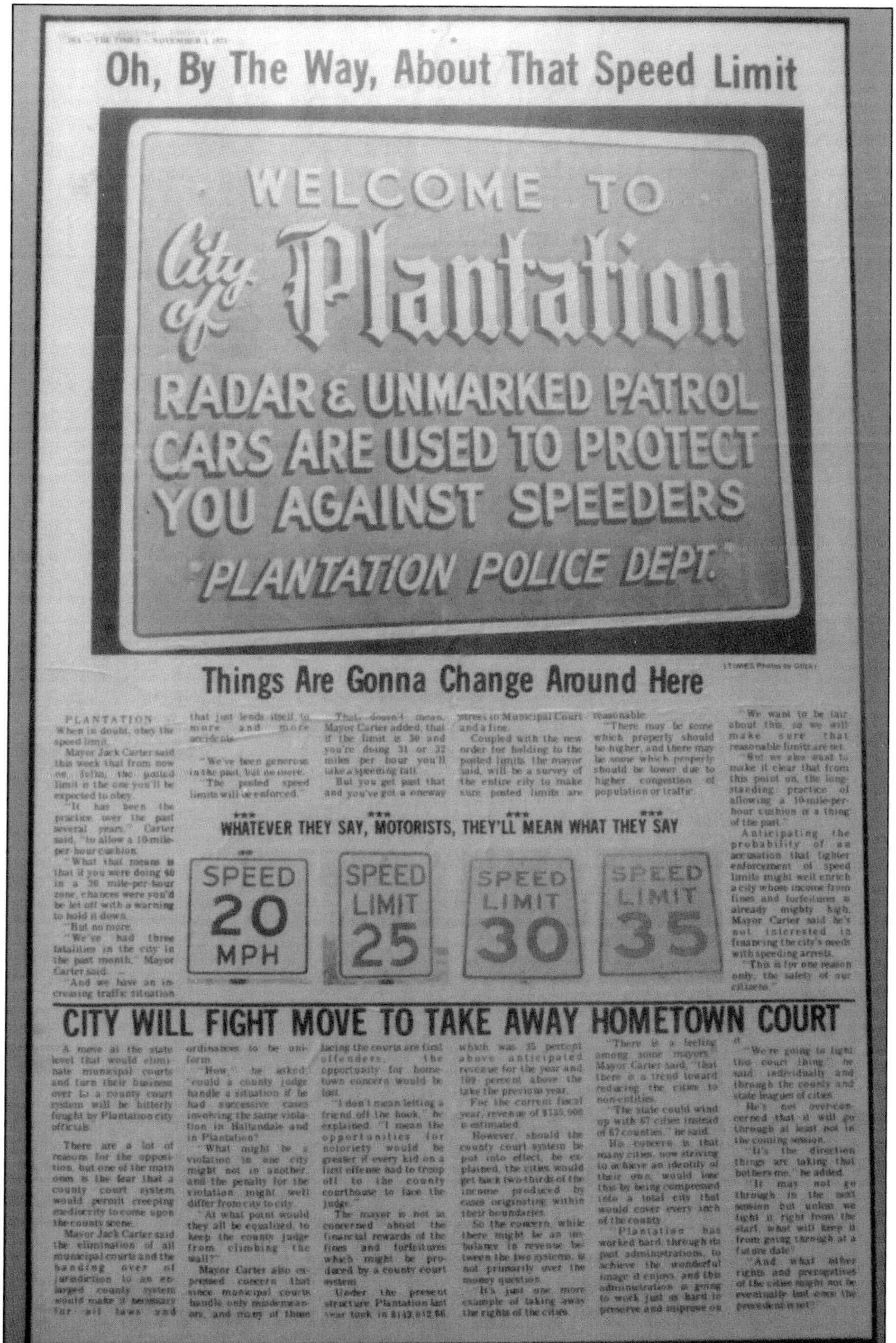

Oh, By The Way, About That Speed Limit

WELCOME TO
City of Plantation
RADAR & UNMARKED PATROL CARS ARE USED TO PROTECT YOU AGAINST SPEEDERS
"PLANTATION POLICE DEPT."

Things Are Gonna Change Around Here

PLANTATION — When in doubt, obey the speed limit.

Mayor Jack Carter said this week that from now on, folks, the posted limit is the one you'll be expected to obey.

"It has been the practice over the past several years," Carter said, "to allow a 10-mile-per-hour cushion.

"What that means is that if you were doing 40 in a 30 mile-per-hour zone, chances were you'd be let off with a warning to hold it down.

"But no more.

"We've had three fatalities in the city in the past month," Mayor Carter said.

"And we have an increasing traffic situation that just lends itself to more and more accidents.

"We've been generous in the past, but no more.

"The posted speed limits will be enforced."

That doesn't mean, Mayor Carter added, that if the limit is 30 and you're doing 31 or 32 miles per hour you'll take a speeding fall.

But you get past that and you've got a oneway street to Municipal Court and a fine.

Coupled with the new order for holding to the posted limits, the mayor said, will be a survey of the entire city to make sure posted limits are reasonable.

"There may be some which properly should be higher, and there may be some which properly should be lower due to higher congestion of population or traffic.

"We want to be fair about this, so we will make sure that reasonable limits are set.

"But we also want to make it clear that from this point on, the long-standing practice of allowing a 10-mile-per-hour cushion is a thing of the past."

Anticipating the probability of an accusation that tighter enforcement of speed limits might well enrich a city whose income from fines and forfeitures is already mighty high, Mayor Carter said he's not interested in financing the city's needs with speeding arrests.

"This is for one reason only, the safety of our citizens."

*** WHATEVER THEY SAY, *** MOTORISTS, THEY'LL *** MEAN WHAT THEY *** SAY

SPEED 20 MPH
SPEED LIMIT 25
SPEED LIMIT 30
SPEED LIMIT 35

CITY WILL FIGHT MOVE TO TAKE AWAY HOMETOWN COURT

A move at the state level that would eliminate municipal courts and turn their business over to a county court system will be bitterly fought by Plantation city officials.

There are a lot of reasons for the opposition, but one of the main ones is the fear that a county court system would permit creeping mediocrity to come upon the county scene.

Mayor Jack Carter said the elimination of all municipal courts and the handing over of jurisdiction to an enlarged county system would make it necessary for all laws and ordinances to be uniform.

"How," he asked, "could a county judge handle a situation if he had successive cases involving the same violation in Hallandale and in Plantation?

"What might be a violation in one city might not in another, and the penalty for the violation might well differ from city to city.

"At what point would they all be equalized, to keep the county judge from climbing the wall?"

Mayor Carter also expressed concern that since municipal courts handle only misdemeanors, and many of those facing the courts are first offenders, the opportunity for hometown concern would be lost.

"I don't mean letting a friend off the hook," he explained. "I mean the opportunities for notoriety would be greater if every kid on a first offense had to tromp off to the county courthouse to face the judge."

The mayor is not as concerned about the financial rewards of the fines and forfeitures which might be produced by a county court system.

Under the present structure, Plantation last year took in $1[illegible] which was 35 percent above anticipated revenue for the year and 109 percent above the take the previous year.

For the current fiscal year, revenue of $135,[illegible] is estimated.

However, should the county court system be put into effect, he explained, the cities would get back two-thirds of the income produced by cases originating within their boundaries.

So the concern, while there might be an imbalance in revenue between the two systems, is not primarily over the money question.

It's just one more example of taking away the rights of the cities.

"There is a feeling among some mayors," Mayor Carter said, "that there is a trend toward reducing the cities to non-entities.

"The state could wind up with 67 cities instead of 67 counties," he said.

His concern is that many cities now striving to achieve an identity of their own would lose this by being compressed into a total city that would cover every inch of the county.

"Plantation has worked hard through its past administrations to achieve the wonderful image it enjoys, and this administration is going to work just as hard to preserve and improve on it.

"We're going to fight this court thing," he said, individually and through the county and state leagues of cities.

He's not over-concerned that it will go through at least not in the coming session.

"It's the direction things are taking that bothers me," he added.

"It may not go through in the next session but unless we fight it right from the start, what will keep it from going through at a future date?

"And what other rights and prerogatives of the cities might not be eventually lost once the precedent is set?"

Citing the safety of Plantation's residents, Mayor Jack Carter declared war on speeders in the city in 1971. Warnings to obey the speed limits from the Plantation Police Department were added to welcome signs, and the article above appeared in the *Plantation Times* newspaper, warning drivers there would no longer be a "10-mile-per-hour cushion" added to posted speed limits.

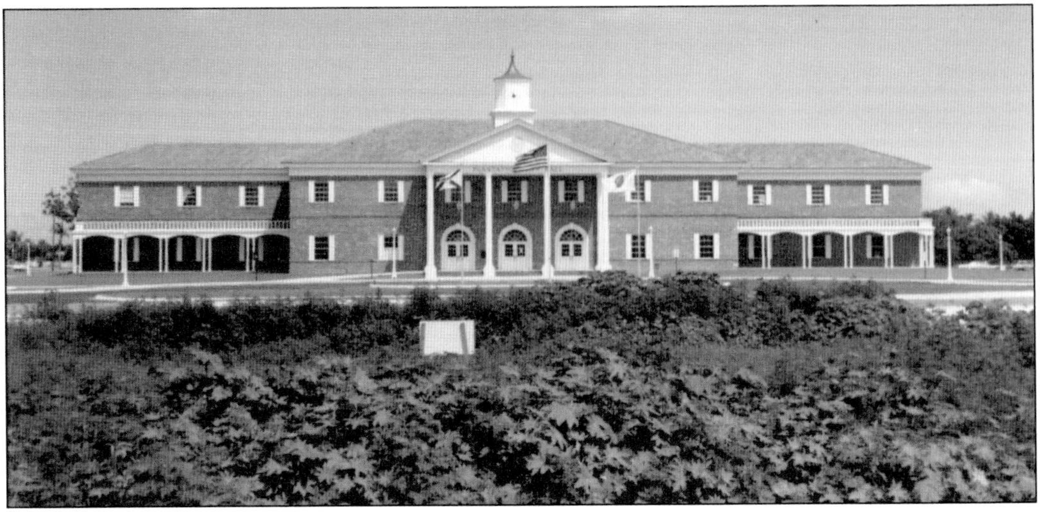

In 1964, the city purchased 12 acres of land adjacent to the police department and city offices on Fifth Street from Frederick C. Peters for $10,000 an acre. Peters generously donated $5,000 an acre back to the city. In 1972, a $1,036,500 bid was accepted to build the New Colonial–style city hall, designed by architect William G. Crawford, on the property. The building was dedicated on December 2, 1973.

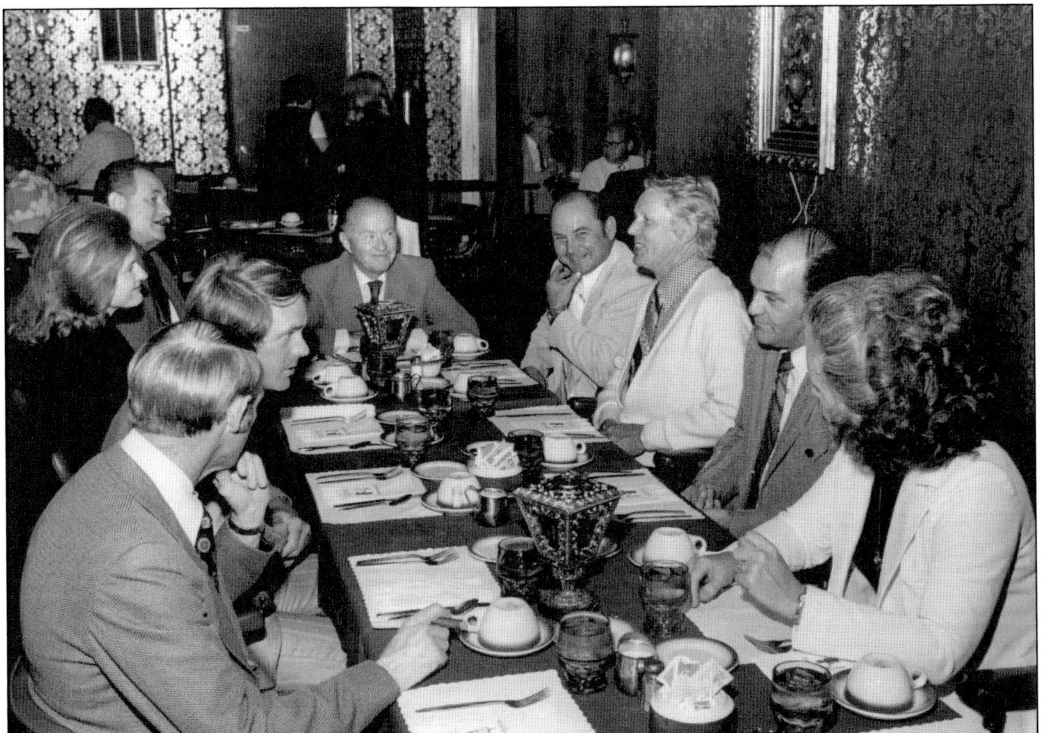

Located on US 441/SR 7 and Northwest Fifth Street, the Gaslight Inn was a restaurant popular with the business lunch crowd. Mayor Jack Carter, seated at the head of the table with city administrator Stu Campbell (on his left) and Bob Blakely of Old Plantation Farms Inc., attend an early 1970s business luncheon.

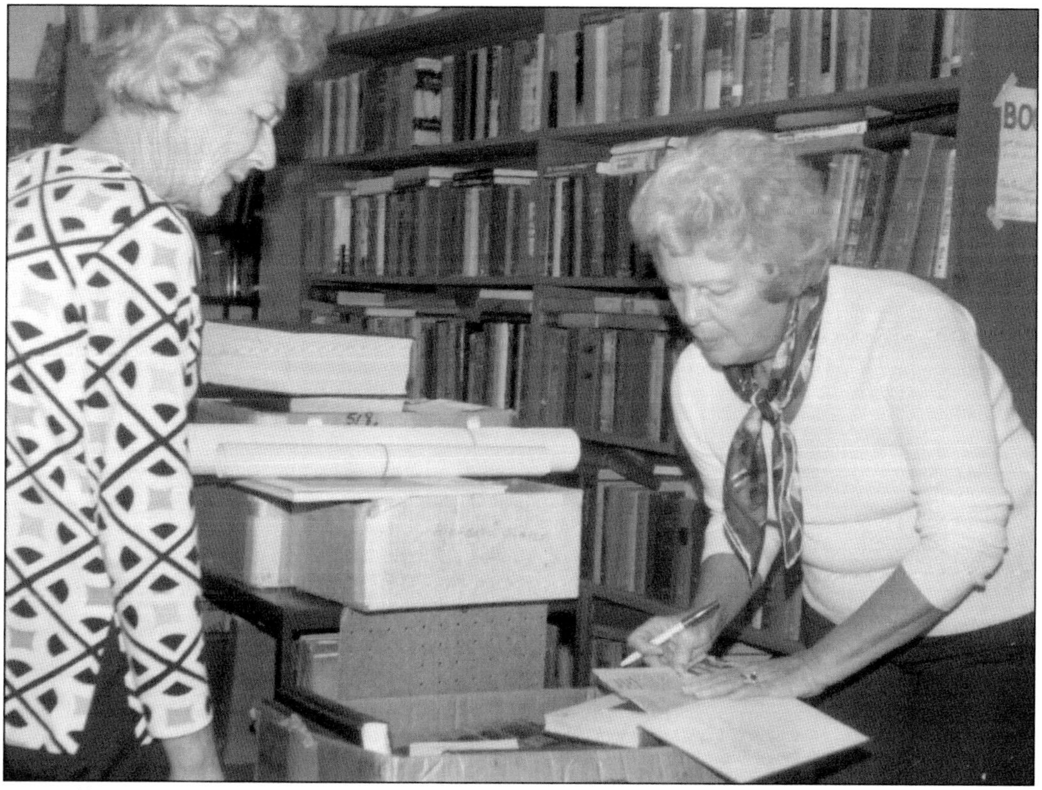

A small group of friends who shared a common interest in books formed the Friends of the Plantation Library on October 22, 1970, to support the growing city library, which moved into its own building on North Fig Tree Lane in 1968. It was expanded in 1974 and 1979. The Friends of the Plantation Library fundraising book sales and luncheons continue to support the library today. Above, Dorothy O'Hare works at a book sale. Below, hostesses at the 1974 Friends of the Library golf tournament and luncheon are, from left to right, Helen Bigney, Estelle Clark, Millie Young, Betsy Foltz, Dorothy O'Hare, and Peg Strickland.

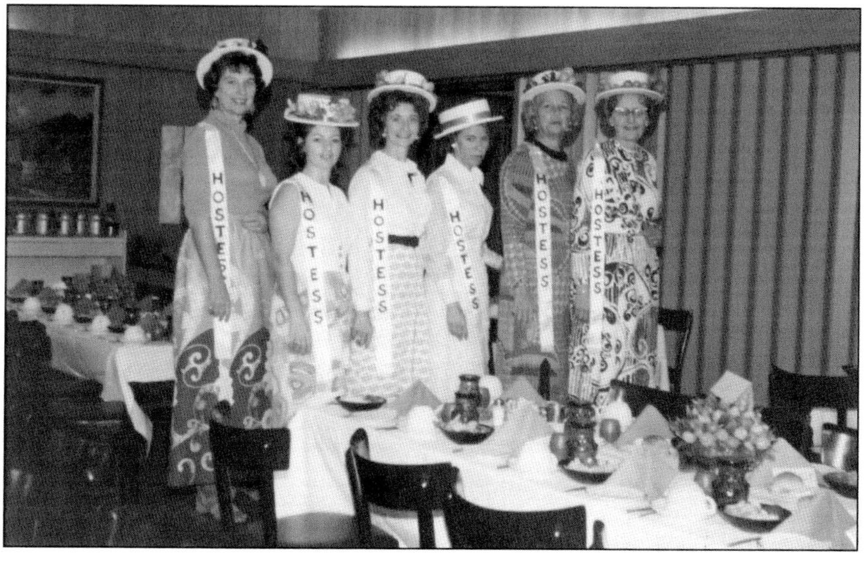

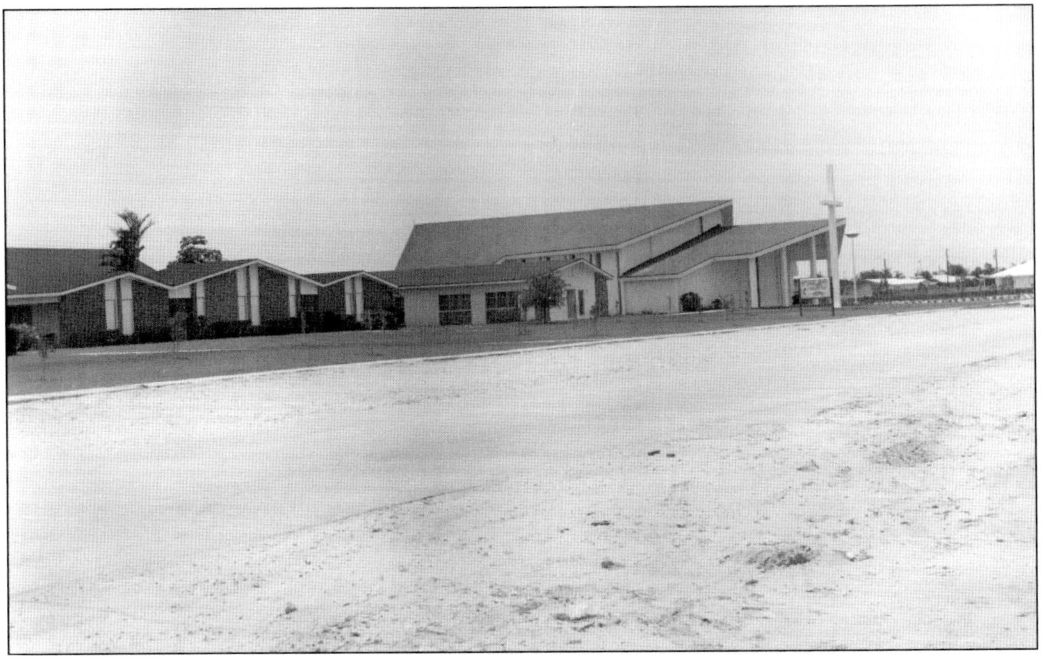

With 155 members, Plantation United Methodist Church opened on February 28, 1960, on Northwest 70th Avenue. Generations of Plantation children started their education in the church's preschool program, which began in 1963. The church is pictured in 1974.

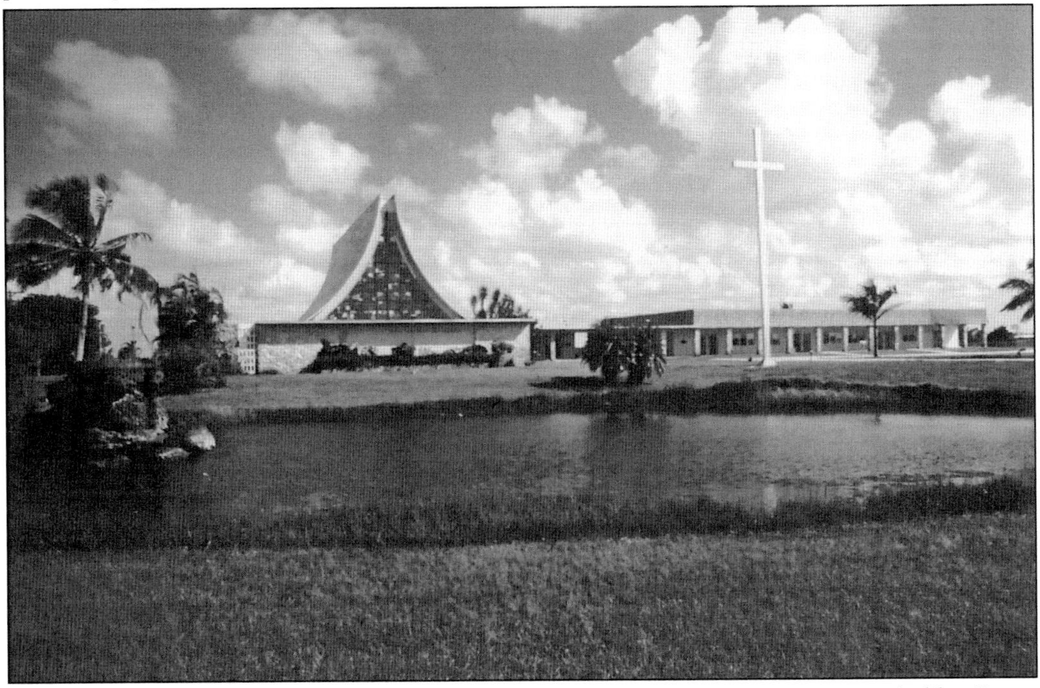

Pastor Robert Grunow founded Our Savior Lutheran Church in 1961. Services were held at Peters Elementary School until the church on Northwest Fifth Street was dedicated on April 8, 1962. The church's school has been serving the Plantation area since 1963, and a new educational wing was added in 1971.

Temple Kol Ami Emanu-El was chartered by the state of Florida in 1975. Rabbi Dr. Sheldon J. Harr was engaged as its first rabbi in June 1976 and continues to serve until his anticipated retirement in June 2013. The temple has grown into a congregation of close to 1,000 families. Rabbi Harr is pictured at the 1977 ground breaking on Peters Road.

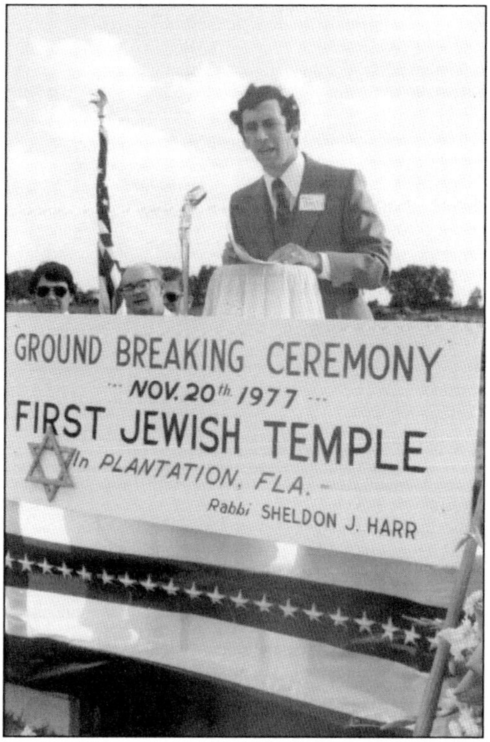

Valencia Retirement Center was constructed in 1970 on West Broward Boulevard. Covenant Retirement Communities purchased the facility and opened Covenant Village of Florida in 1977. The 20-acre community features both active and passive lifestyles for seniors.

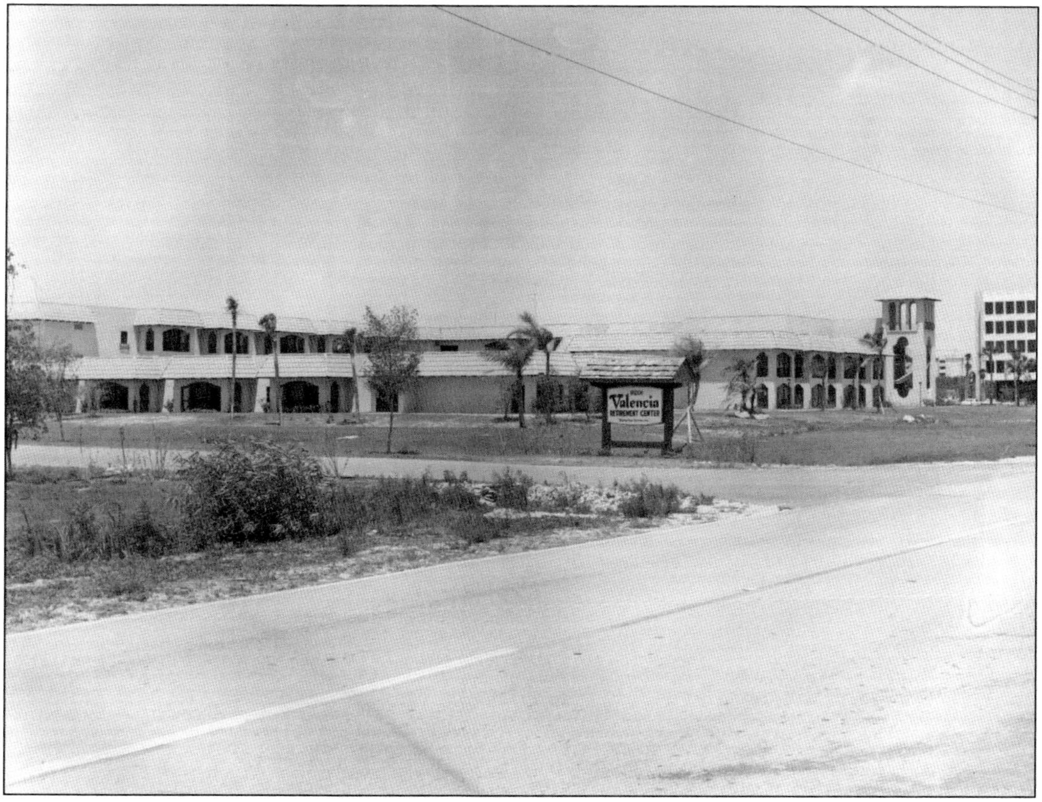

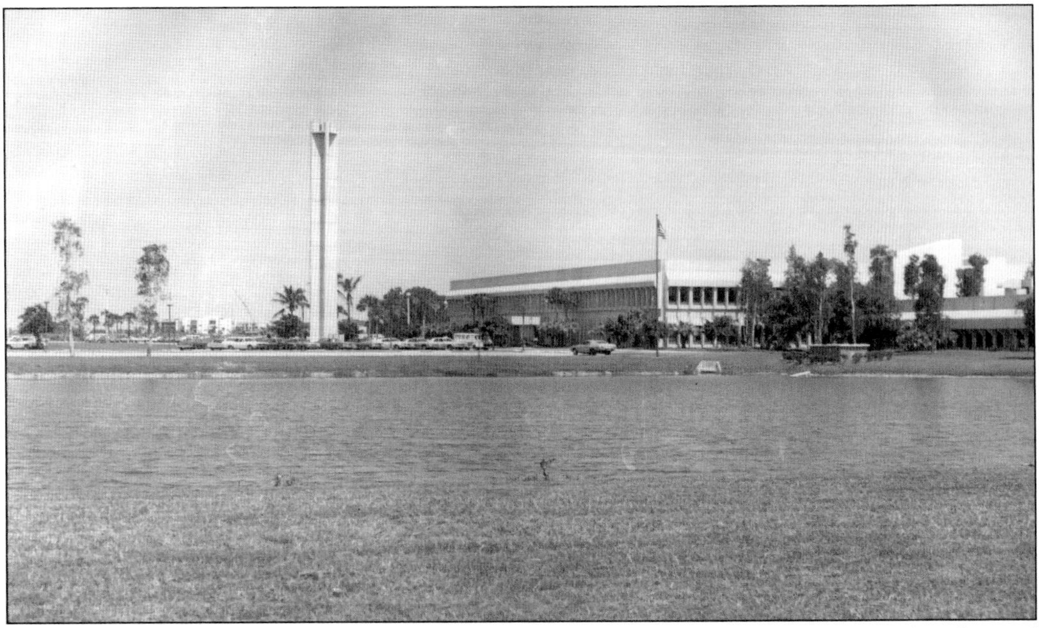

Motorola, pictured here in 1974, began construction on its new 240,000-square-foot plant located on Sunrise Boulevard and University Drive in 1969. A one-ton granite boulder from Motorola's Illinois headquarters was placed on the site "symbolizing a permanent foundation for Motorola's continued growth in Florida."

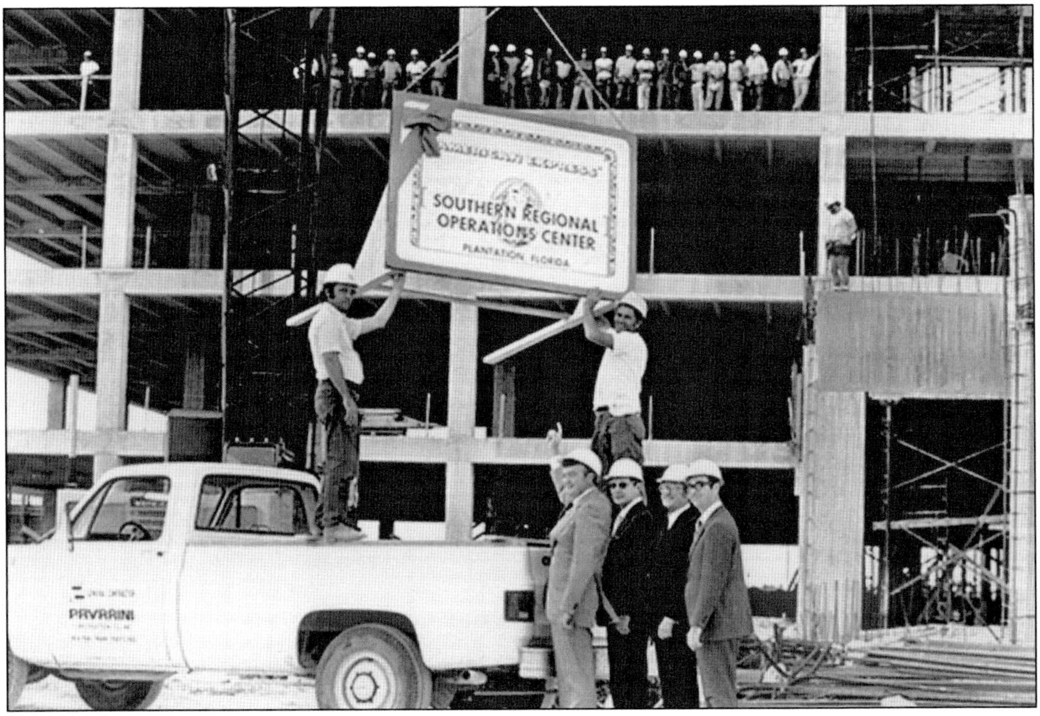

American Express opened its 50-acre Southern Regional Operation Center in 1975 on Cleary Boulevard and Pine Island Road and continues to be one of Plantation's largest employers. (Courtesy of Florida Memory Project.)

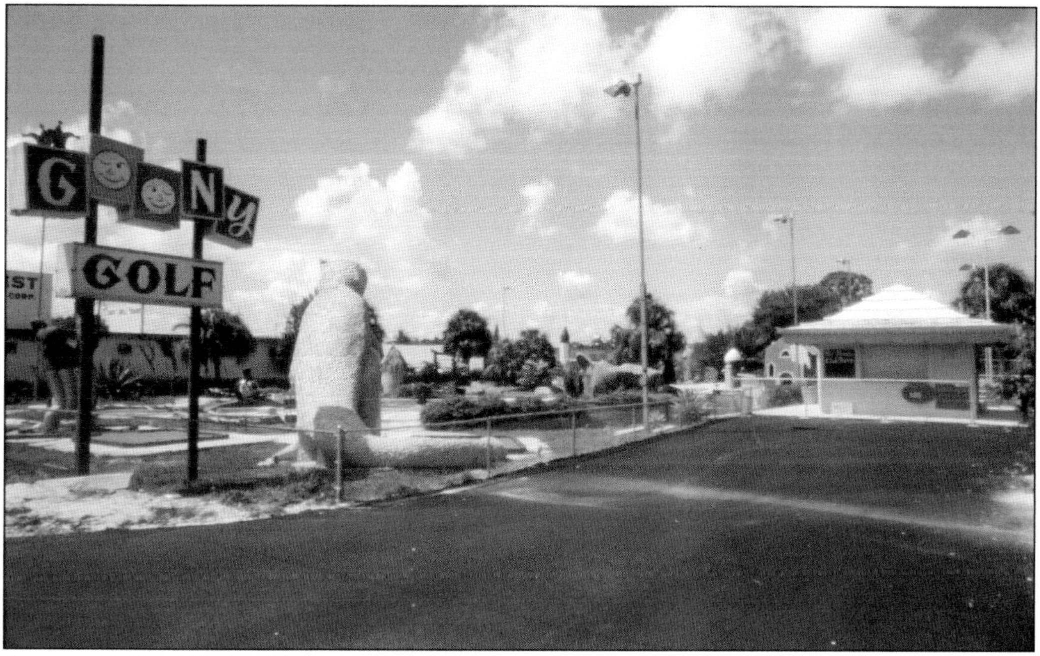

Gooney Golf on US 441/SR 7 was a popular destination for Plantation families in the 1970s. The state-of-the-art miniature golf course included animated dinosaurs and a chance to win a free game at the final skee-ball hole. The large, yellow tyrannosaurus rex was a unique landmark for residents giving directions.

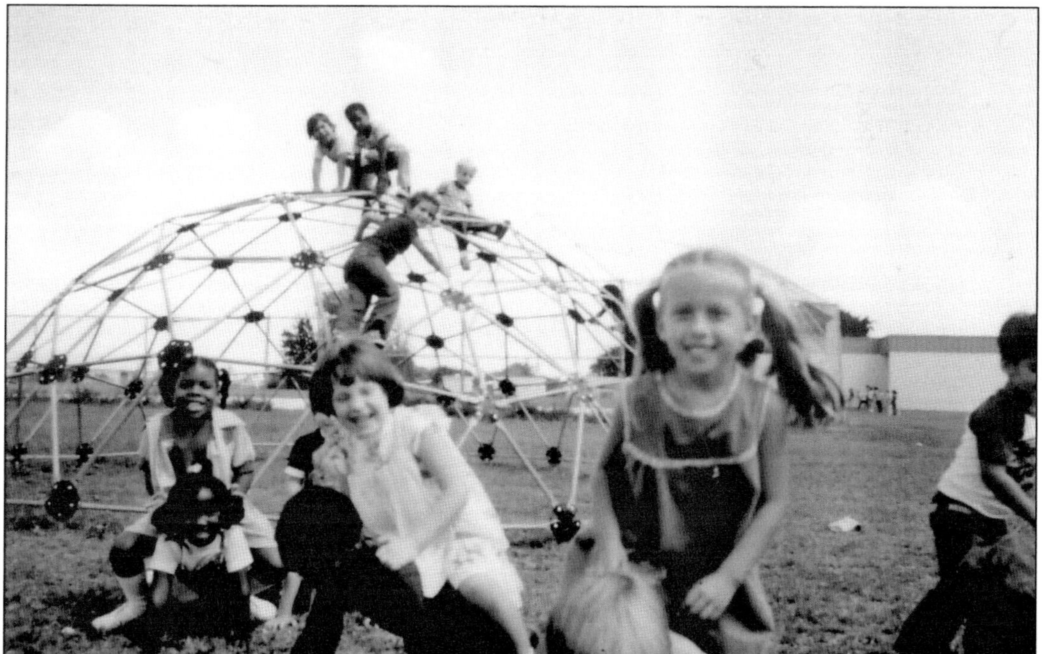

This 1978 photograph shows students at Peters Elementary School, Plantation's first school, enjoying recess on the playground. The school that was named for Berenice Peters, wife of Frederick C. Peters, has been updated and expanded several times since opening in 1959.

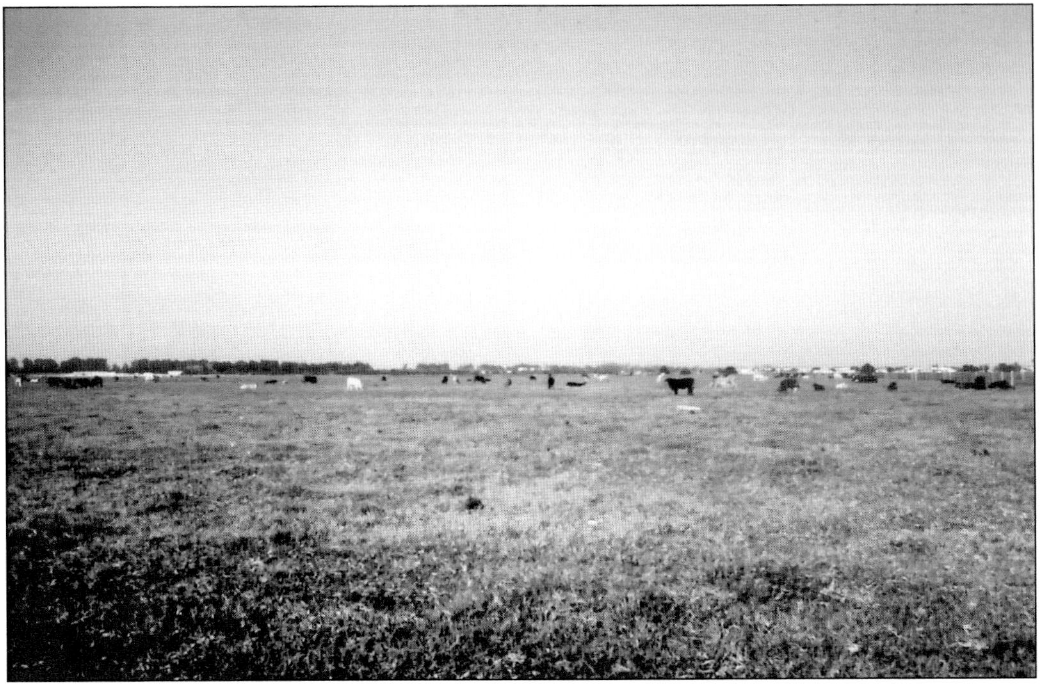

Once the site of cow pastures, the Broward Mall opened on University Drive on August 10, 1978. At the time, it was the largest mall in the southeastern United States. The mall was acquired by Westfield Group in 2007 and underwent a multi-million-dollar renovation and was renamed Westfield Broward.

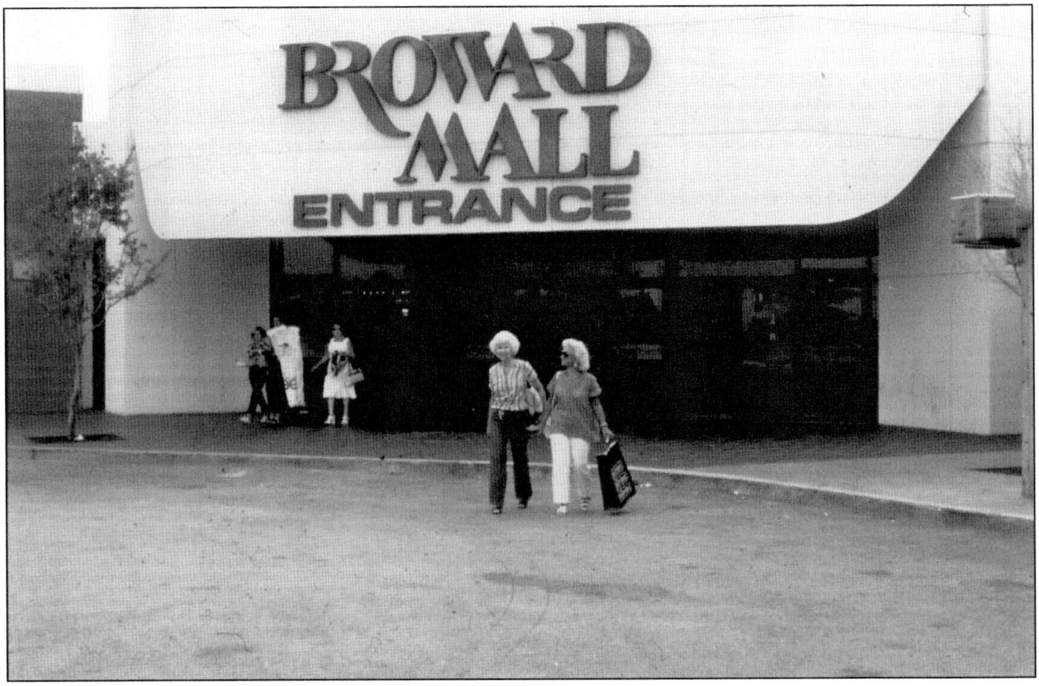

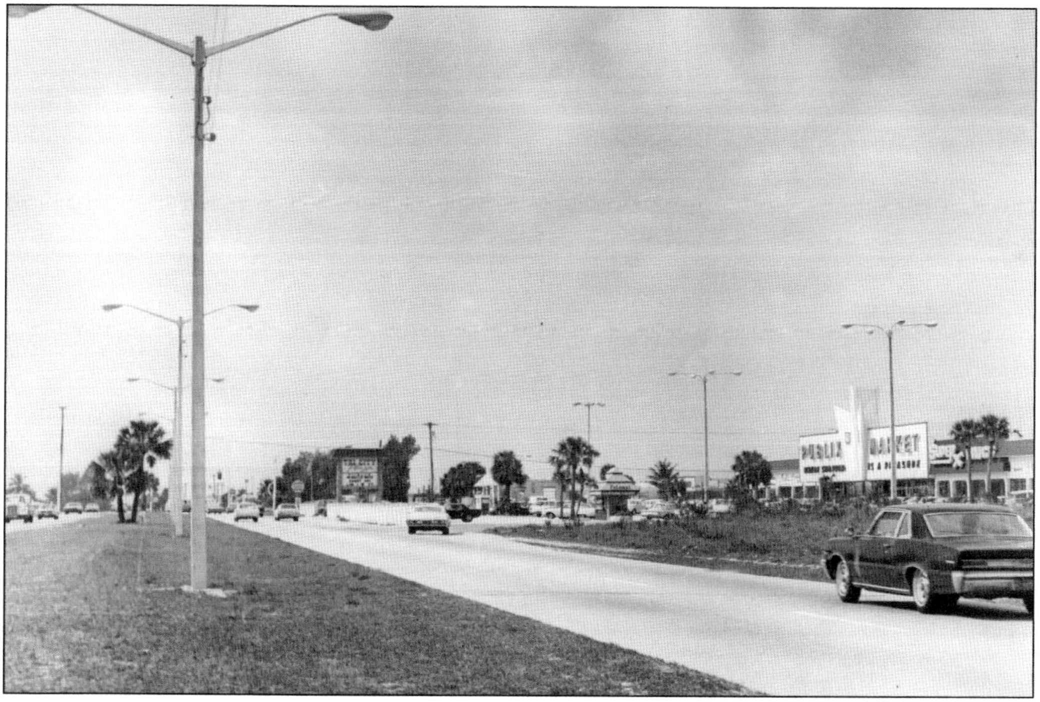

The Tri City Plaza, pictured in the 1970s, on West Sunrise Boulevard, was named for the three cities surrounding it: Plantation, Sunrise, and Lauderhill. Once anchored by a Publix Super Market, the plaza is now home to a Neighbors IGA Market.

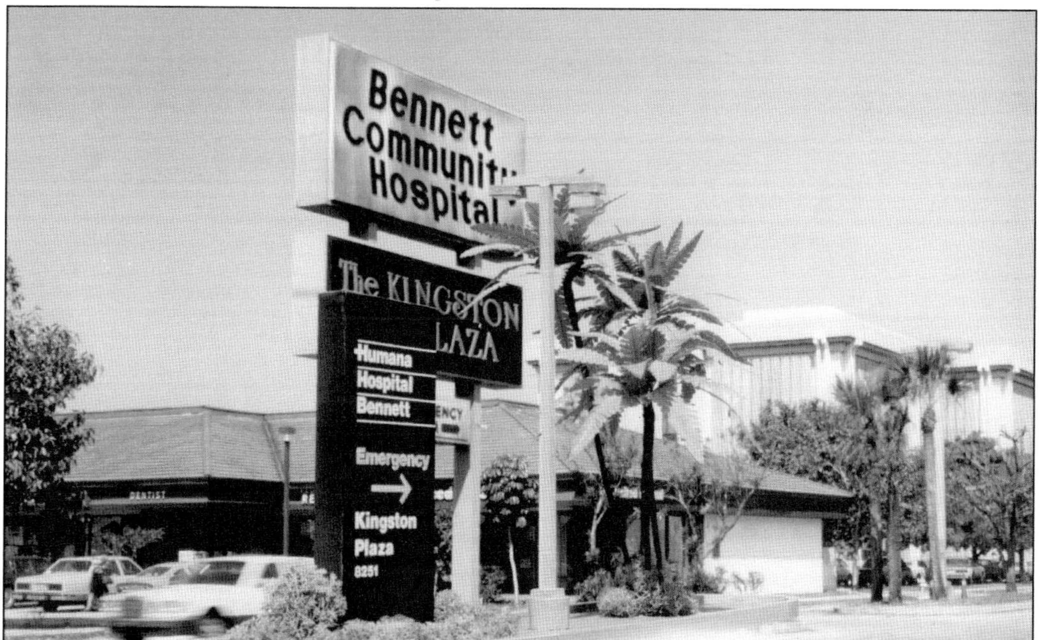

Bennett Community Hospital was dedicated December 8, 1974. The hospital was named for Dr. Grant Miles Bennett, a Plantation physician, who died with his wife and infant son in a plane crash in July 1973. The hospital became Westside Regional Medical Center in 1993.

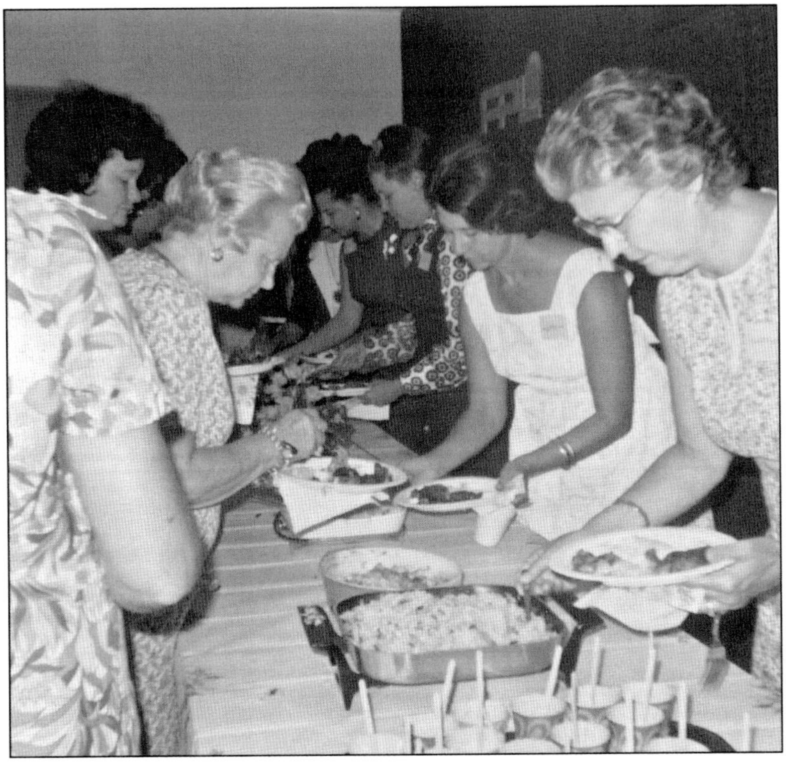

The Plantation Woman's Club, the oldest civic organization in the city, continues to meet monthly at Deicke Auditorium. In the image at left, the ladies are enjoying a potluck luncheon.

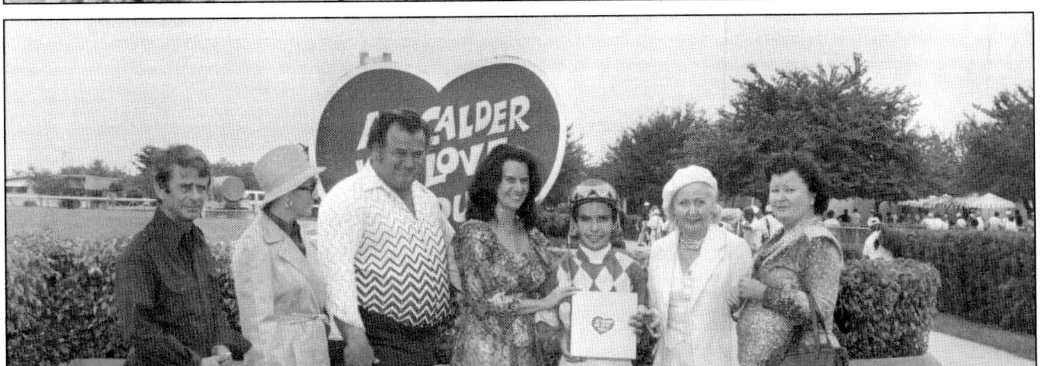

"A Day at the Races" was a popular club fundraiser held annually at Calder Race Course. Pictured here are, from left to right, horse owners Nathan and Barbara Kelly; trainer G. Stidham; unidentified guest; jockey William Rodriguez; Plantation Woman's Club member Ruth Miller, and club president Eleanor Armitage on November 9, 1978.

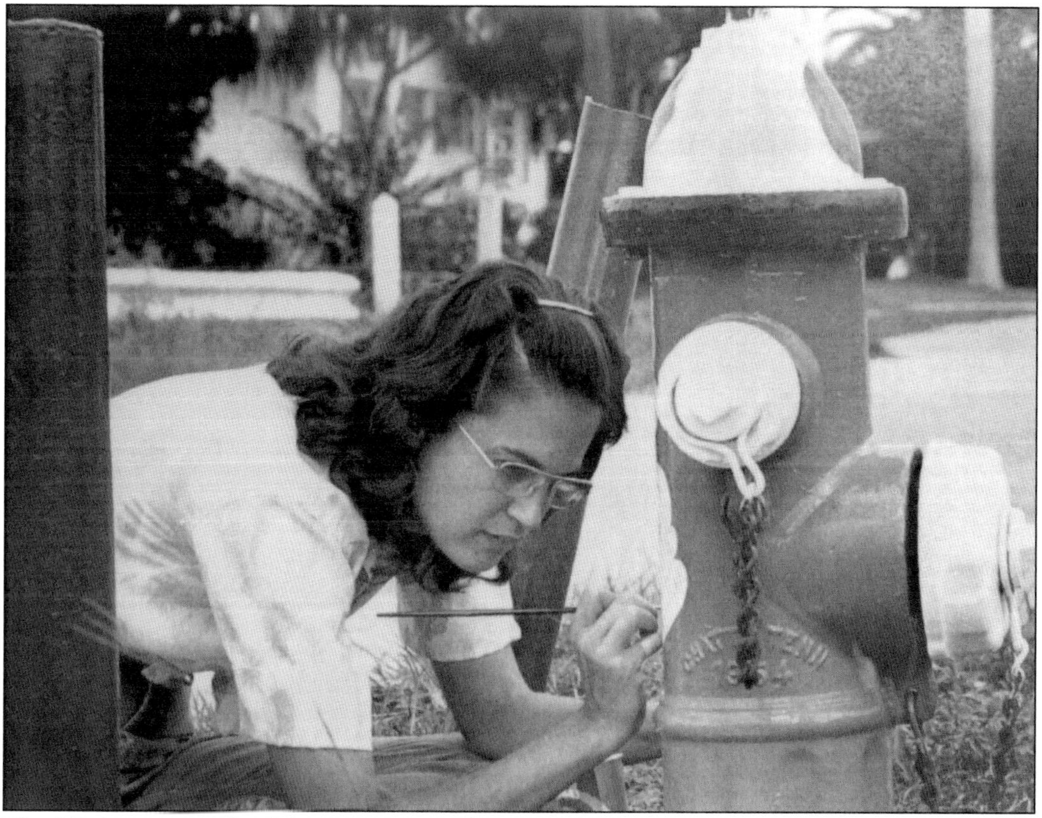

The US bicentennial celebration in 1976 began with a reenactment of Paul Revere's ride and "the shot heard 'round the world" at city hall. Other festivities included concerts, the traditional Fourth of July parade, and the planting of a tree symbolizing the original Liberty Tree at Fifth Street Park. Volunteer Kay Ellington is pictured above painting a patriotic theme on a hydrant during the yearlong national celebration.

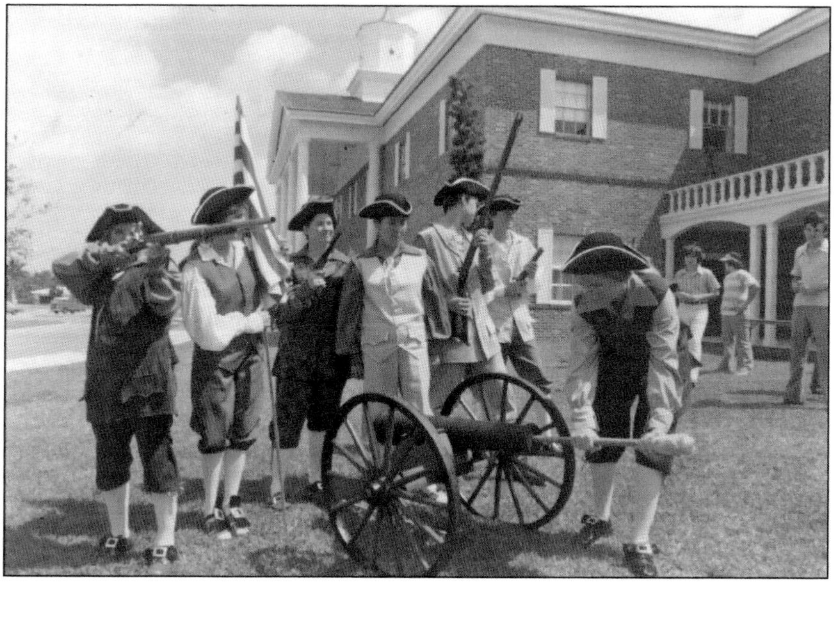

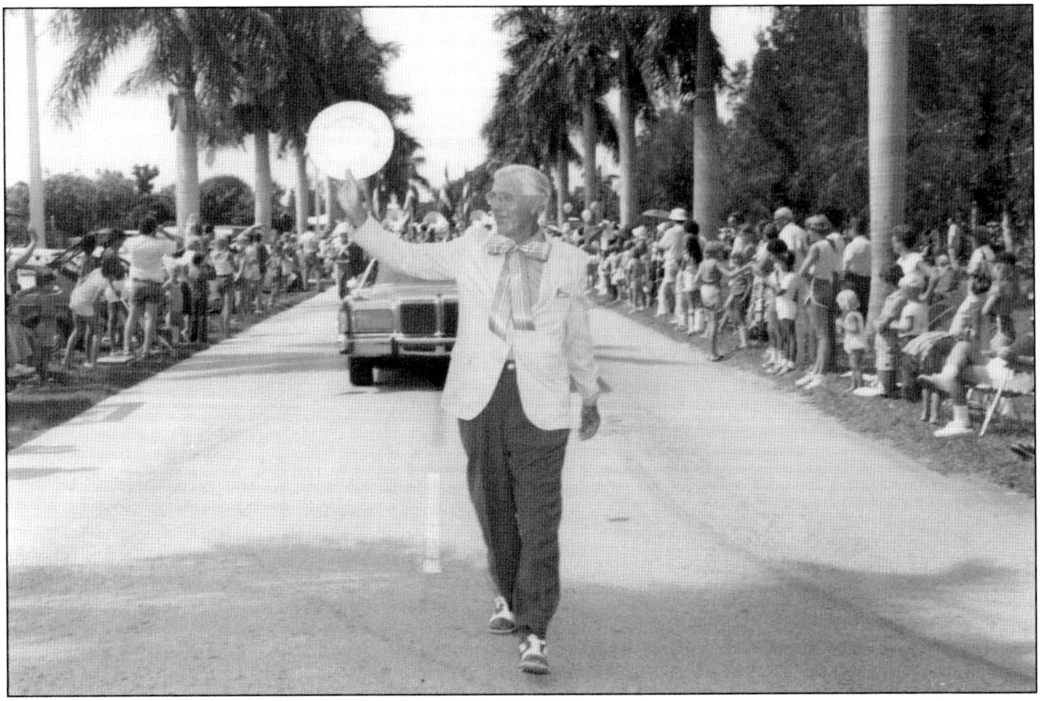

From Plantation's beginning, residents have gathered to celebrate Independence Day with picnics, parades, and neighborhood celebrations. For 24 years, Mayor Frank Veltri led the Fourth of July parade on foot. Pictured here in 1978, he is wearing his famous red, white, and blue shoes. Below, the Plantation Elks present a prize-winning float complete with bathing beauties at the Fourth of July parade in 1979.

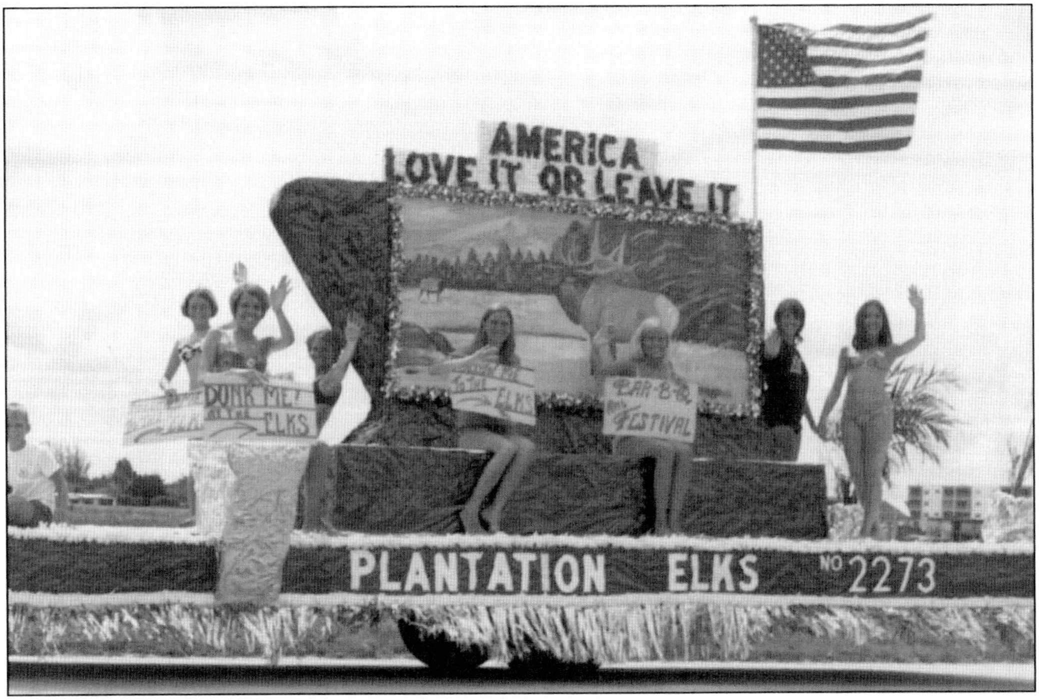

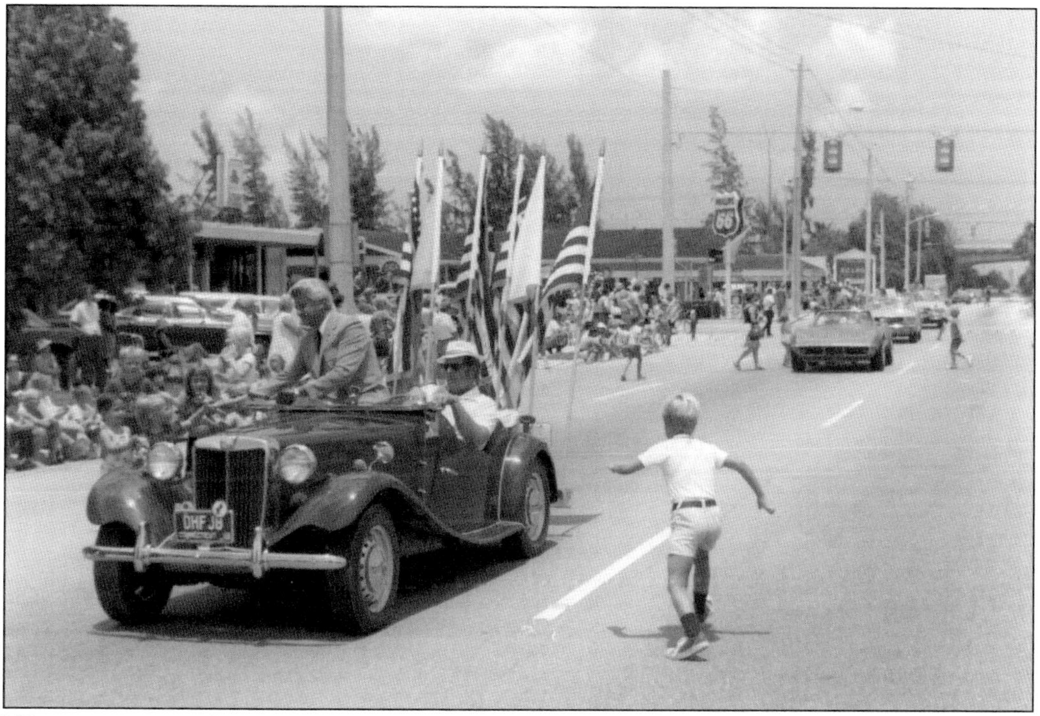

US representative from Florida, Edward John Stack, grand marshal of the 1976 Fourth of July parade, throws candy to eager children along Broward Boulevard just west of East Acre Drive (above). Plantation's Fourth of July parade traditionally ends at city hall with an awards ceremony. Pictured below in 1979 are, from left to right, Mayor Frank Veltri, Genevieve Veltri, Lois Deicke, and Edwin Deicke, grand marshal.

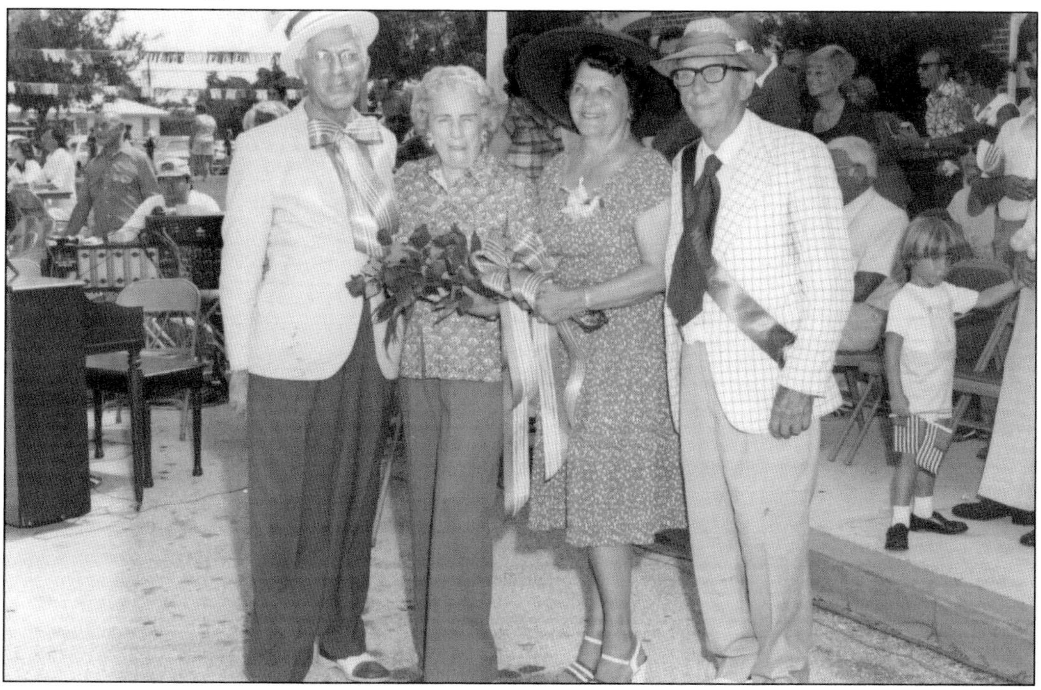

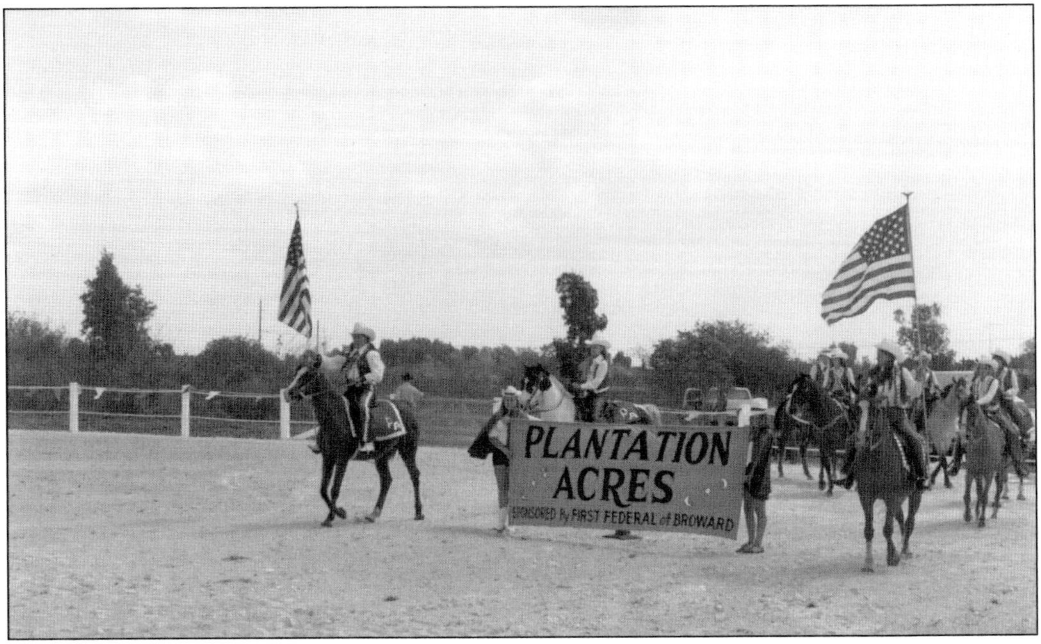

The Plantation Historical Society was selected to plan the city's 25th anniversary in 1978. The Plantation Silver Anniversary Celebration featured three days of events, including band and chorus concerts, barbershop singers, square dancing, a puppet show, and a commemorative church service at the Plantation Community Church. Shown above is the Horse Arena in Plantation Acres. The arena's dedication and horse show were part of the festivities.

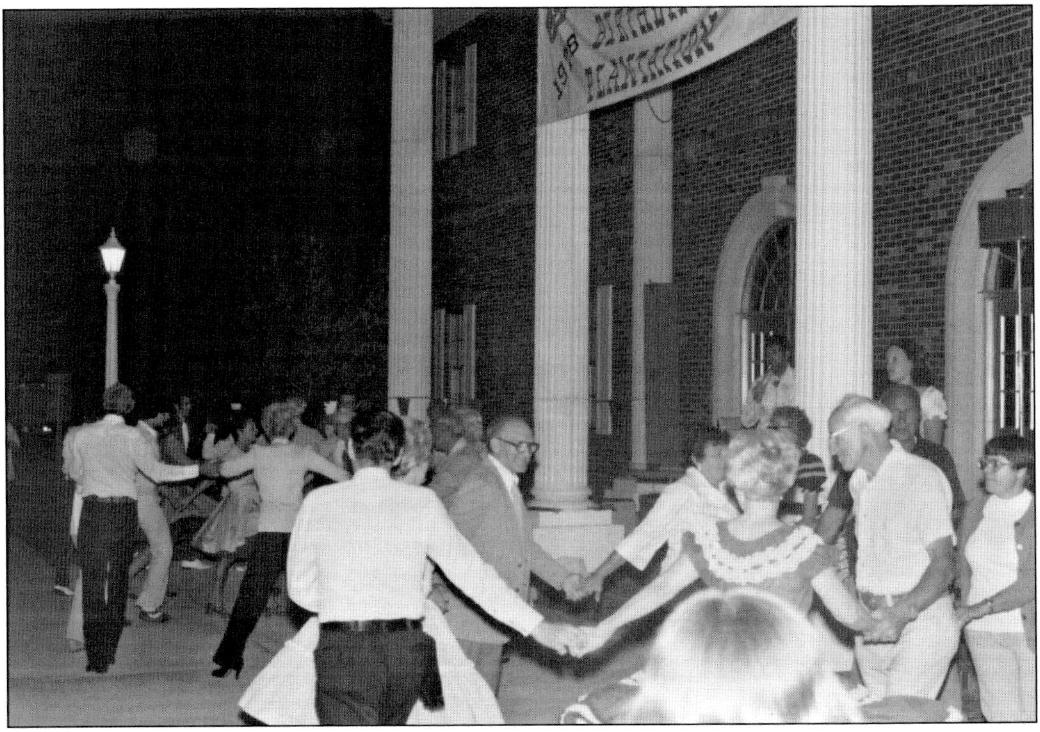

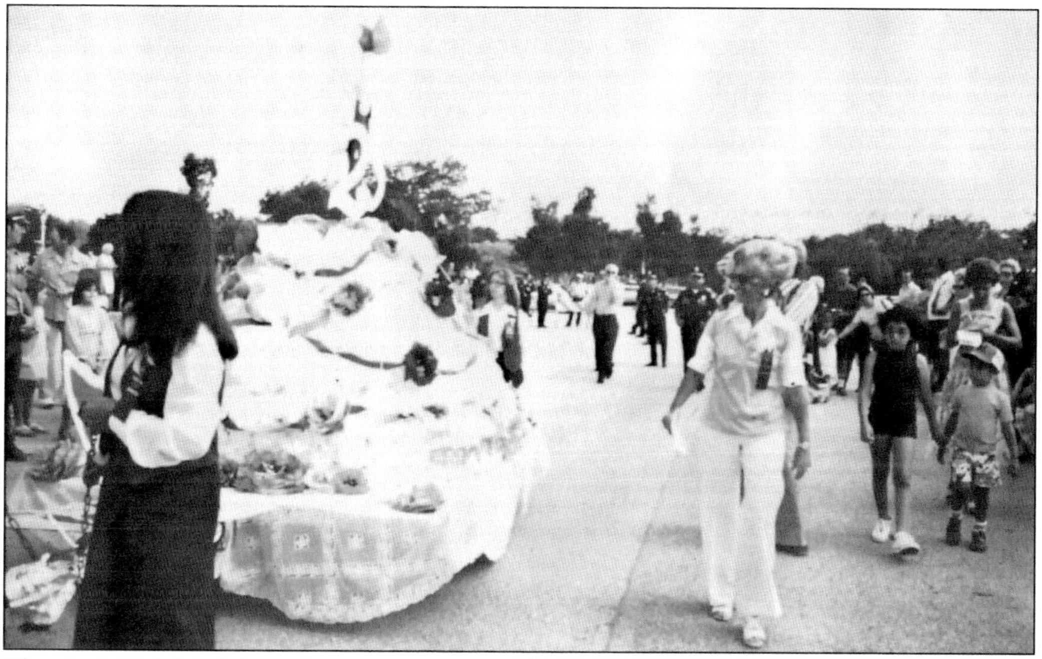

The city's 25th birthday cake was constructed by Plantation High School seniors, under the direction of Plantation Historical Society member Phyllis Napp (pictured right of cake). When the cake popped open, 25 white doves were to fly out. As doves were unavailable, 100 pigeons were placed inside the cake. It was mating season, and when the cake opened, none of the birds wanted to leave. A police officer had to climb aboard and encourage them with his cap. Included in the bicentennial celebration was a cornerstone ceremony held at city hall on July 4, 1976. Pictured below with the stone are, from left to right, Councilman Ralph Merritt III; Judge John Camilla, presenting the stone; Mayor Frank Veltri, setting the stone; Dorothy O'Hare; Genevieve Veltri; and Larry Abbate, cornerstone donor.

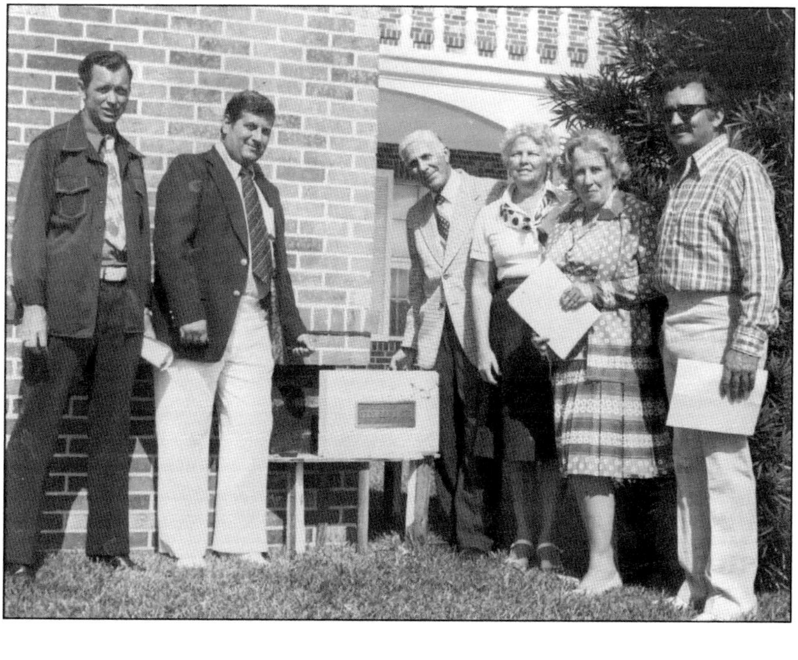

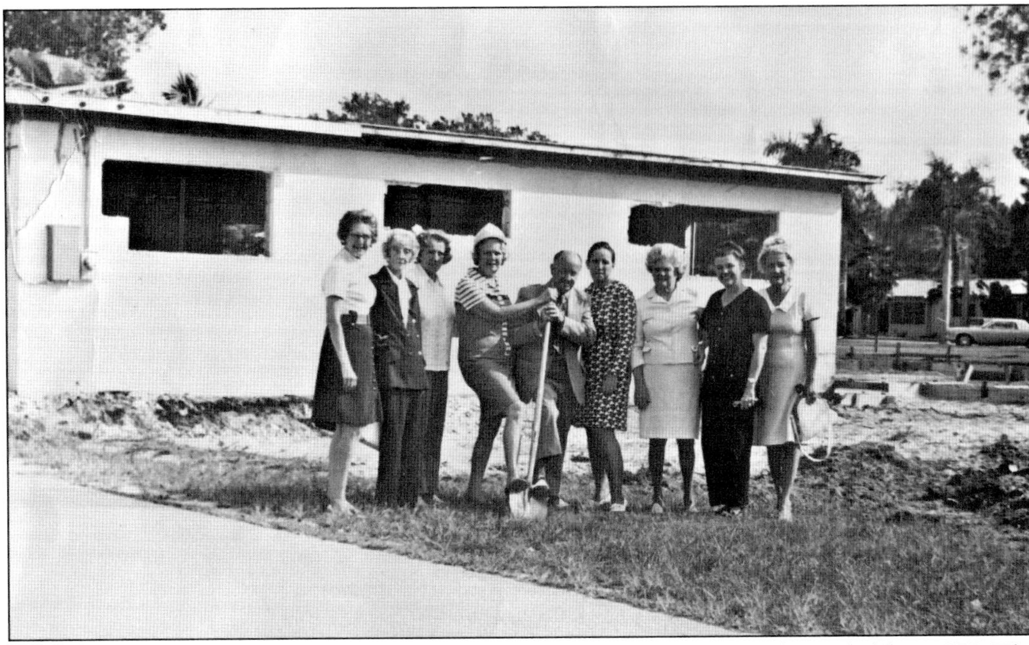

The ground breaking ceremony for Deicke Auditorium at Hoffman Park was held in 1972. The building in the background, the original community center for residents during the city's early years, was incorporated into the new building and is currently the small-meeting room west of the central foyer. Pictured are, from left to right, Peg Strickland, Edna Armstrong, Genevieve Veltri, Dottie O'Hare, Mayor Jack Carter, Donna Gilmore, Bertha Brisch, Betty Cobb, and Ruth Miller.

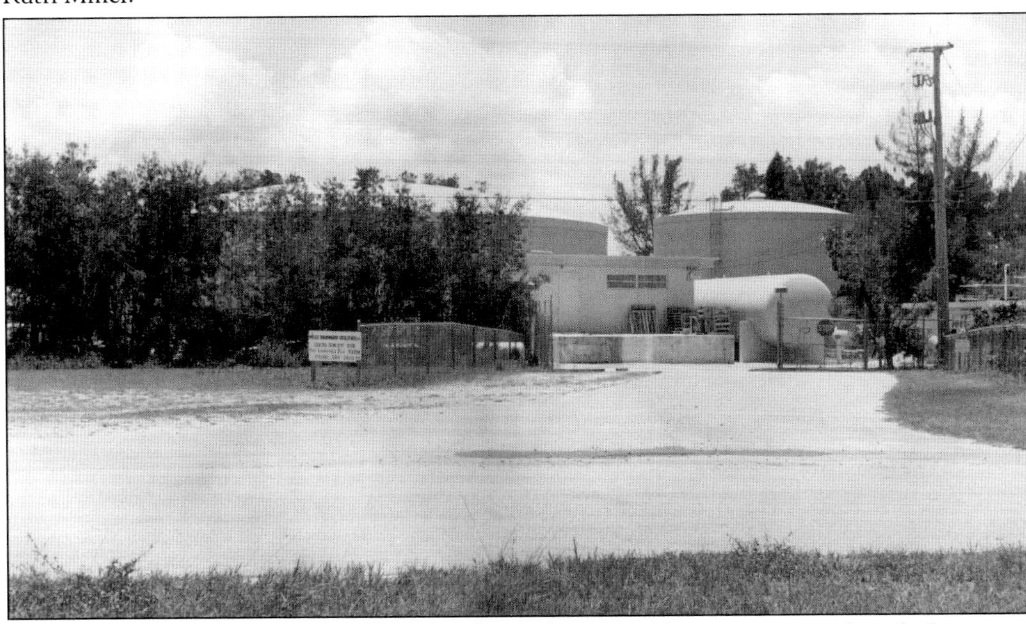

In 1974, city council authorized $10.5 million of water and sewer revenue bonds for system improvements. Additional bonds were issued to pay $3.5 million for West Broward Utilities, which operated utilities in the Plantation Acres, Melaleuca Isles, and areas west and south of the city covering approximately 19 square miles.

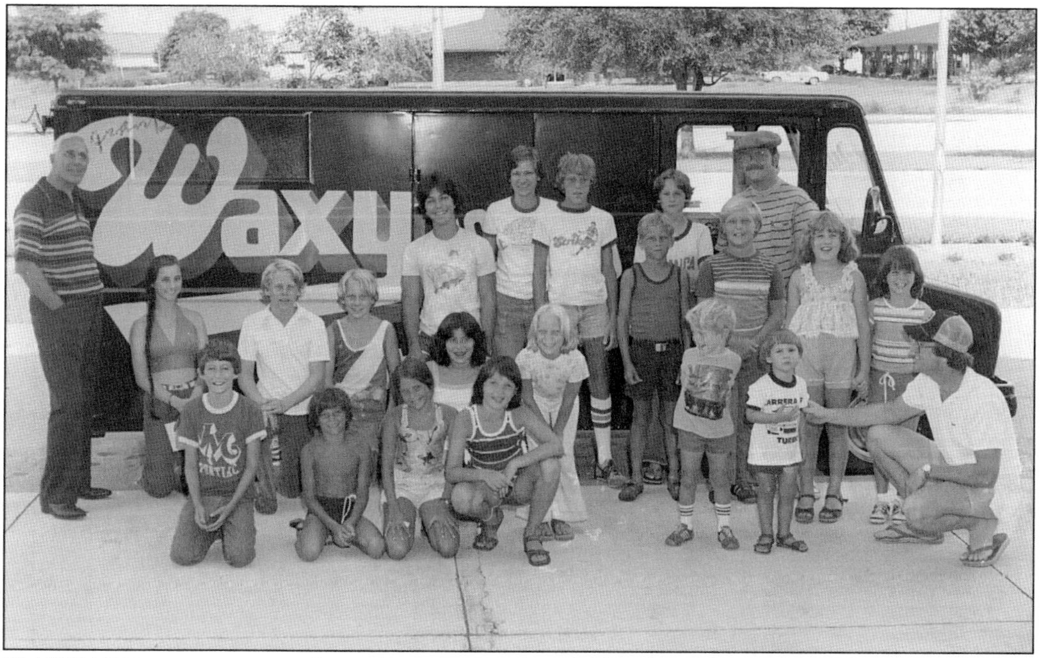

WAXY 105.9 was a very popular radio station in South Florida in the 1970s with a Top 40 format. Mayor Frank Veltri is pictured here in 1975 with local children and the WAXY radio van at city hall.

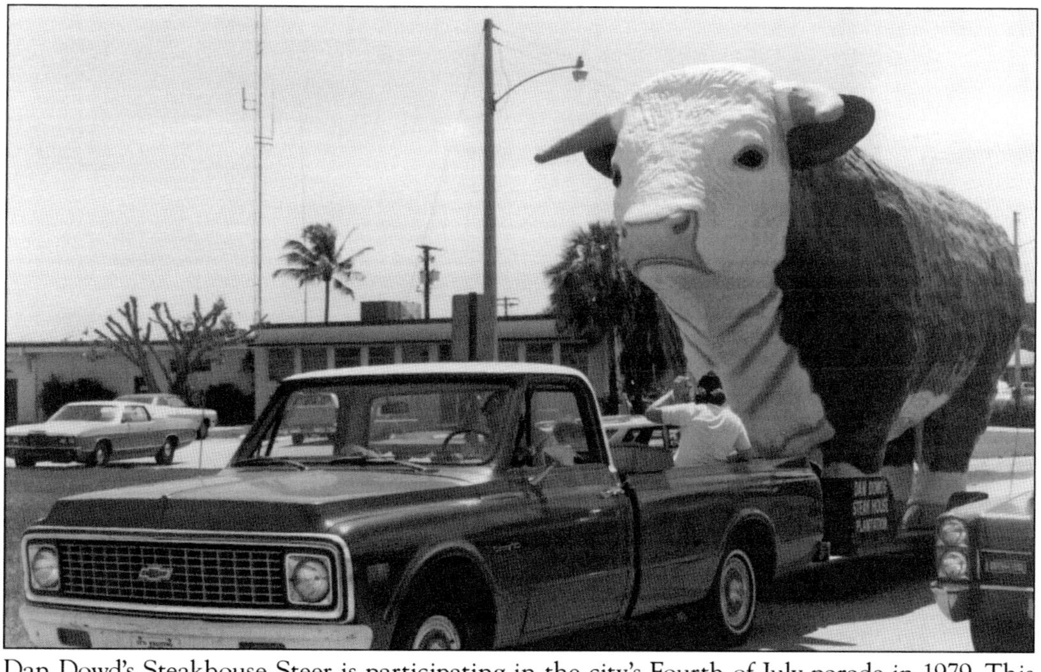

Dan Dowd's Steakhouse Steer is participating in the city's Fourth of July parade in 1979. This noble steer made its public debut in the 1961 Macy's Thanksgiving Day Parade. The owner of Dan Dowd's Restaurant and Meat Market on US 441/SR 7 purchased it for $3,000 and parked it outside the restaurant. The steer, an attractive target for pranksters since it was mounted on wheels, was forever showing up in front yards, parking lots, and even at Plantation High School.

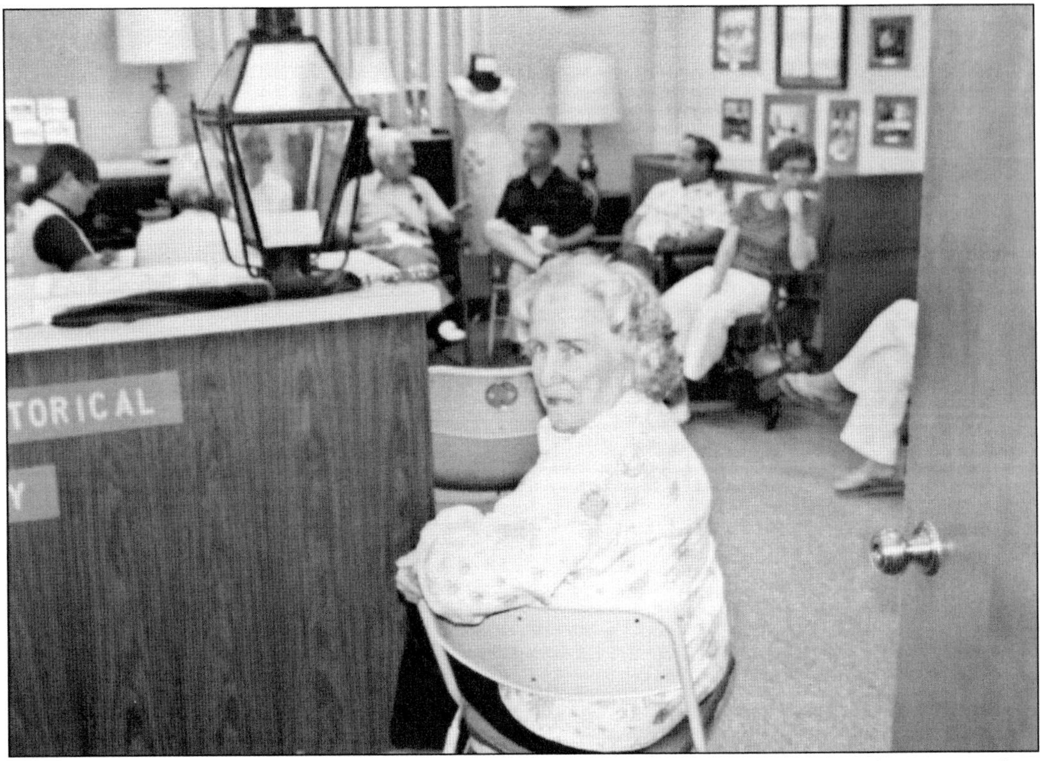

The Plantation Historical Society found a home at city hall while funds were being raised to build a permanent museum on the property behind the Helen B. Hoffman Plantation Library on Fig Tree Lane. Pictured above at a society meeting in the "mini museum" in October 1979 are, from left to right, (foreground) Genevieve Veltri; (background) Clarence Strickland, Bill Allen, R. Woodward, and Carolyn Woodward. Pictured below are, from foreground and then from left to right, Dottie O'Hare, Barbara Hoeltzel, Helen Bigney, Beverly Grant, Jean Hanes, and Ginny Allen.

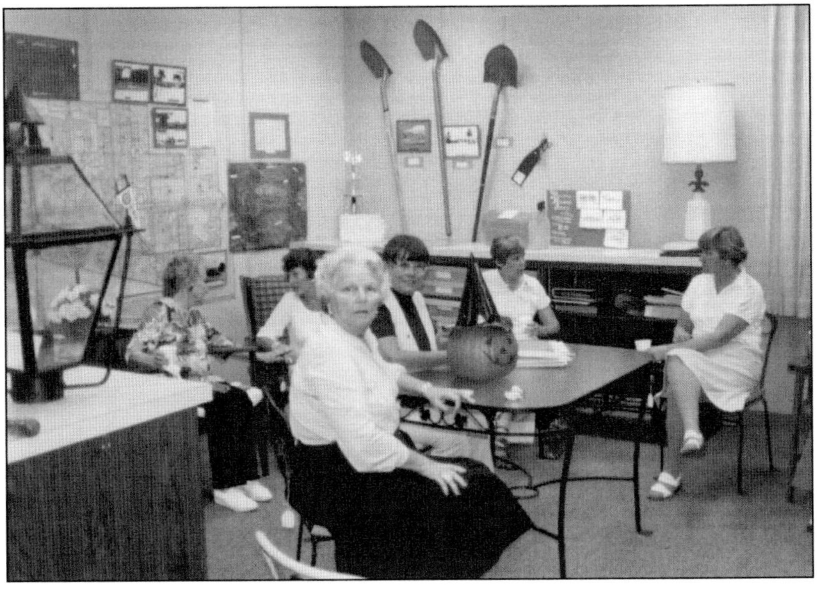

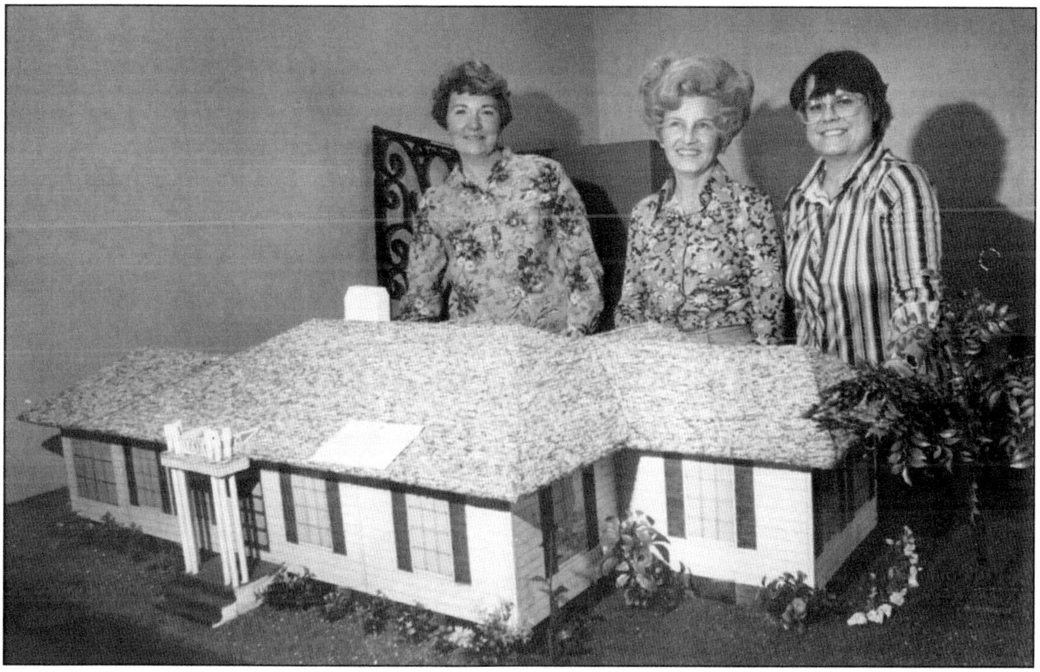

In 1979, the Plantation Historical Society attempted to move the summer home of Frederick C. Peters from the north side of Peters Road to the south side to start a museum. The house had been abandoned for years, and unfortunately, considerable termite damage and the jostling truck ride made it unsalvageable. A few architectural details from the home were salvaged and are on display at the Plantation Historical Museum, which also includes the model of the Peters home pictured above. The model was built by Bill and Jean Hanes and Dan and Beverly Grant. Lois Brickhouse, Phyllis Napp and Beverly Grant are pictured with the model. Pictured below, standing beside their boarded up house, are Frederick T. Peters and his mother, Berenice.

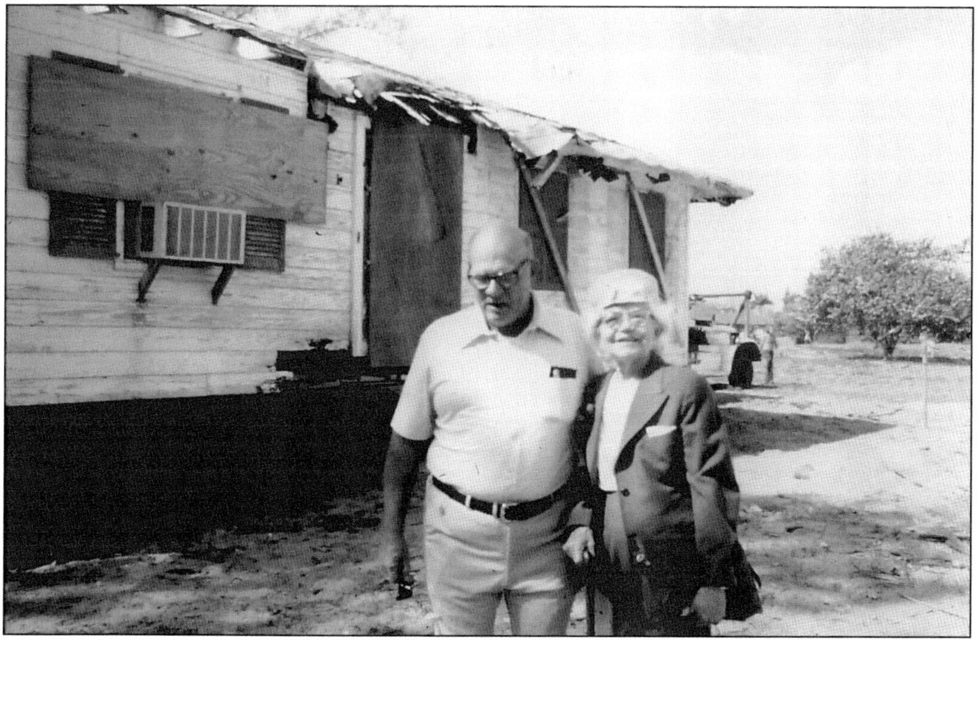

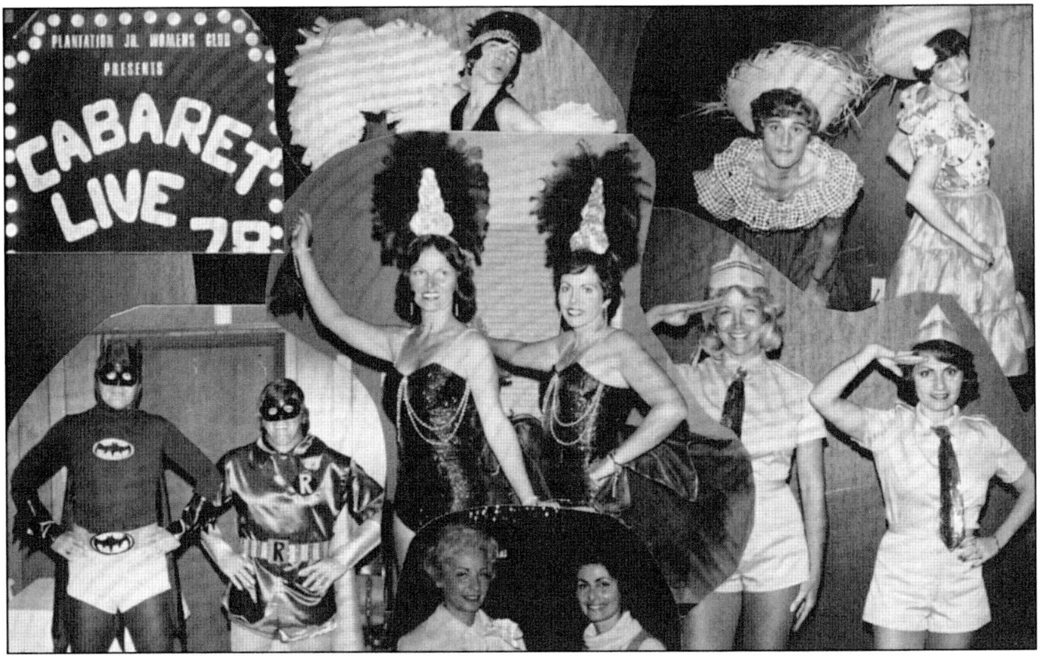

The Plantation Junior Woman's Club organized the first of 21 annual cabaret fundraisers in April 1960. Pictured above is a collage from their "Cabaret Live" in 1978. "Unpollute Plantation Day," an annual clean-up campaign by the Plantation Junior Woman's Club, first began in April 1972. Pictured below in 1977, members wait for residents to drop off unwanted items.

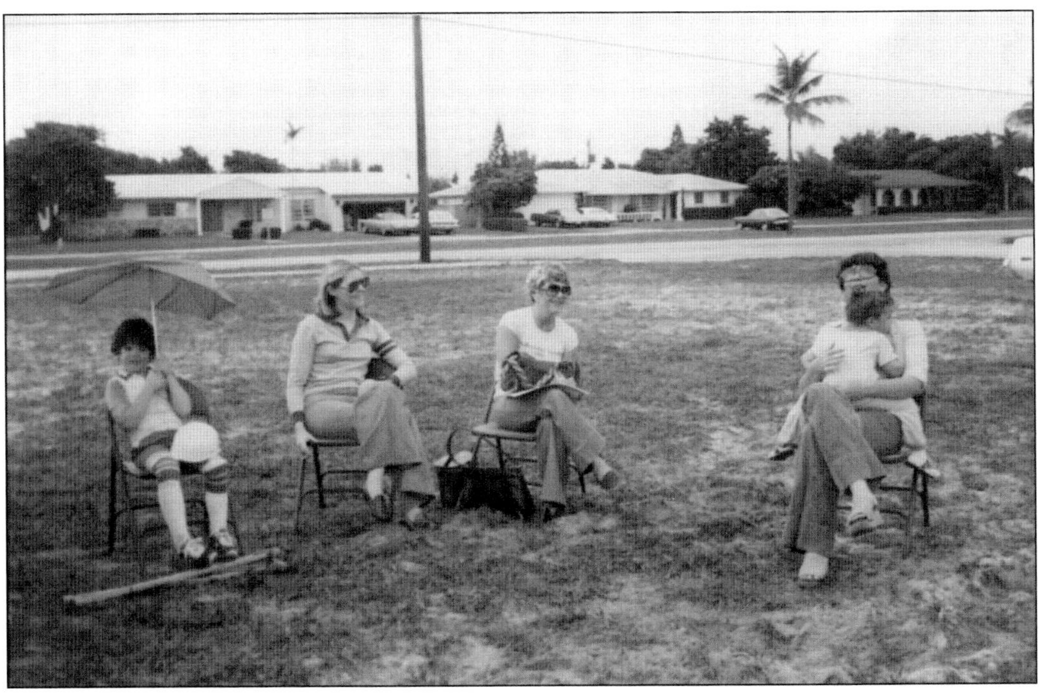

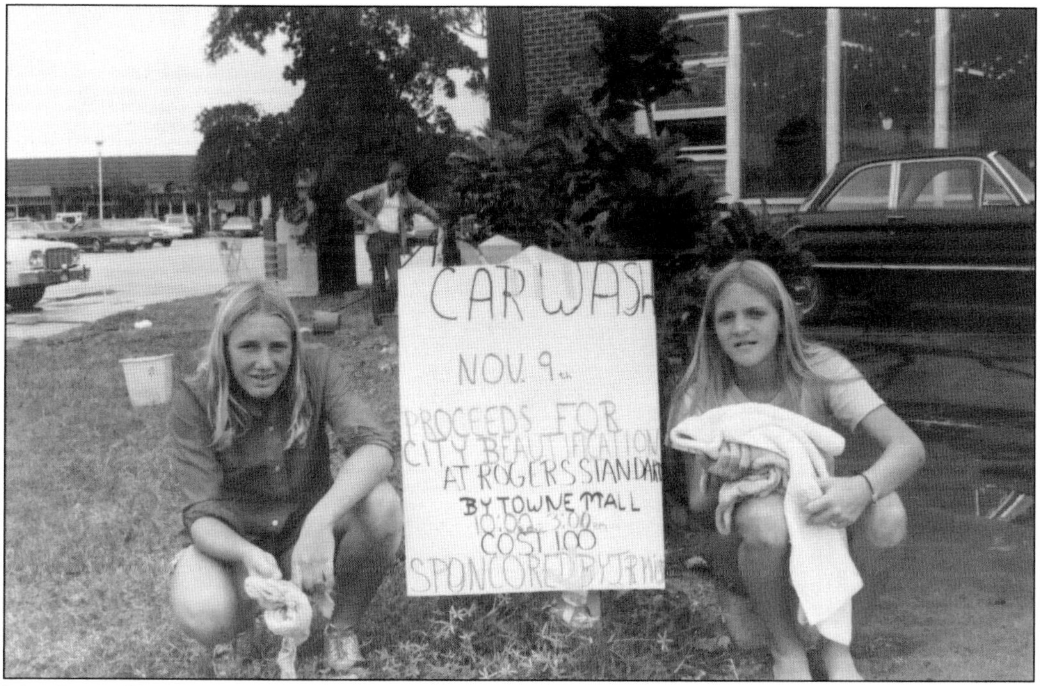

Members of Junior Miss, a group sponsored by the Plantation Junior Woman's Club, hold a $1 car wash fundraiser at Rogers Standard Gas Station near the Towne Mall in 1975.

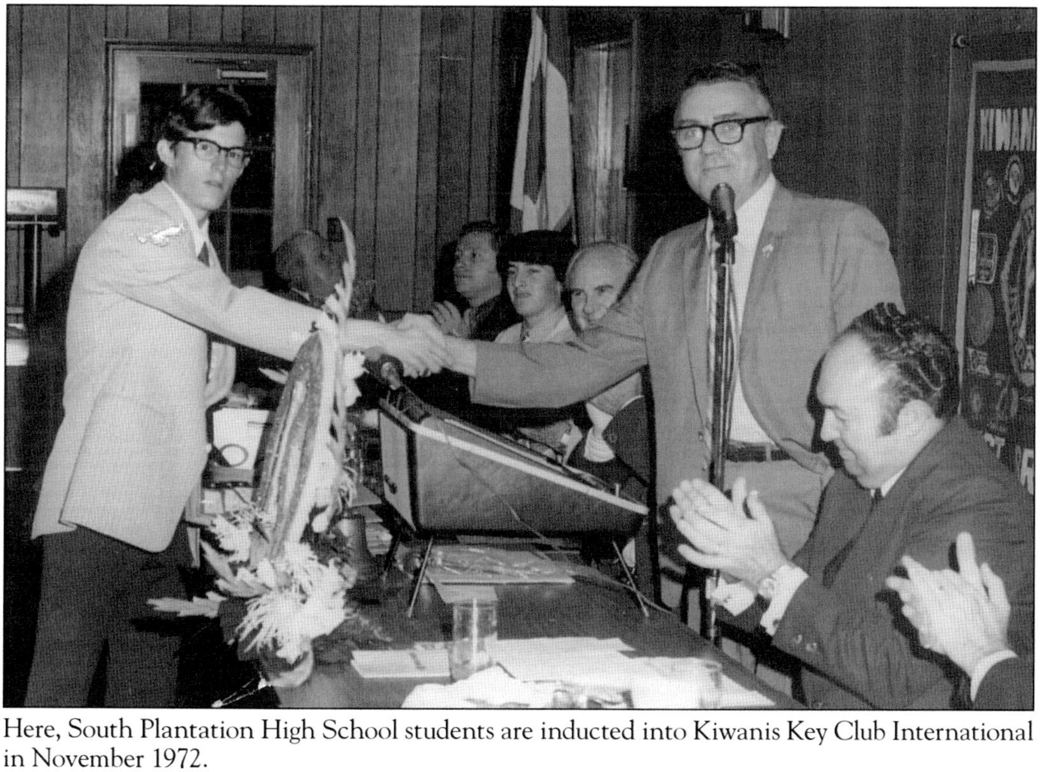

Here, South Plantation High School students are inducted into Kiwanis Key Club International in November 1972.

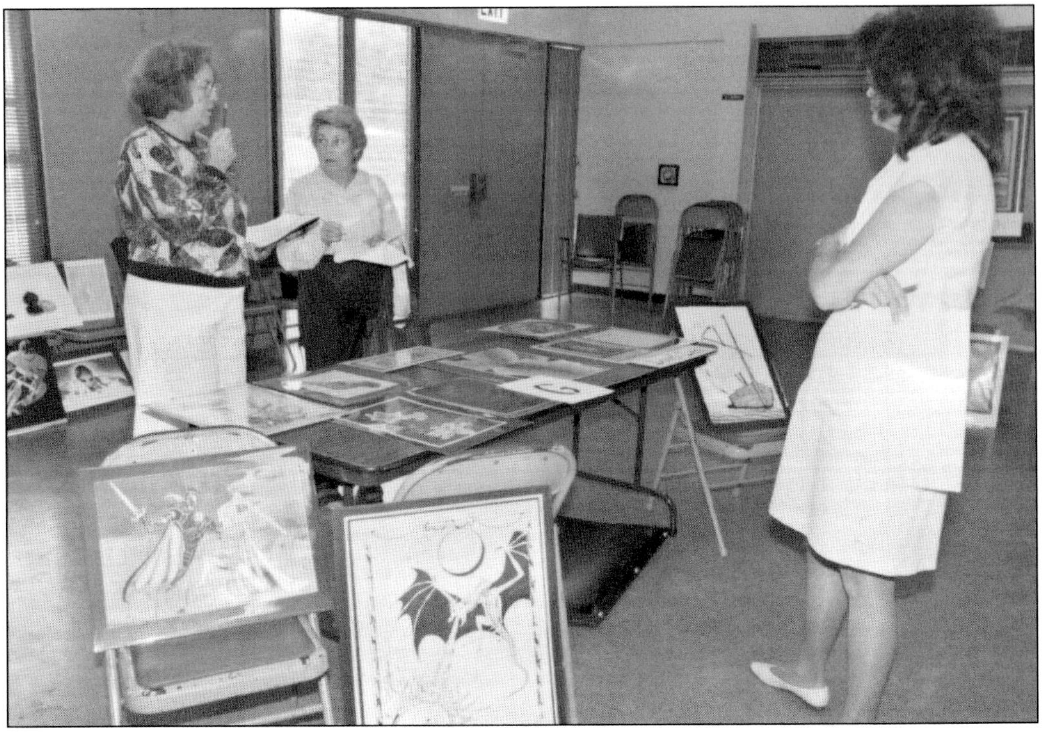

The Plantation Art Guild has supported the visual arts in Plantation since 1973 with demonstrations, exhibits, workshops, and scholarships. Lillian Ragland and Jean Hanes of the Plantation Art Guild are pictured with artwork entered in a show at the Plantation Community Center.

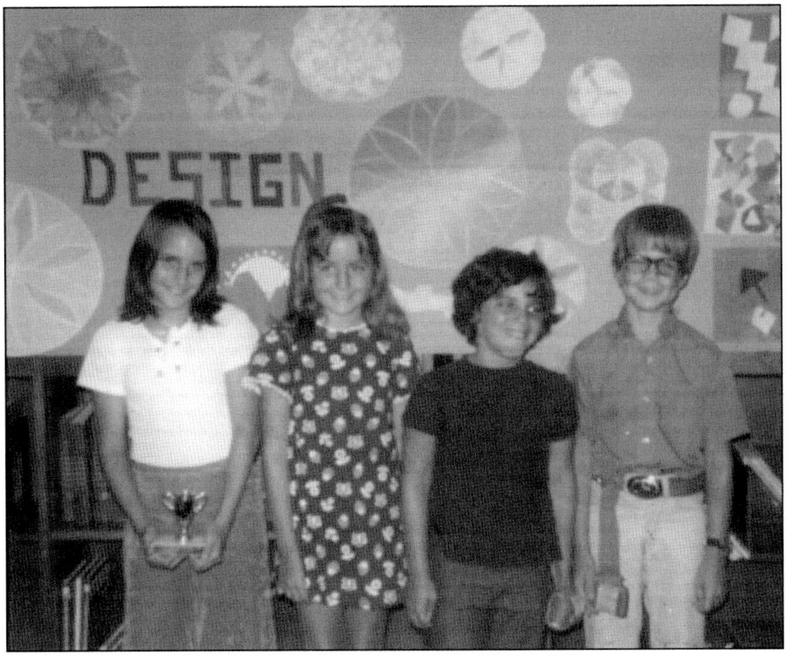

The Plantation Junior Woman's Club sponsored a spelling bee for over 300 fourth-graders in Plantation public schools. The winning student from each school received a $100 savings bond, and the school was given a trophy. Pictured are Mirror Lake Elementary School students, from left to right, Robin Gilbert (school winner), Susan Lovo, Jeff Herman, and Richard Shlakman.

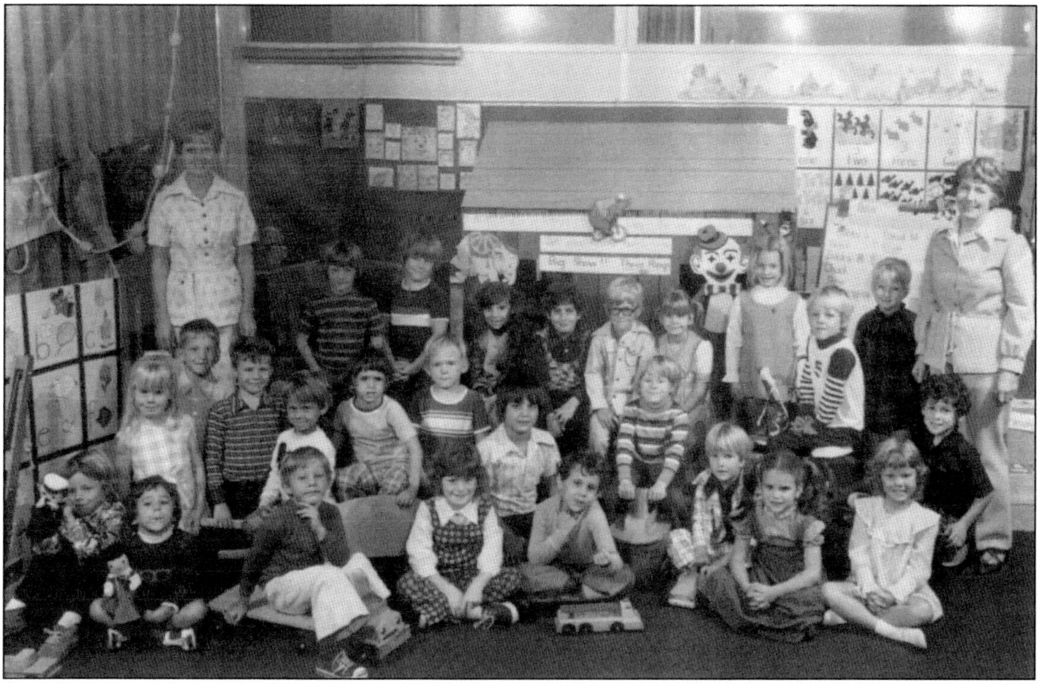

Plantation Park Elementary opened in 1966. Pictured here are kindergarten teacher Janet Y. Knapp and her aide Vesta Malloy with their 1974 class.

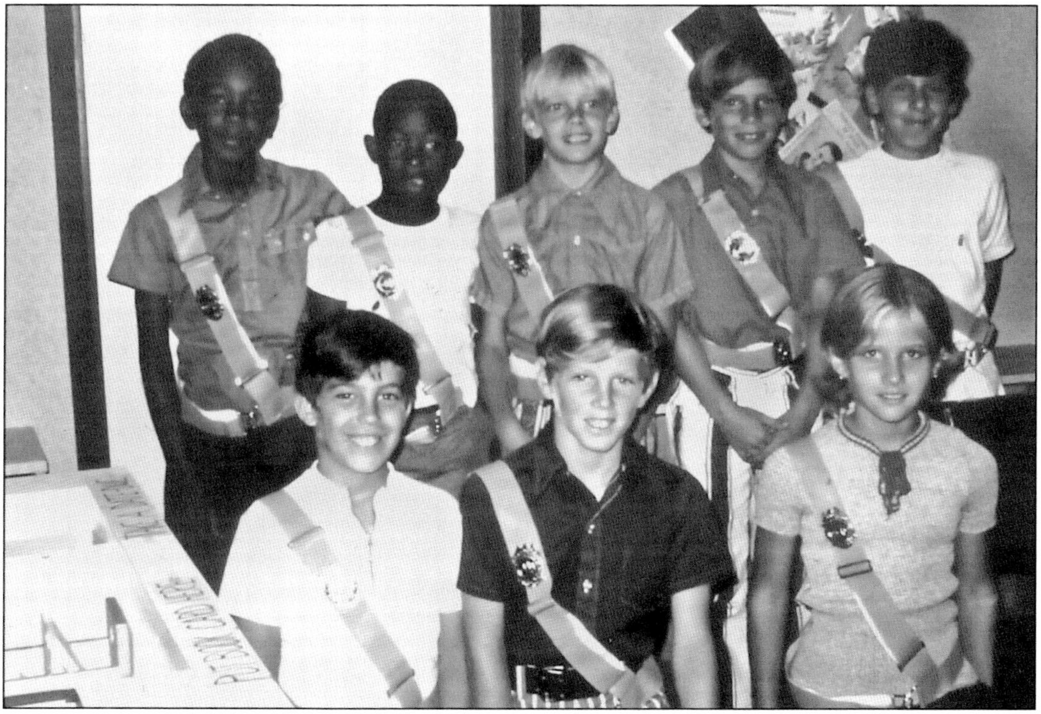

Another elementary school opened in 1970, Tropical Elementary School. Pictured are the members of the 1971 Safety Patrol. The fifth-graders were selected on the basis of maturity, leadership, and dependability.

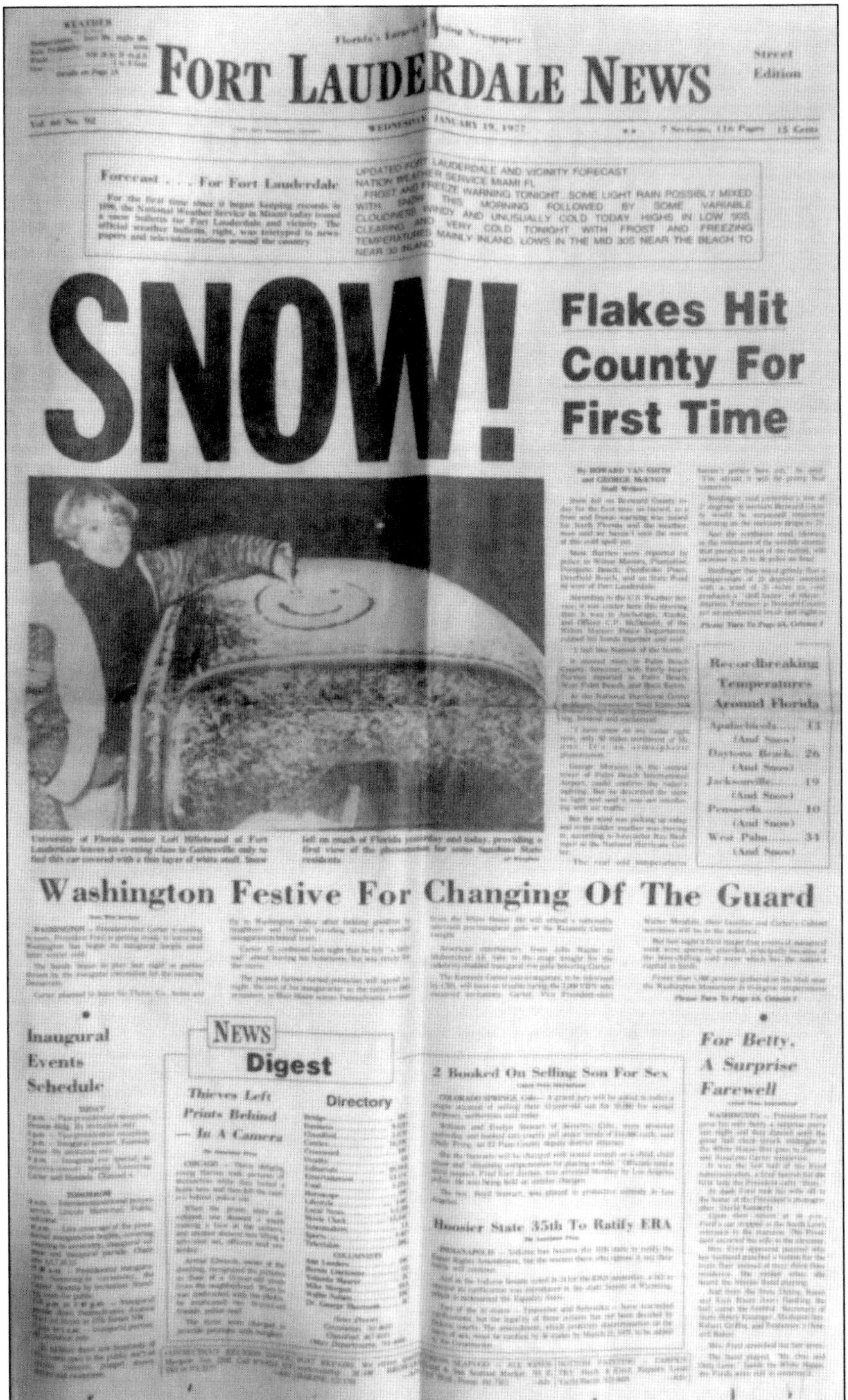

The *Fort Lauderdale News* evening edition of Wednesday, January 19, 1977, reported that the first snowflakes ever to be seen in South Florida fell in Wilton Manors, Plantation, and several other cities. Forecaster Noel Risnychok of the National Hurricane Center in Miami reported, "I have snow on my radar right now, only 50 miles northwest of Miami. It's an atmospheric phenomenon."

Six

The 1980s

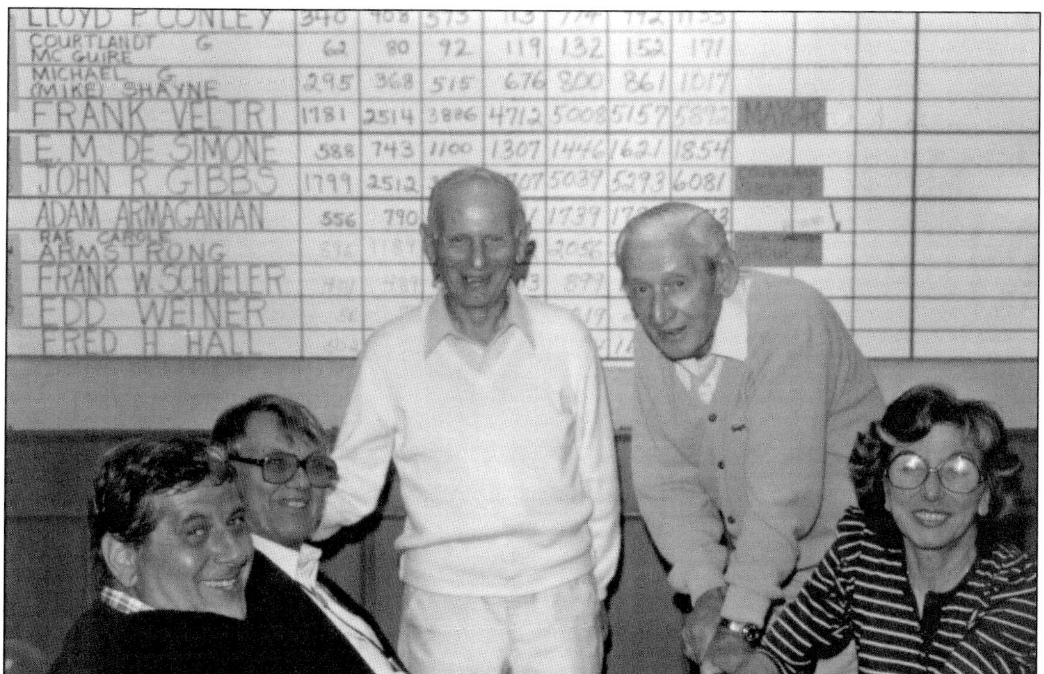

From the mid-1970s through the 1990s, city hall would open on the city's election night and candidates and their supporters would gather while the votes were tallied. Pictured on election night 1983, from left to right, are John Camilla, Gene Stoner, Murry Conister, Hy Baron, and Mella Stoner.

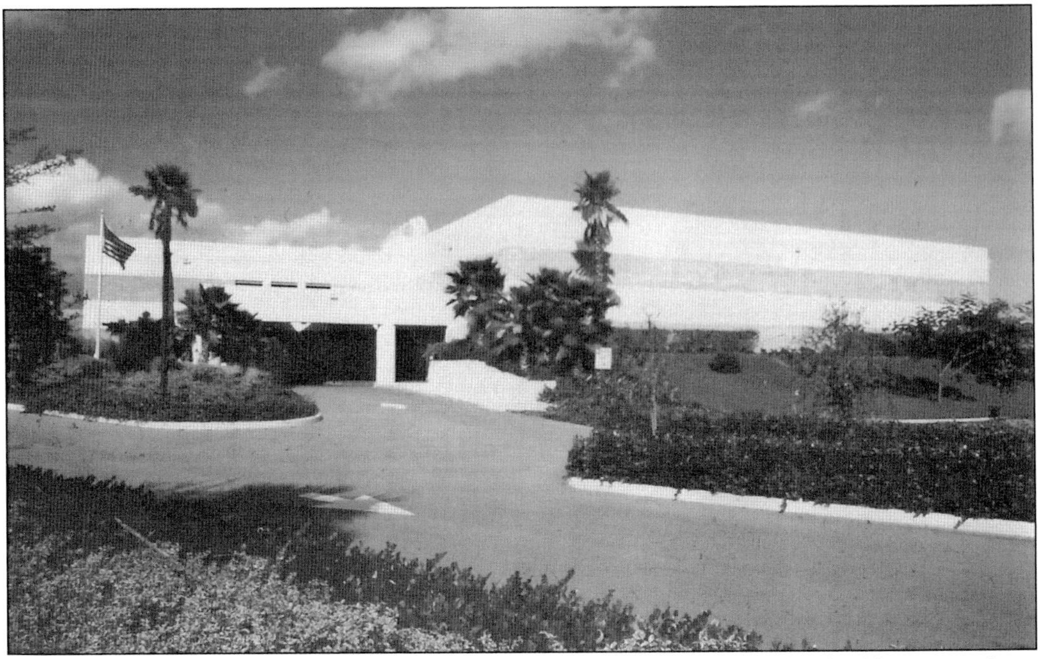

In the late 1970s, Plantation's elected officials approved a $6 million bond to build a new park on 77 acres in the center of the city. Plantation Central Park opened on February 20, 1983. These photographs show the main entrance to the recreation building in 1984 and an aerial view of the park in 1982. The tennis complex was completed first and opened prior to the recreation center, swimming pool, and ball fields.

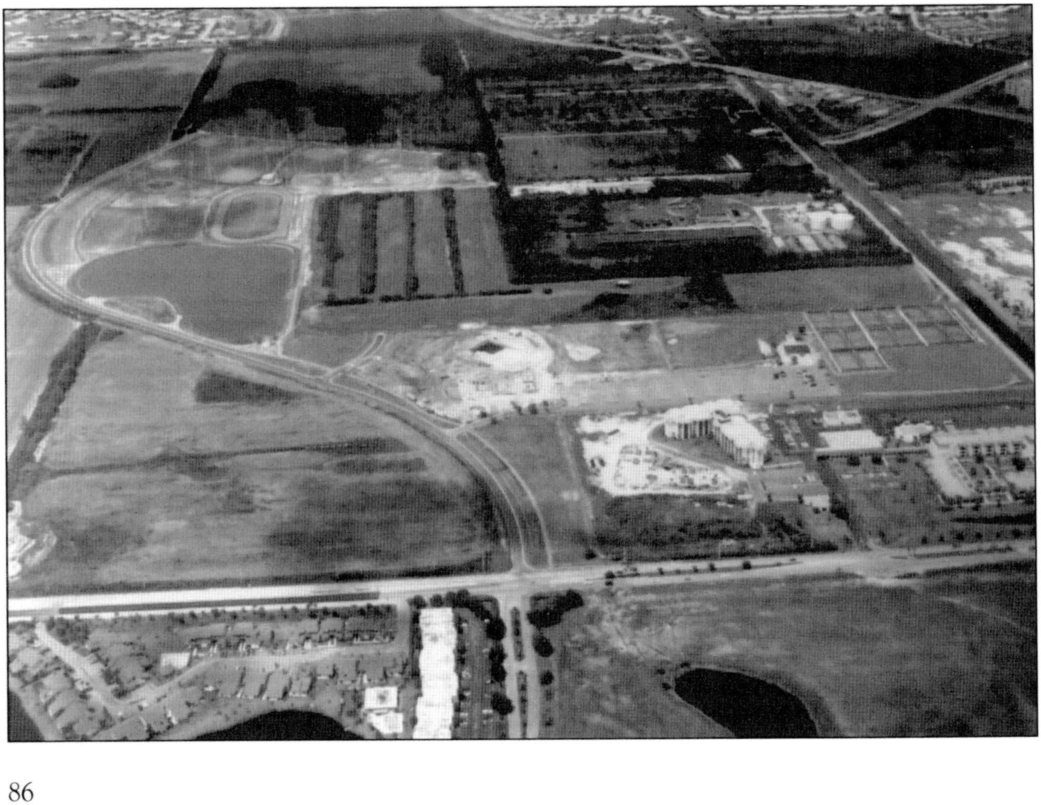

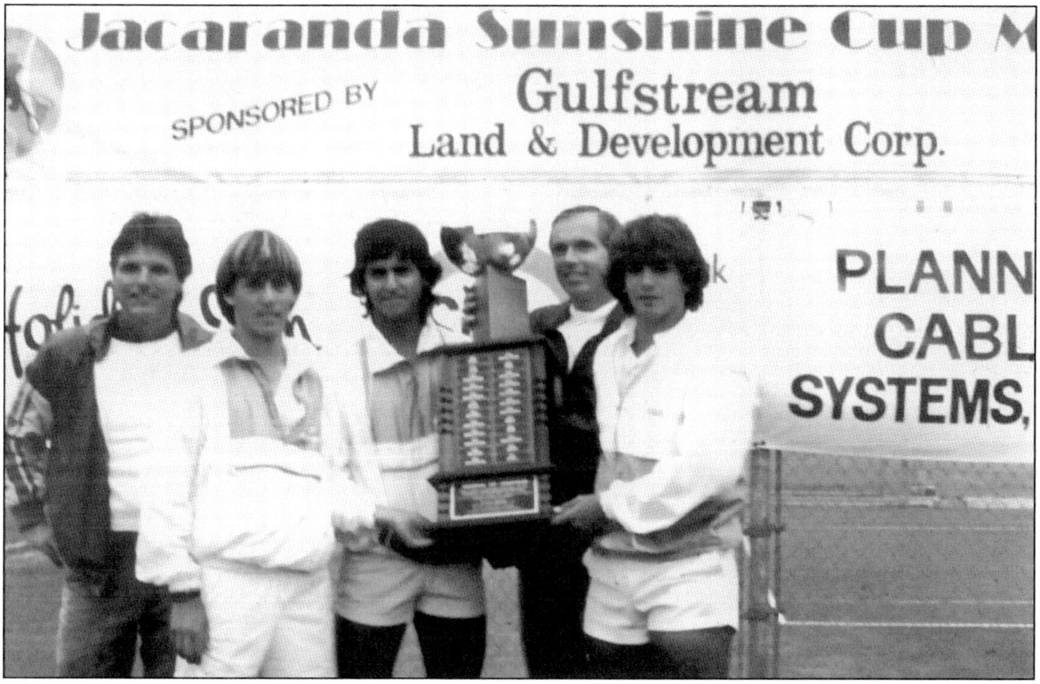

The international Sunshine Cup tennis match was first held at Plantation's tennis center in 1983 and included a young, unknown Boris Becker on the West German team. The 1986 tournament winners from Spain are pictured here with Plantation tennis pro Bob Cooper (far left) and Larry Justice (second from right) of Gulf Stream Land & Development Corporation, the tournament's sponsor.

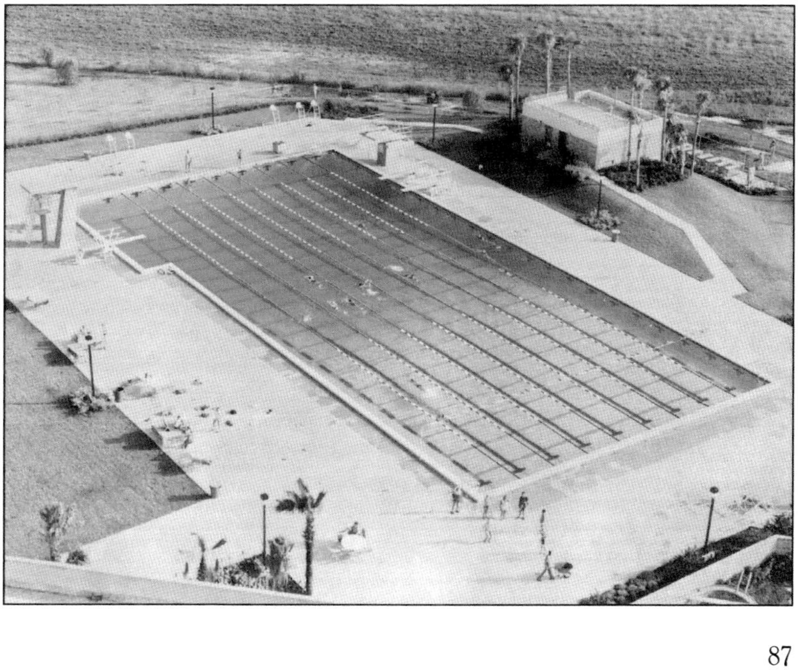

Pictured is the Central Park pool in 1983. Today, the Aquatic Center has two Olympic-sized pools and a hydro-playground. The pools are home to the nationally ranked Plantation swim and dive teams. The center is also used as a training site for the US Navy Seals and local law enforcement, and as a host site for the Junior Olympics.

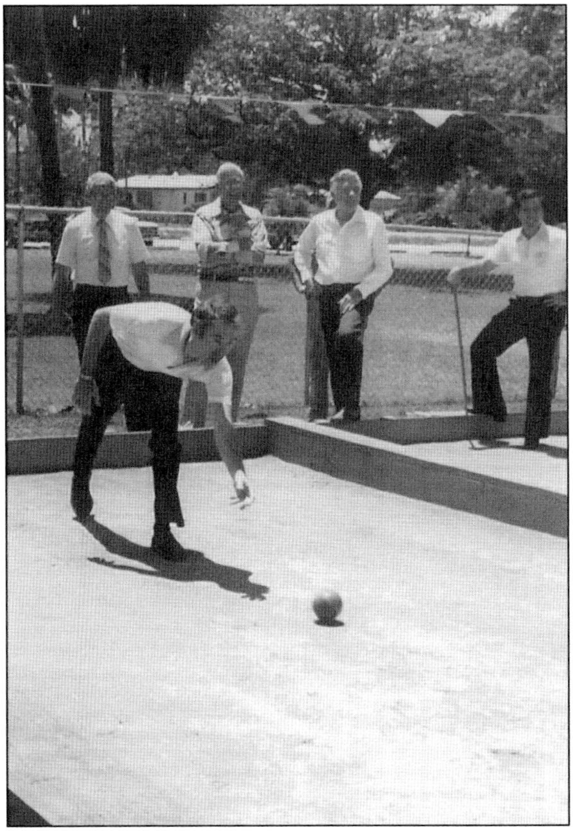

The Plantation Community Center on Palm Tree Road featured many amenities for activities and programs for adults including shuffleboard, horseshoes, tennis, and bocce ball. This photograph from the early 1990s shows, from left to right, Councilman Don King, Mayor Frank Veltri, Councilman John Gibbs, and recreation superintendent Ed Fernandez watching parks and recreation director Pete Zelinke playing bocce.

On February 16, 1987, Mayor Veltri and members of the city council gathered to officially open Veterans Park, a five-acre park featuring a memorial wall with dedication plaques and a memorial sculpture, *Eagle in Flight*. Today, the park is home to the annual Memorial Day and Veterans Day services. Pictured from left to right are council members Larry Freilich, John Gibbs, and Rae Carole Armstrong; Mayor Veltri; Martin Dishowitz; Congressman E. Clay Shaw; and Councilman Ralph Merritt.

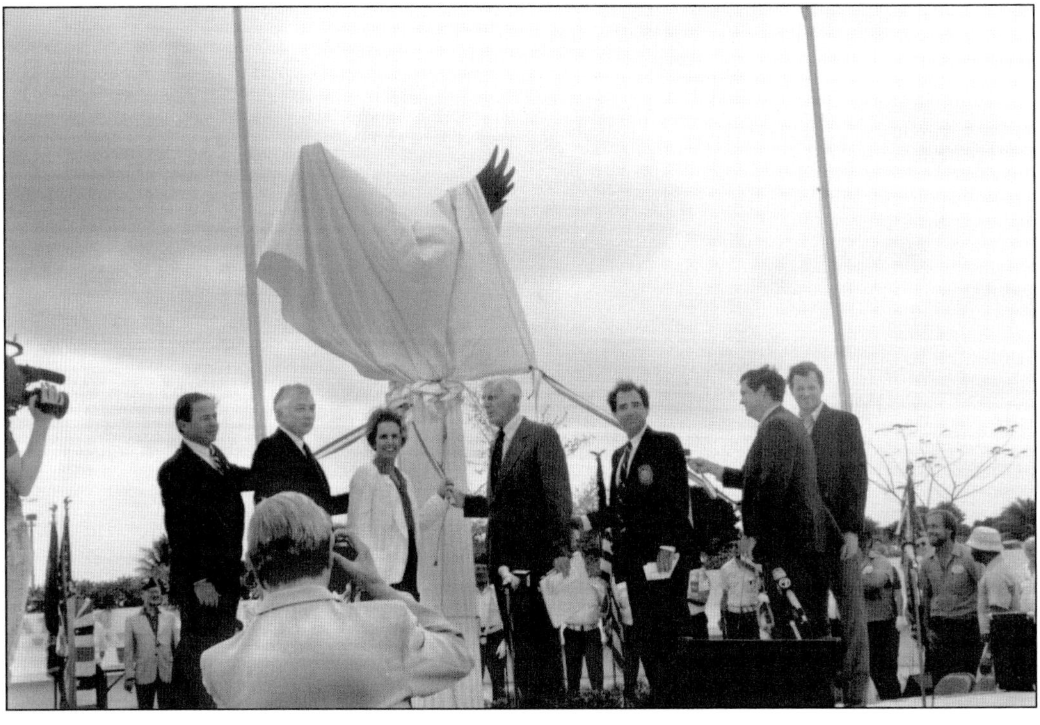

Lauderdale West members and their "Showboat Float" are ready for the Fourth of July parade. Mayor Frank Veltri is on the far right of the first row.

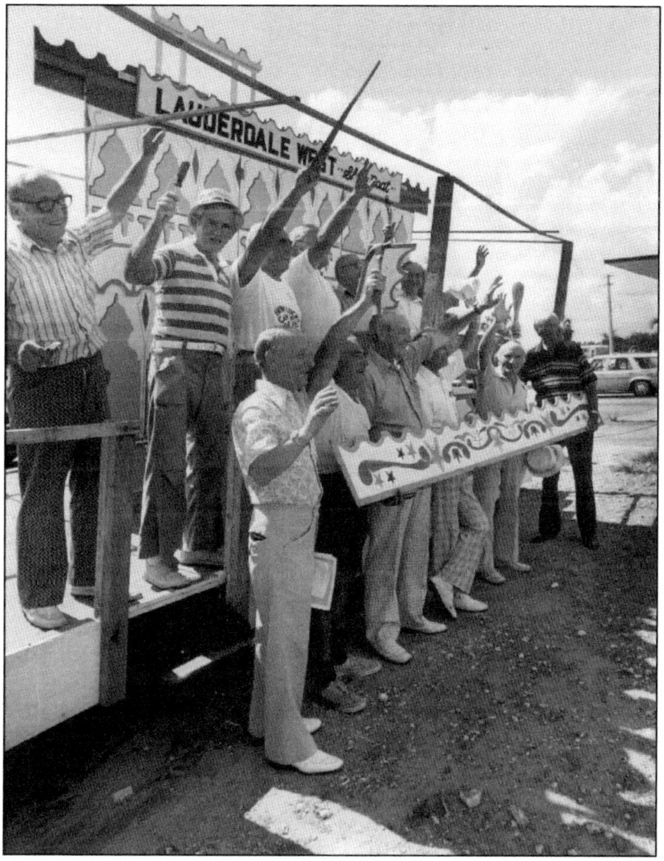

In 1977, the city and Broward County jointly acquired land that was once part of the Peters farm using grant funding from the Federal Land and Water Conservation Fund to create a new county park. In December 1984, Plantation Heritage Park opened.

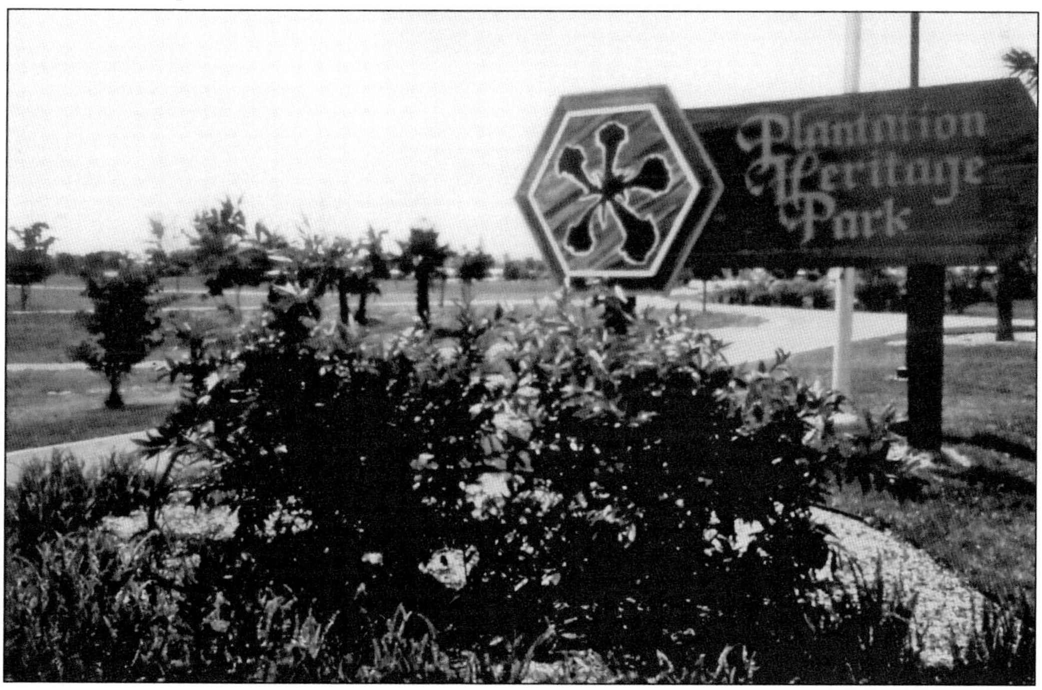

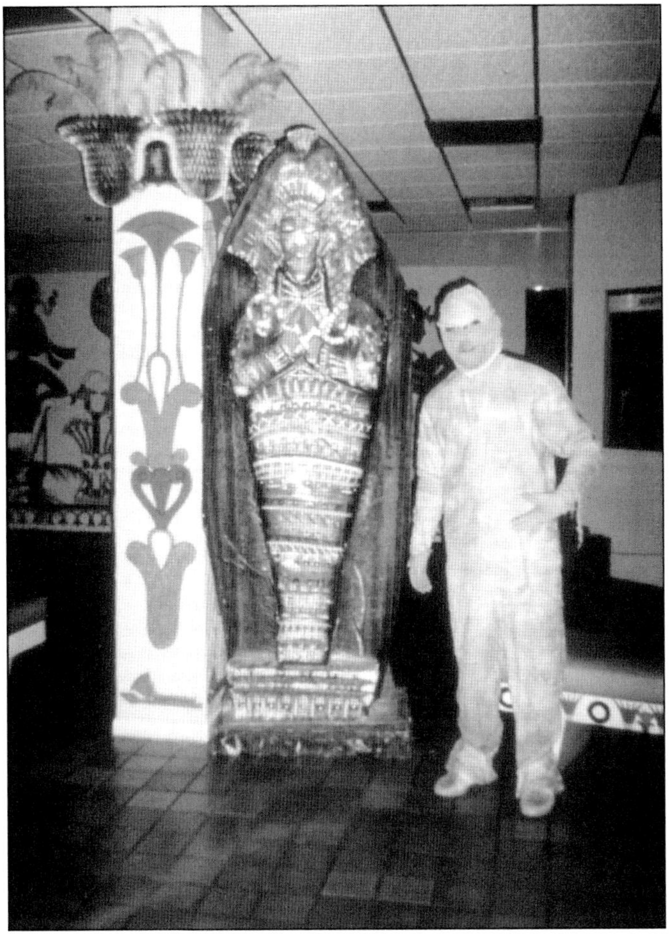

The city's annual haunted house began in the 1980s with the opening of Central Park. During the 1980s and 1990s, residents would wait up to 90 minutes for a chance to be frightened at this wildly popular Halloween event. Pictured is Neal Trafford as "The Mummy" in the lobby of Central Park in 1987.

During the mid-1980s, Jazzercise was all the rage. The city's parks and recreation department offered jazzercise and aerobic classes to all ages. Pictured here are aerobic instructor Kelli Carry and her 1986 "Mousercise" class.

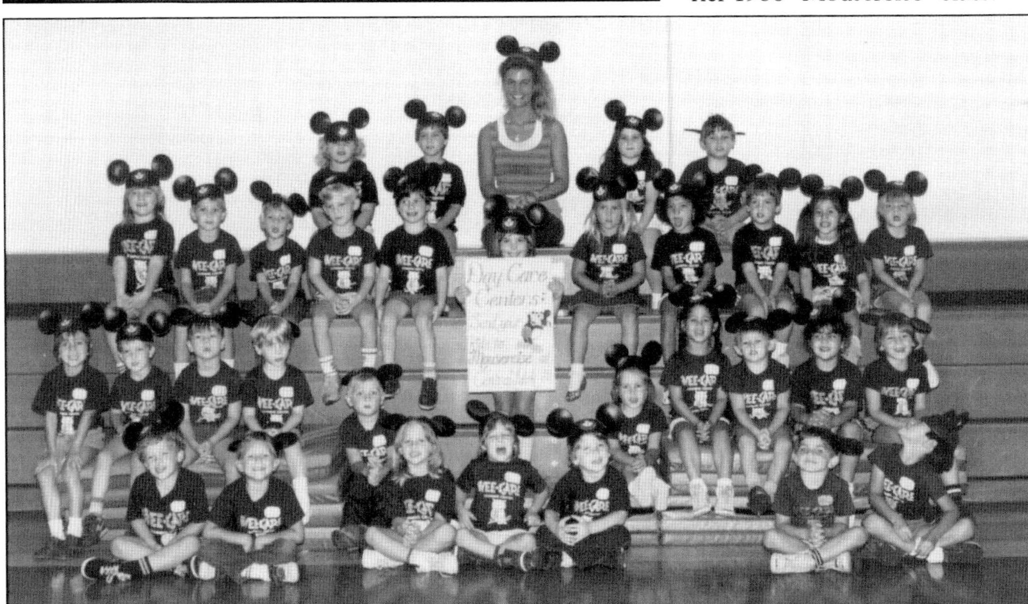

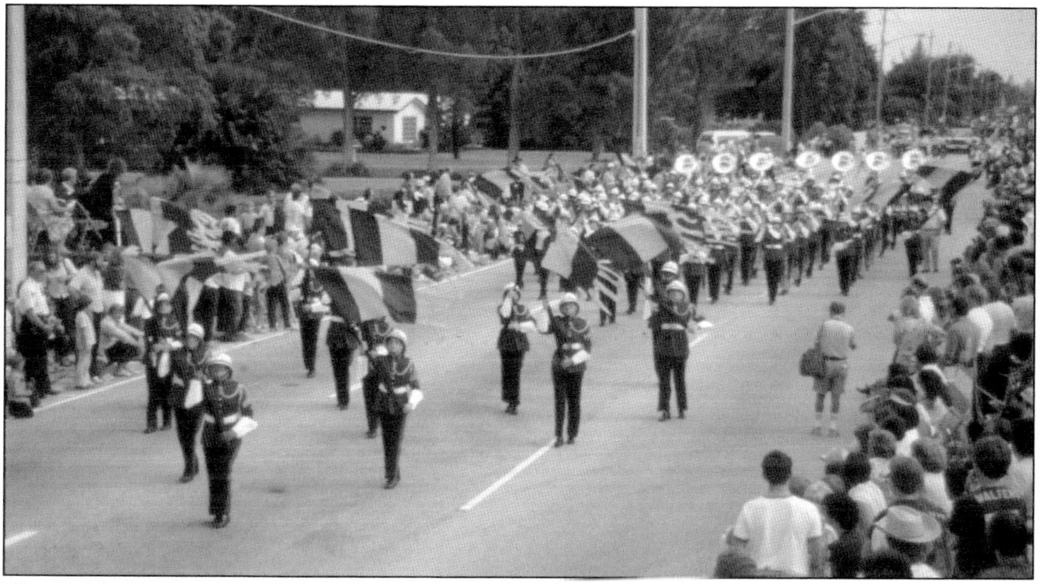

The Gold Coast Holiday Parade began as a small parade in the 1960s called the Jaycee's Christmas Parade. By the 1980s, it had grown into a large event that was covered by local television stations. The parade's big attraction was a competition between local high school marching bands. The Deerfield Beach High School band is pictured in the 1981 parade. The Greater Plantation Chamber of Commerce continues this tradition today with the "It's a Wonderful Life in Plantation" Holiday Parade.

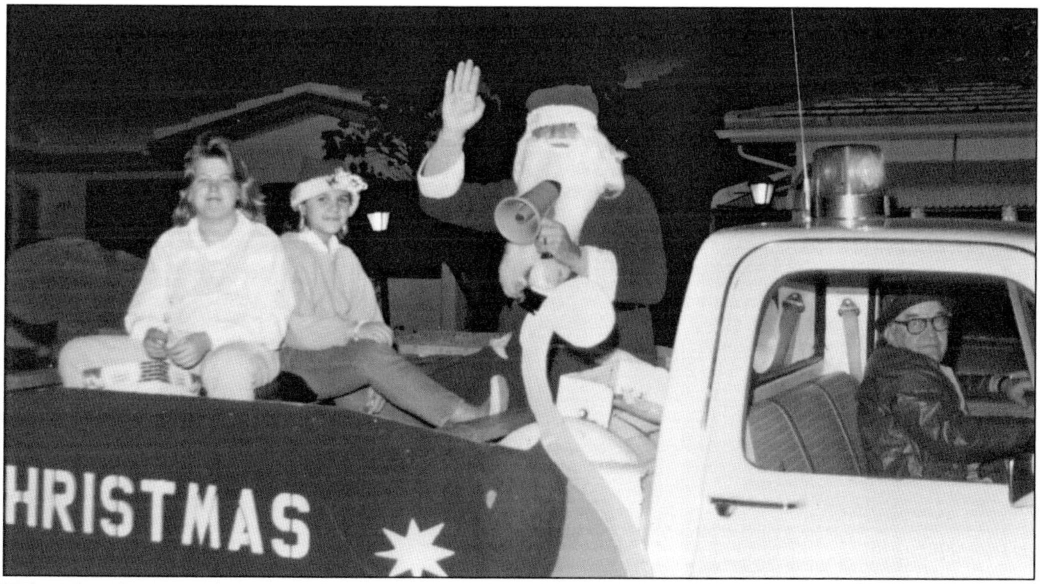

What has become known throughout Plantation as "Santa's Visit" began in the early 1960s. Mayor Jim Ward would dress as Santa and travel Plantation's few blocks on December 24, wishing children and adults a "Merry Christmas." In 1966, the city council agreed to let Santa organize three motorcades so all Plantation children would get to see him. Santa's Visit continues today with Santa visiting the residents of Plantation every Christmas Eve. It now takes 17 Santas, police cruisers, sleighs, and lots of elves to make the yearly visit. Pictured are participants in the 1986 event.

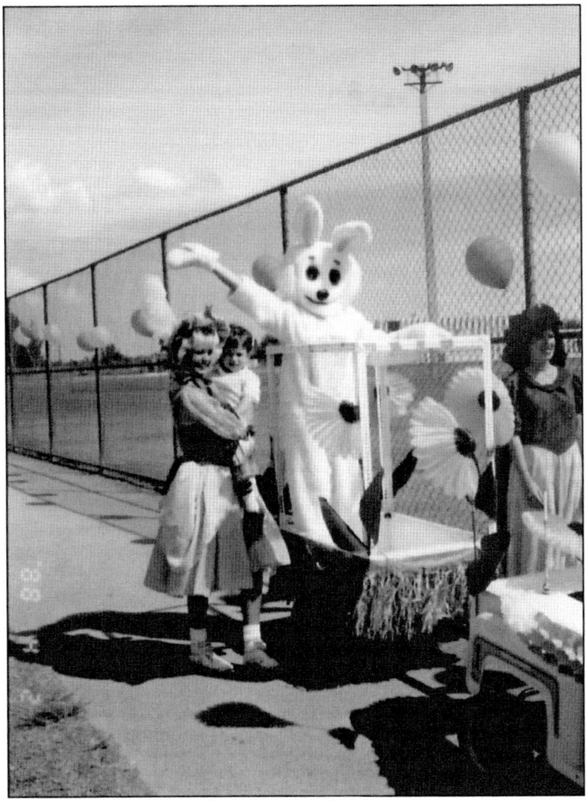

No one remembers what year the city's annual Easter egg hunt began, but it has been held on the Saturday before Easter for a very long time. The event has been held at Pop Travers Field since the 1980s. In 1988, Jennifer Keane dressed as Little Bo Peep and Sheila Smith as Snow White escorted the star of the day as he arrived in the "Bunny-Mobile."

The first annual Kid's Fishing Tournament was held at the Central Park Lake in 1985. The live-release tournament culminated with trophies awarded for categories such as first fish caught, biggest bass, most unusual catch, and best sportsmanship. The last fishing tournament was held in the late 1990s. Pictured is a participant with his catch in the first tournament in 1985.

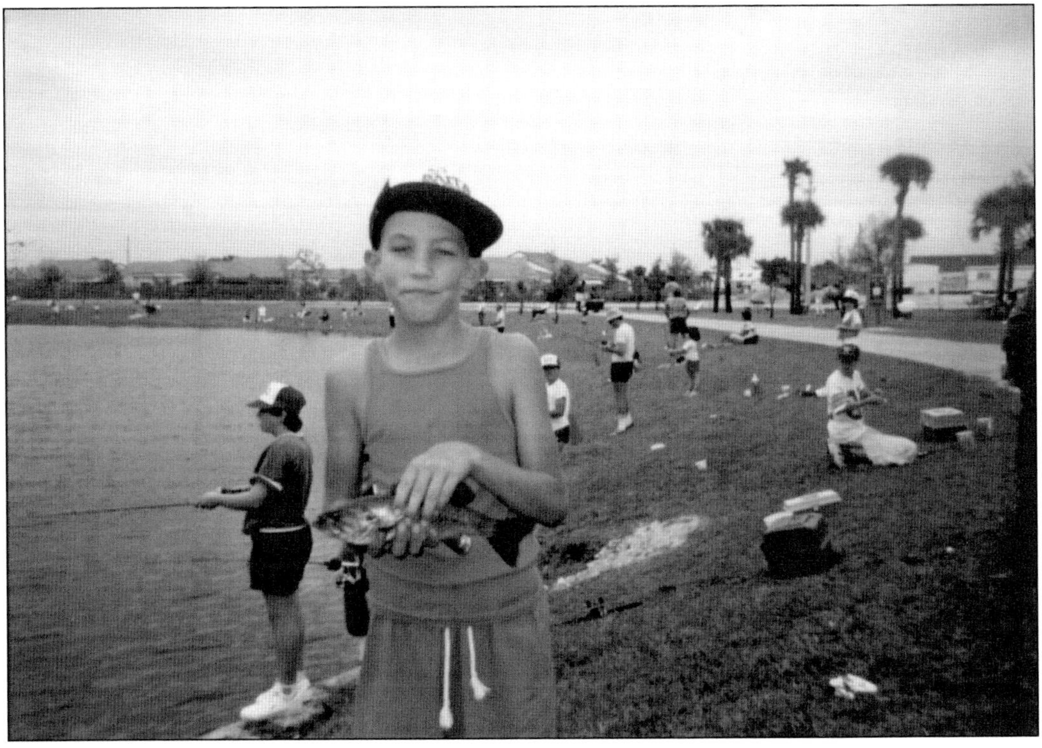

For many years, Plantation children have enjoyed the Winter Wonderland Camp held in December. The program features field trips, crafts, special guests, and fun activities. Pictured are children participating in "Snow Day" at the 1988 camp. Shaved ice would be blown from trucks into a mound for the campers to play in. For many, it was the closest they every came to seeing snow.

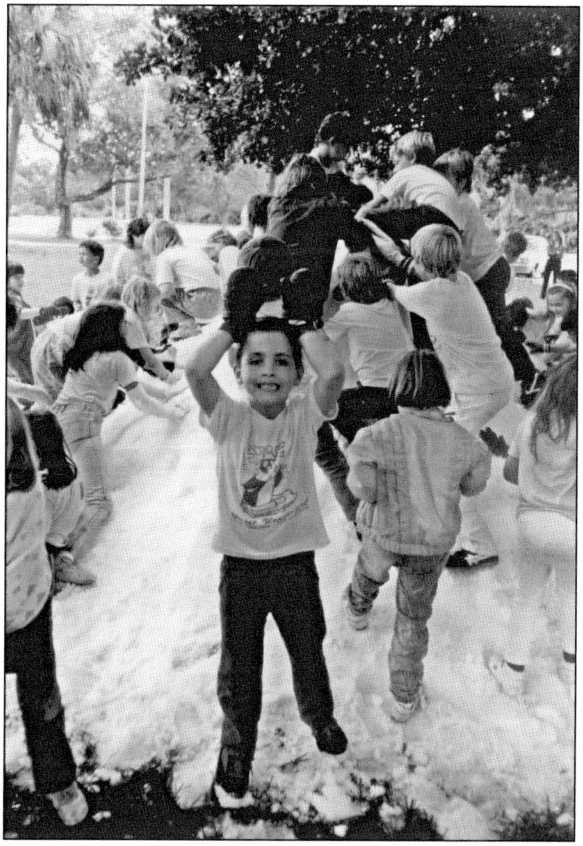

The parks and recreation staff has always sought to find ways to entertain the campers, providing a safe and fun atmosphere while creating memories and nurturing friendships. Long before mousse or hair gel, Plantation campers had fun with "Shaving Cream Hairdos." During the Spring Break Camp of 1988, camp supervisor Dale Dusch creates a special "do" on recreation supervisor Ken Boyce while camp counselor Erin Gallagher and campers look on.

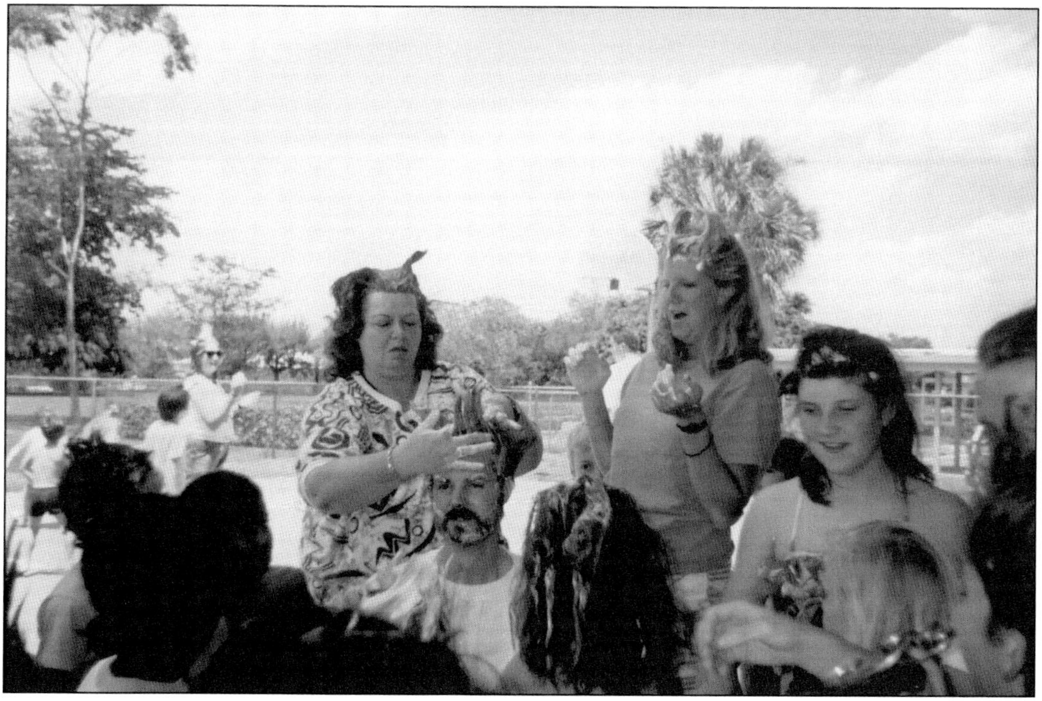

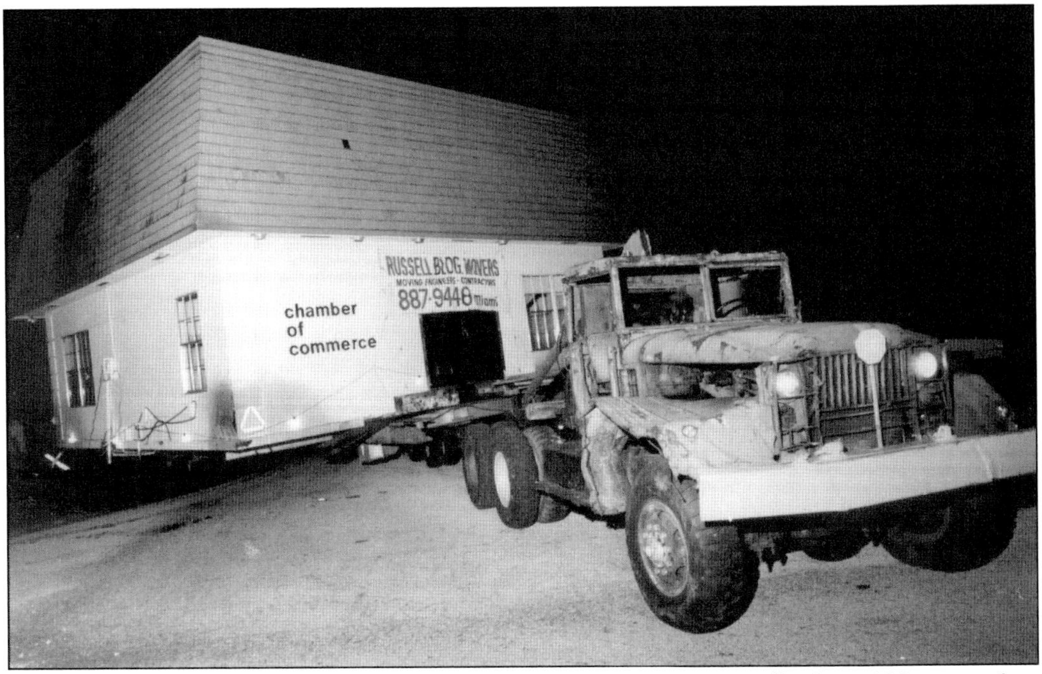

The Greater Plantation Chamber of Commerce building was originally the 1,000-square-foot sales office of the French Quarter apartment complex. The structure was then donated to the Plantation Historical Society to house the museum. At midnight on June 27, 1983, the building was moved from 7401 Northwest Fourth Street to the present site of the museum. Once in place, the museum's new home was vandalized, fell off its cinderblock foundation, and needed to be demolished. The picture below is the present-day chamber of commerce building constructed in 1985 on its original site on Fourth Street.

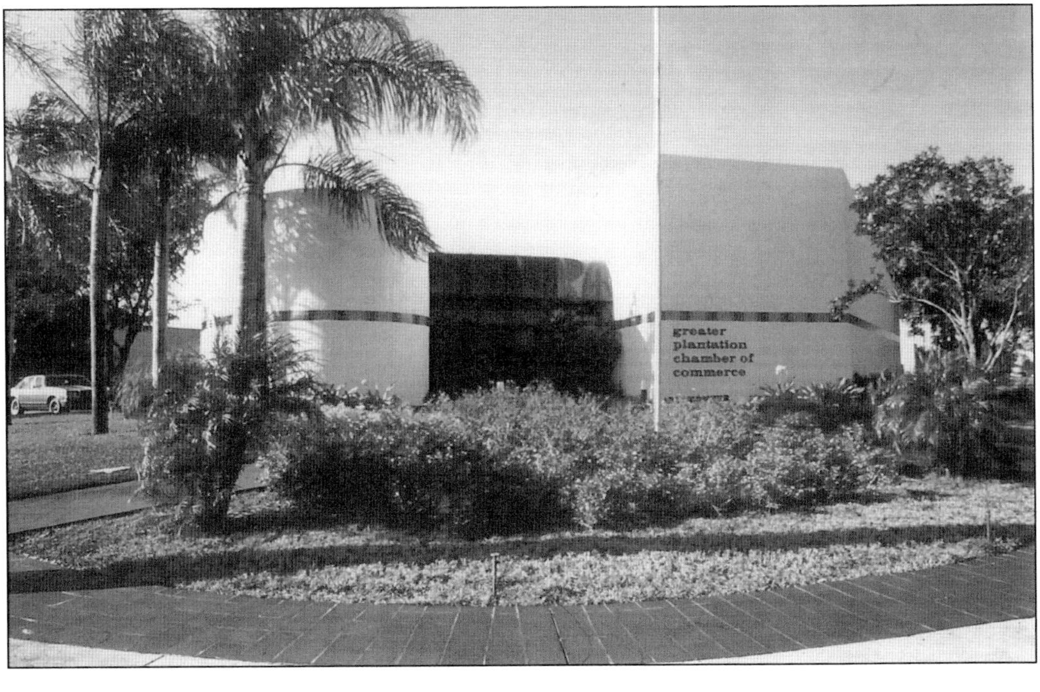

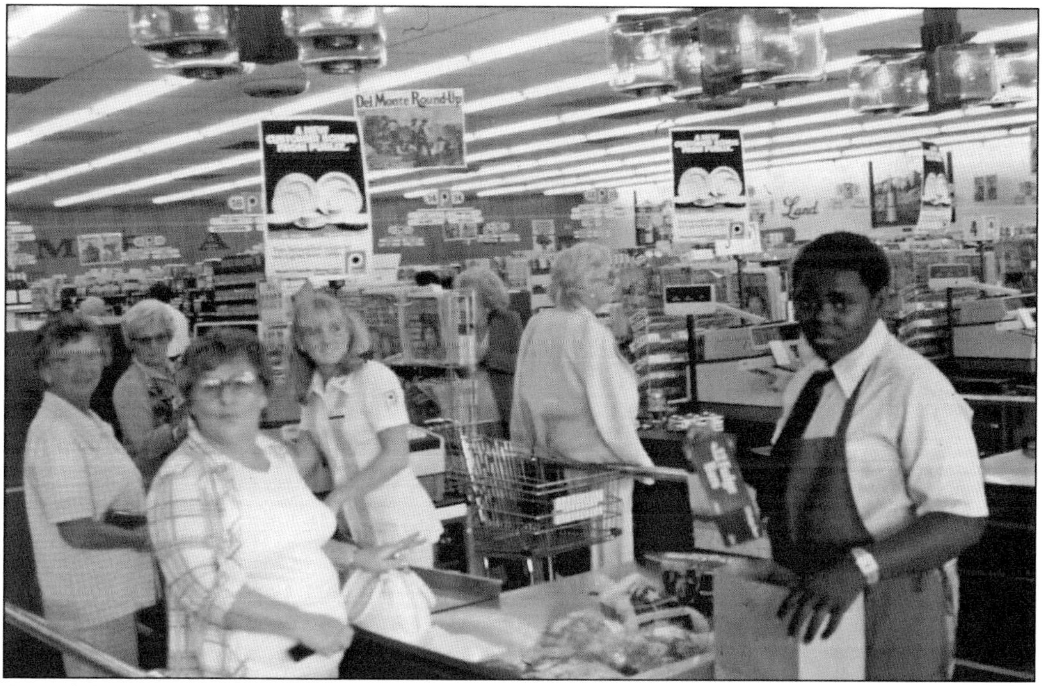

One of Plantation Towne Mall's anchor stores, Publix opened its doors in February 1970. The residents welcomed the neighborhood store. Pictured here in 1984 are customers and personnel.

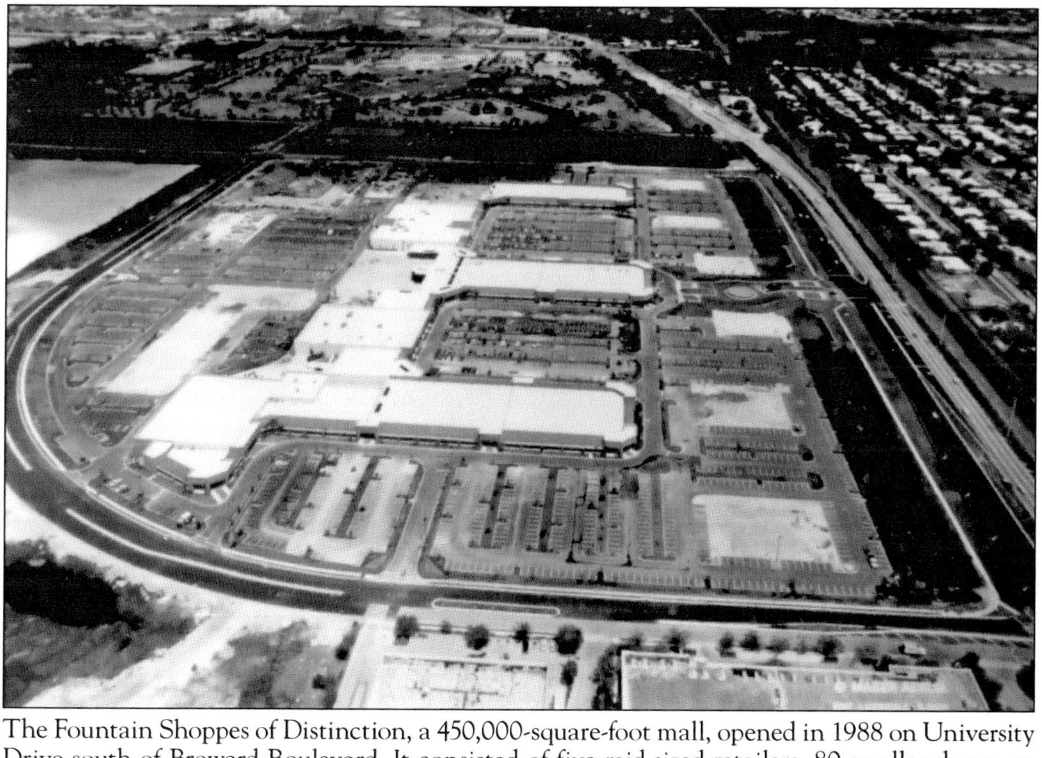

The Fountain Shoppes of Distinction, a 450,000-square-foot mall, opened in 1988 on University Drive south of Broward Boulevard. It consisted of five mid-sized retailers, 80 smaller shops, an eight-screen movie theater, and a 149-room Marriott Hotel.

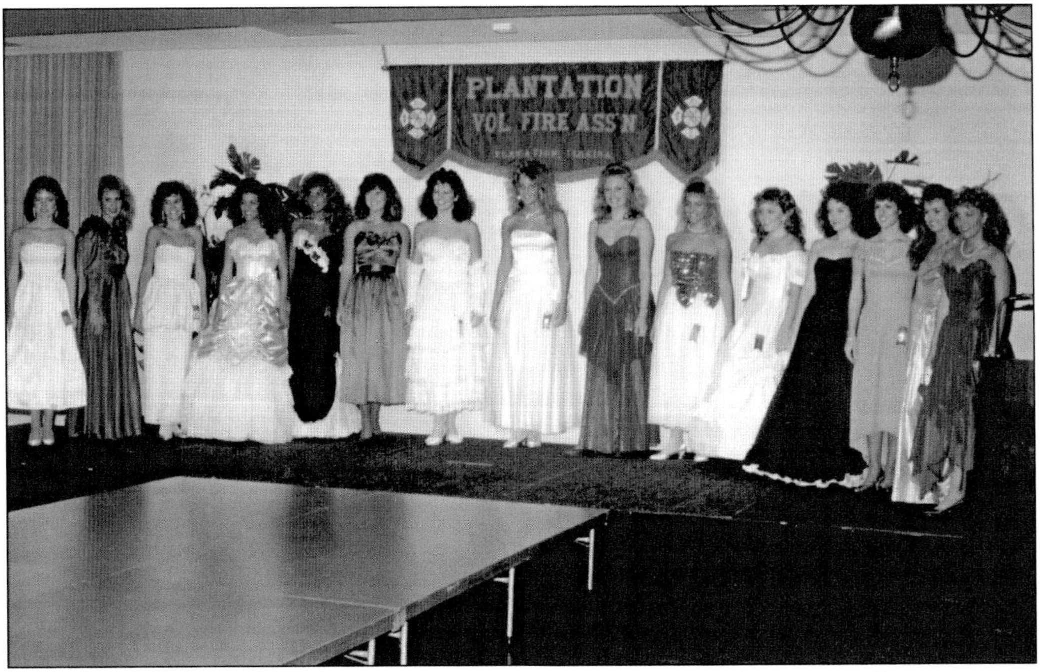

The Miss Flame competition was sponsored by the Plantation Volunteer Fire Department as part of annual Fire Prevention Week until 1989. Pictured are the 1987 contestants competing at Deicke Auditorium.

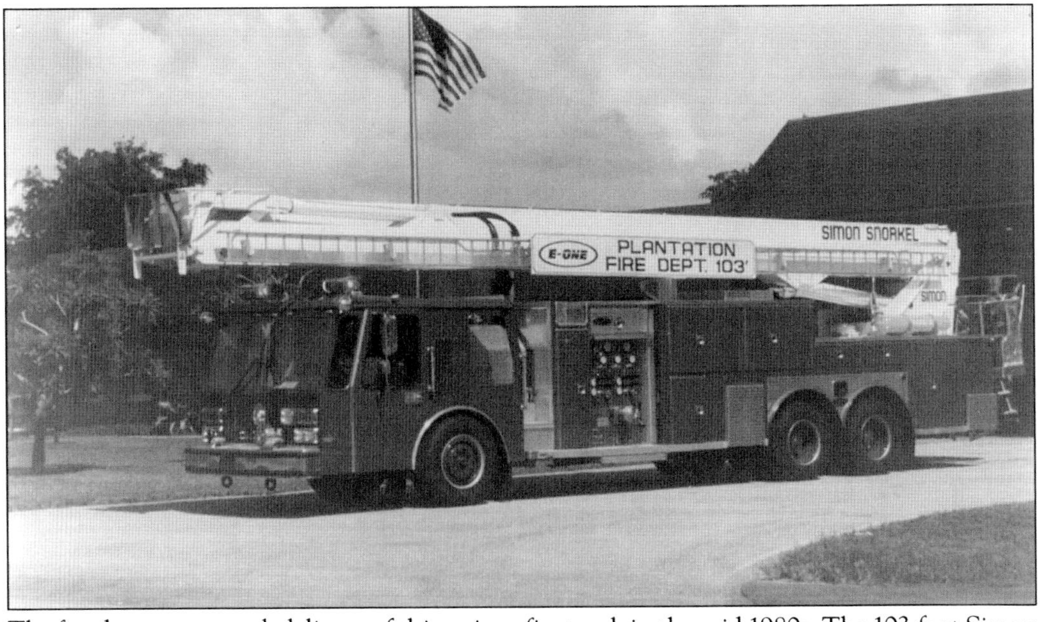

The fire department took delivery of this unique fire truck in the mid-1980s. The 103-foot Simon Snorkel was imported from England and, at the time, was one of only two in the United States. The truck featured three separate, articulating booms, which allowed it to operate similarly to a human arm, technology rarely seen in the United States at that time. "Snorkel 15," now called Snorkel 56, was used extensively throughout Broward County when difficult rescues required specialized apparatus.

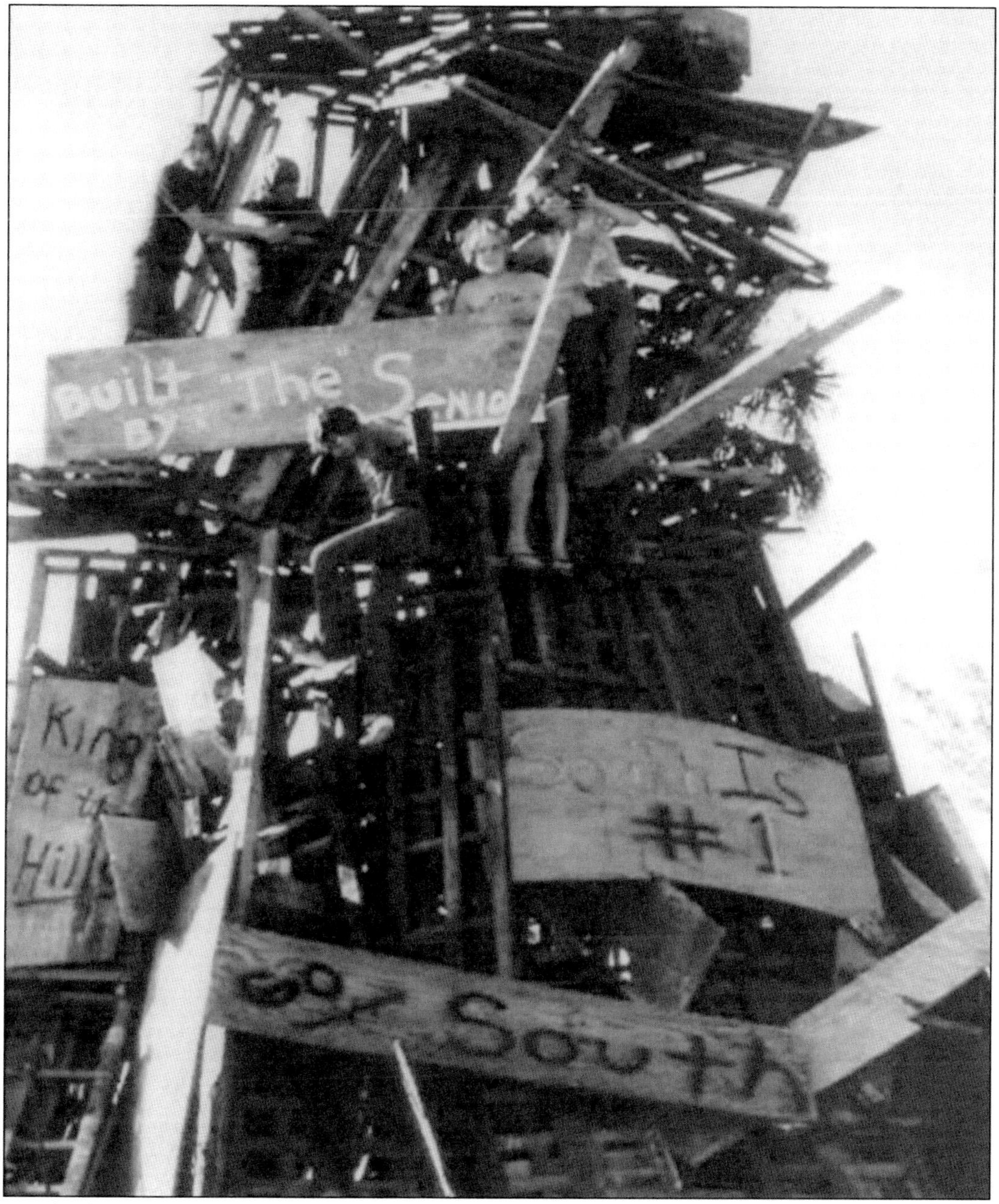

South Plantation High School's homecoming week featured a bonfire and pep rally on school property. This 1984 photograph shows students constructing the bonfire structure from donated scrap wood.

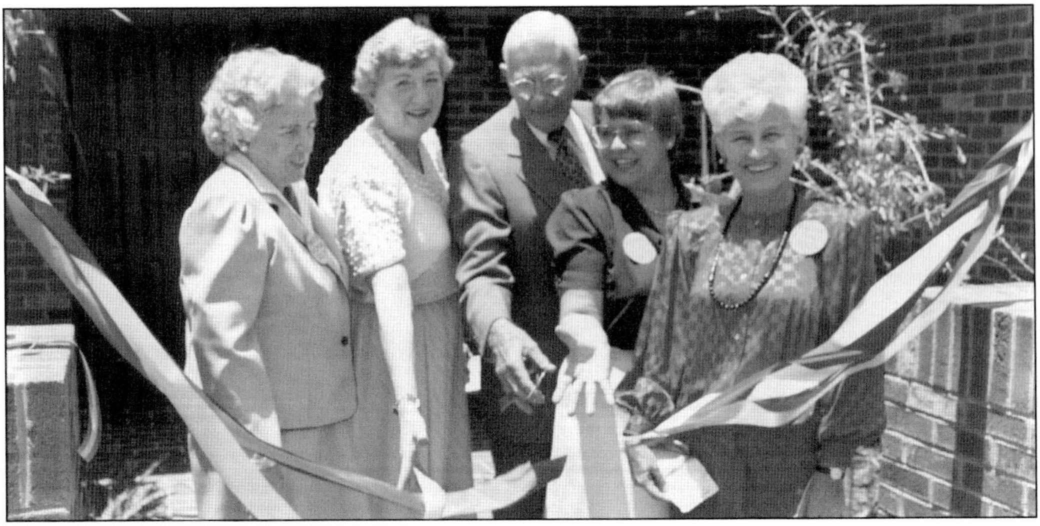

After years of hard work, planning, and fundraising, the Plantation Historical Museum was completed. The dedication took place on June 2, 1985. Above, on hand to cut the ribbon were, from left to right, Genevieve Veltri, Lois Brickhouse, Mayor Frank Veltri, Beverly Grant, and Phyllis Napp. Below, those attending the museum's dedication included, from left to right, Councilman Marty Dishowitz, Mayor Frank Veltri, US congressman E. Clay Shaw, Councilman Neil LaHurd (standing), Genevieve Veltri, and Beverly Grant.

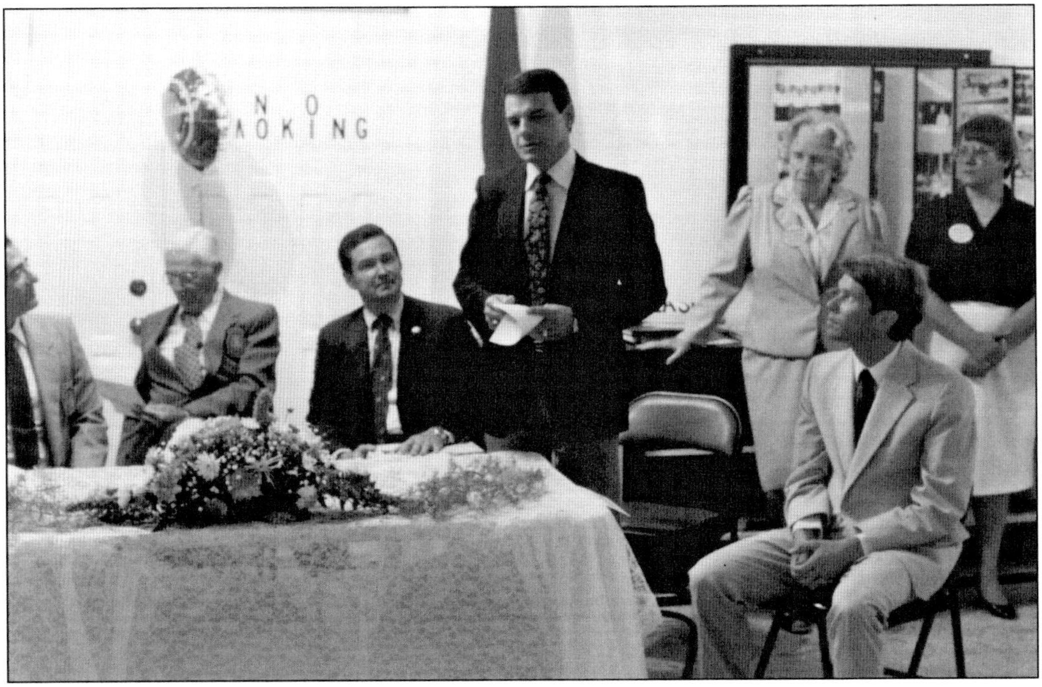

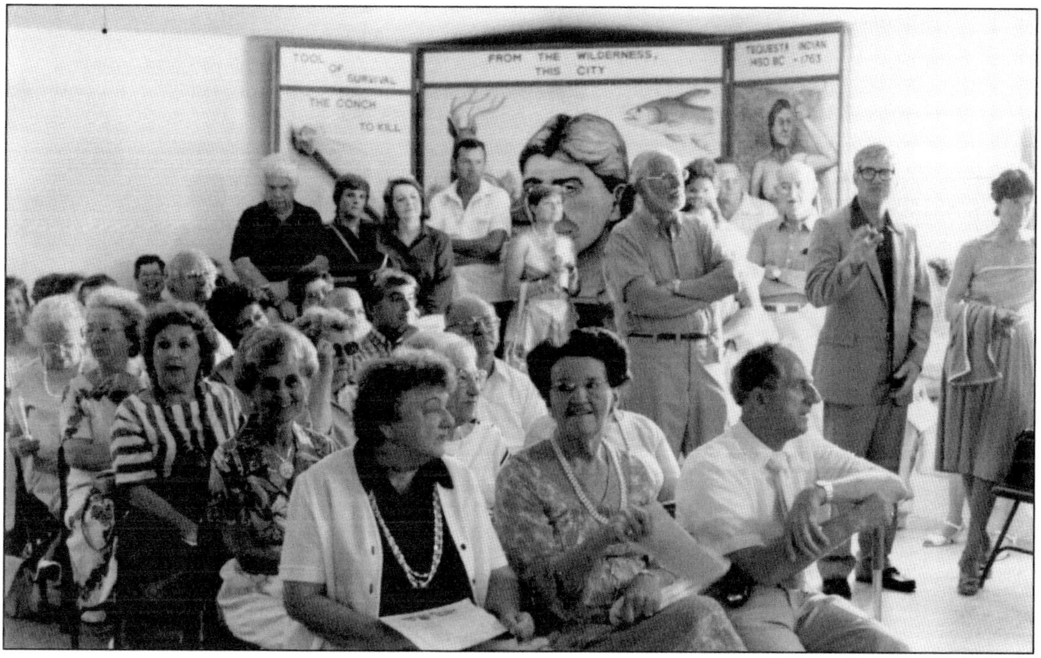

Guests at the historical museum's grand opening enjoy their first glimpse of the new museum. Former city clerk Bea Browning (left) and Helen Hoffman (right) are seated in the first row.

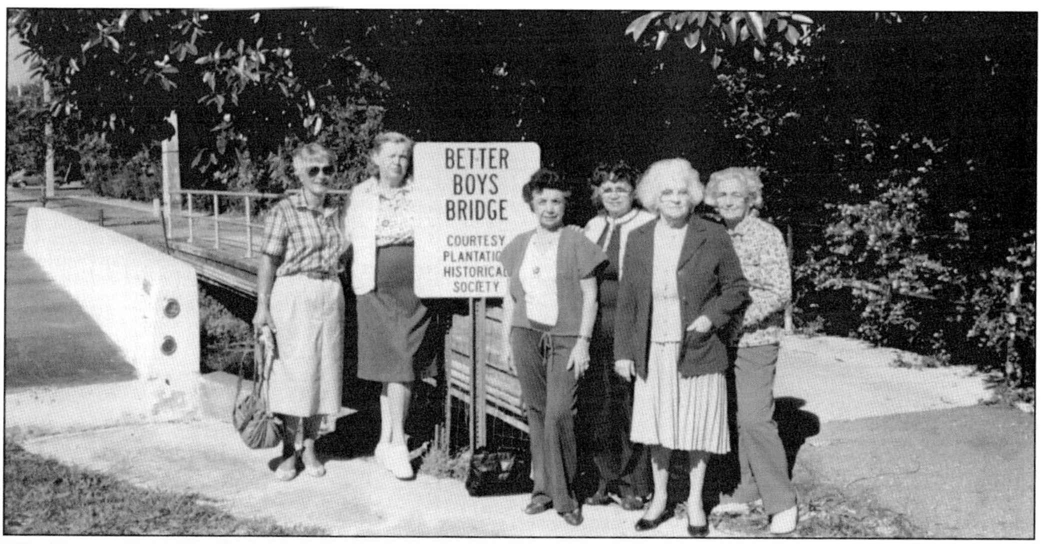

The Better Boys Bridge, just east of Northwest 65th Avenue on Plantation Road, is the site of the Plantation Historical Society's first official historical marker. Pictured at the dedication in April 1986 are, from left to right, Agnes Barrett, Cecile Murphy, Rose Scevola, Betty Crawford, Grace Turner, and Ruth Kaselin. It is believed that a developer put up the bridge in anticipation of the homes and roads to follow. But in the early 1950s, the bridge was far from the existing houses and only the bigger and "better" boys could trek across the open fields to fish on the bridge over the Holloway Canal.

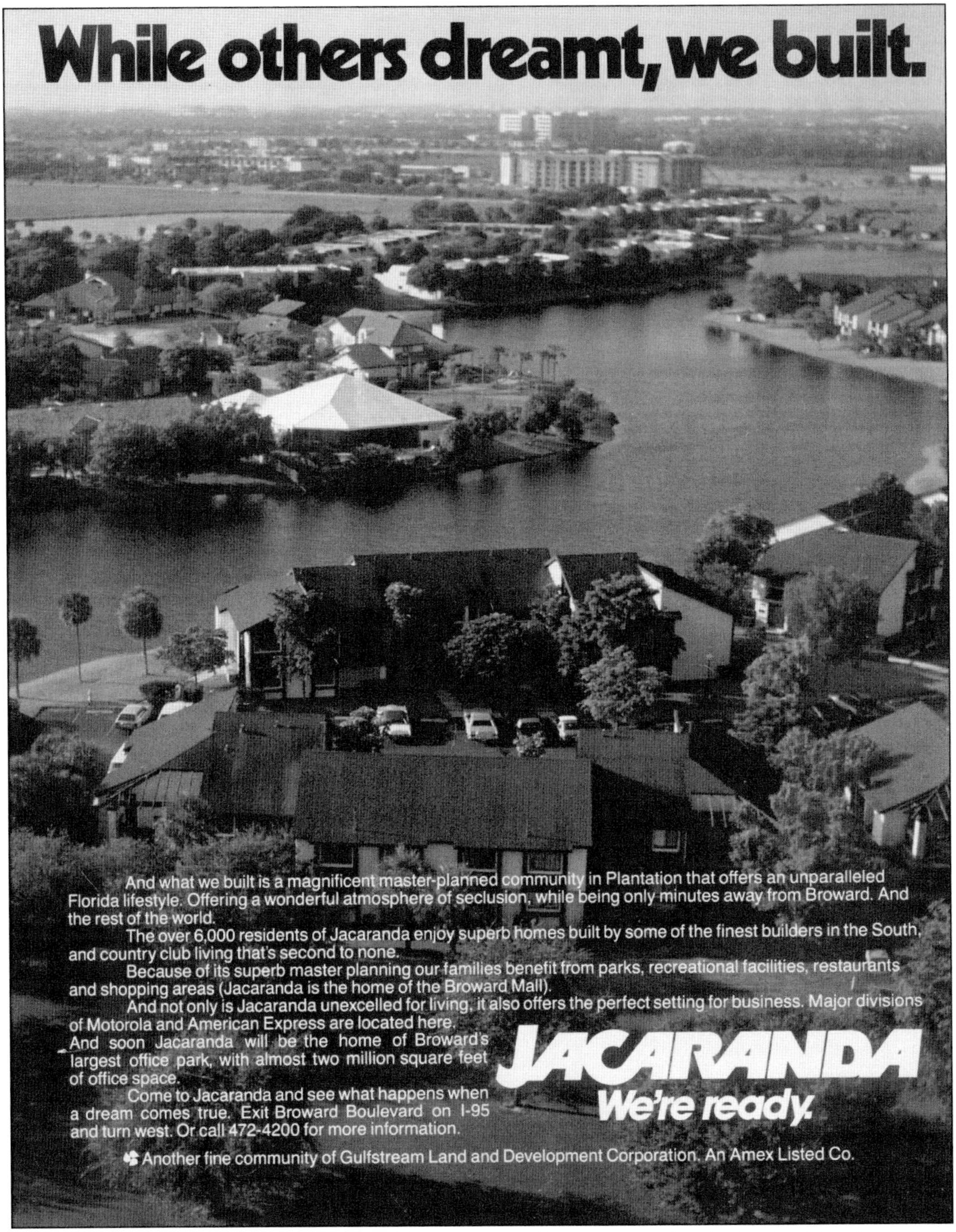

In the early 1970s, Gulfstream Land and Development Company, under the leadership of company president John H. Cleary, developed the remaining half of Fred C. Peters's western property. The intent was to build a Broward County "Coral Gables." The Dade County Coral Gables was where Peters settled upon arriving in Florida. The development became known as "Jacaranda." It featured upscale housing, retail stores, commercial businesses, and a country and golf club.

Seven

The 1990s

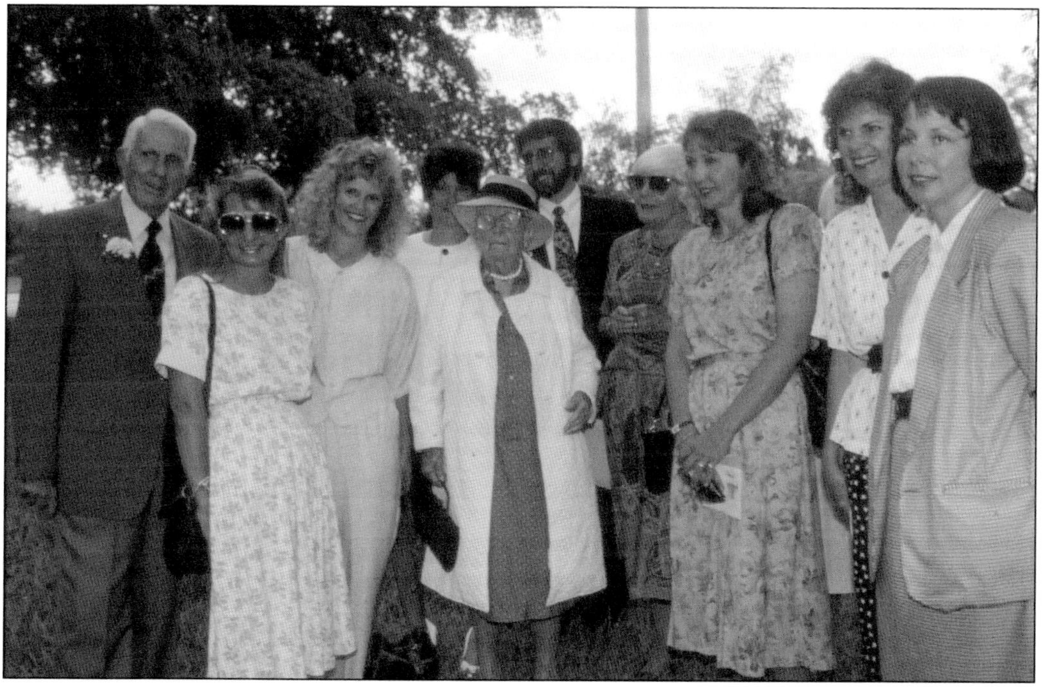

The Plantation Landscaping Award for Nurturing our Town (PLANT) Awards were started by the landscape department in 1984. In 1991, 100-year-old Marjorie Stoneman Douglas was honored at the awards ceremony for being nationally recognized as the "First Lady of Conservation" due to her lifelong commitment to saving the Everglades.

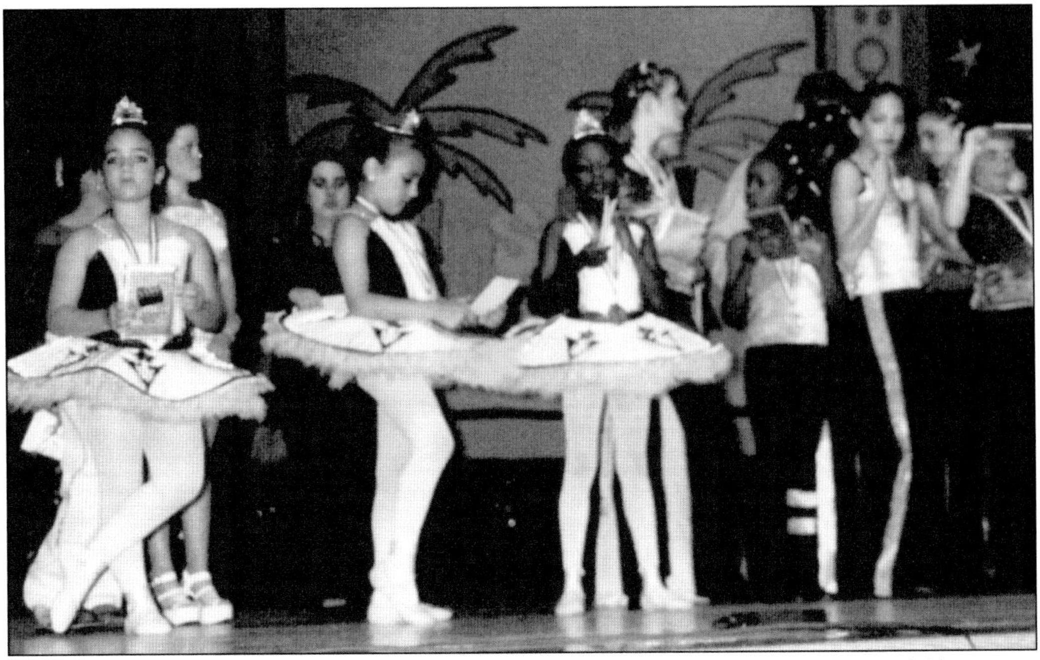

In the early 1980s, the talent show at the Plantation Community Center featured Plantation residents of all ages. Then, in the late 1980s, the show moved to Plantation High School auditorium and became known as the Tinsel Town Talent Showcase. In 2008, it moved to Volunteer Park and was given a new name, Tinsel Town Cabaret. Residents perform to a sell-out crowd. Pictured are contestants from the 1999 Tinsel Town Talent Showcase.

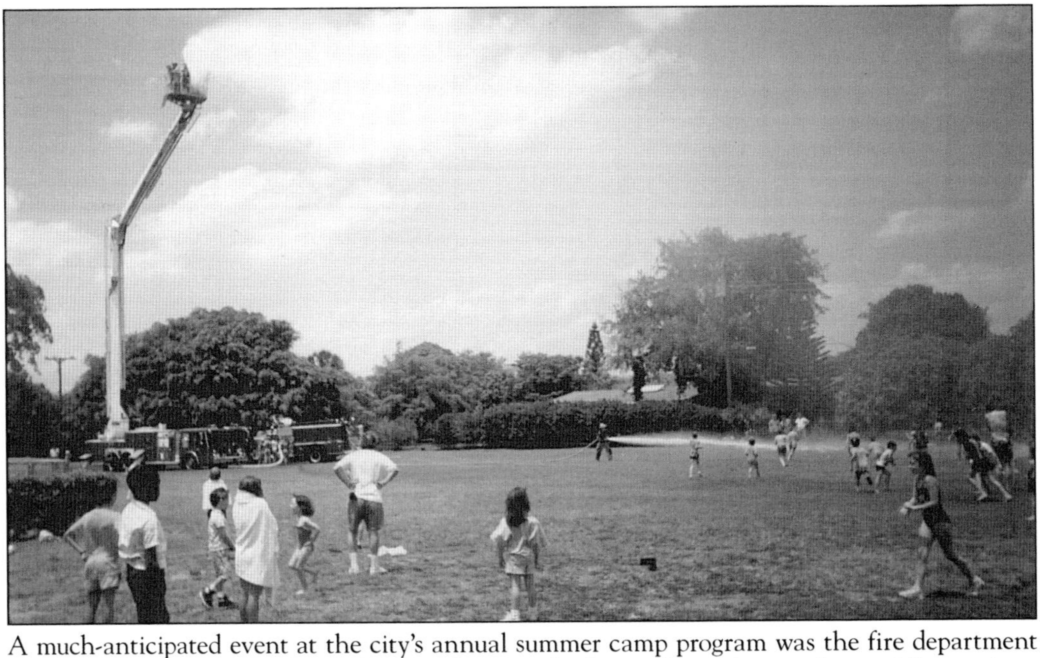

A much-anticipated event at the city's annual summer camp program was the fire department "squirt down." As seen in this mid-1990s photograph, this traditional event featured fire engines, firemen, swimsuit-clad campers, and lots of fun as the children ran through sprays of water shot from both the ground and a bucket truck.

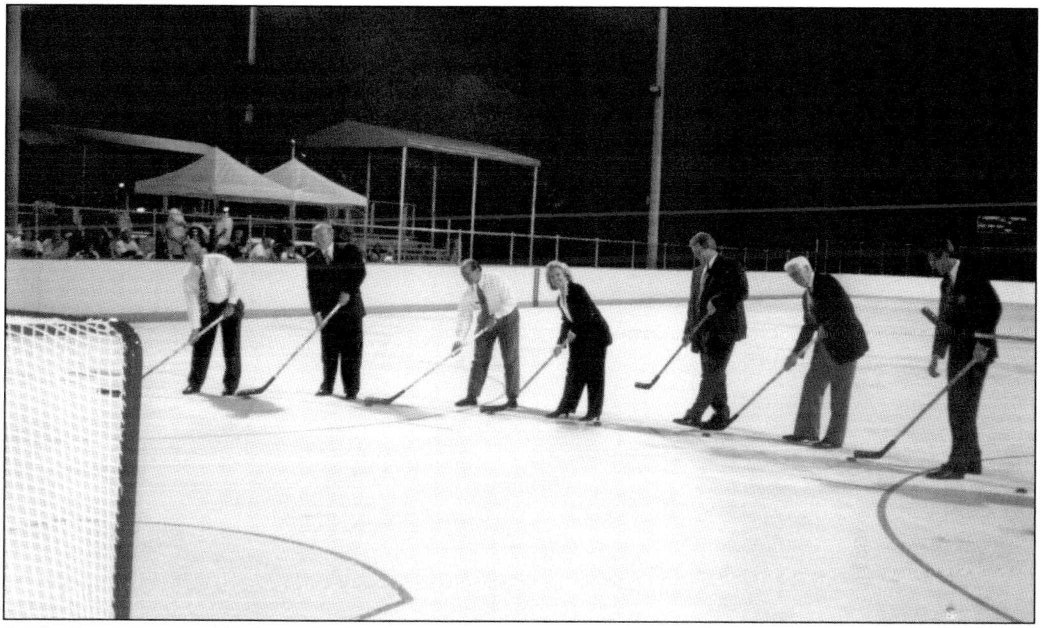

In the late 1990s, roller hockey quickly became one of youth sports' hottest programs. In an effort to keep pace with the trend, the city opened four roller hockey courts at Plantation Central Park on January 27, 1999. This was the first roller hockey complex built in compliance with the National Hockey League regulations in South Florida. Delivering the opening shots are, from right to left, PAL president Laney Stearns, PAL hockey commissioner E.J. Generotti, contractor Jim Fedele, Councilwoman Rae Carole Armstrong, Councilman Bruce Edwards, Mayor Frank Veltri, and Councilman Jerry Fadgen.

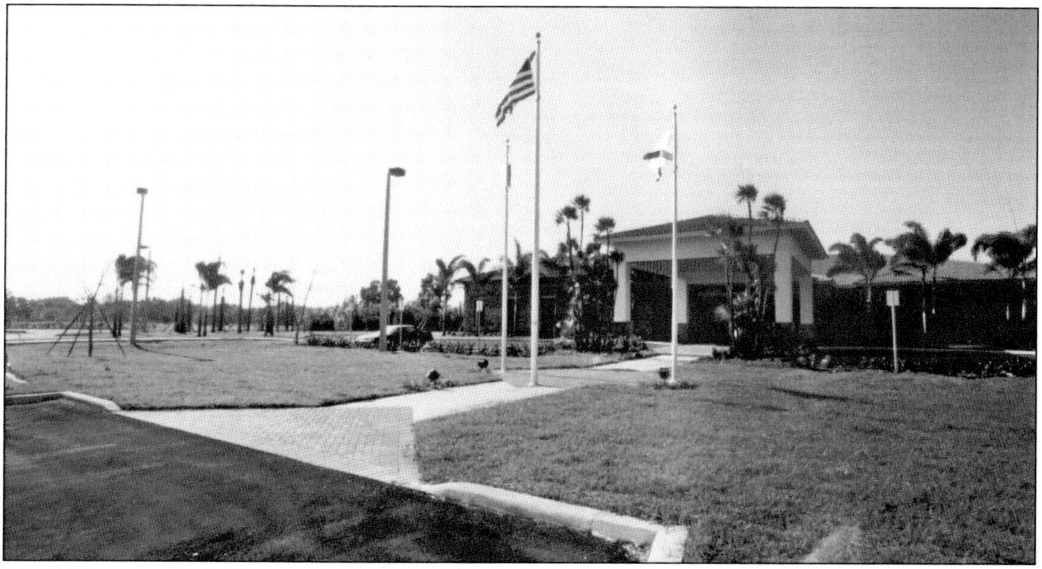

The Volunteer Park Community Center, located in Plantation Acres, was dedicated December 5, 1999. The facility was named for the volunteer efforts of the many civic organizations and individuals that had been so important in Plantation's development. Since its opening, the property has added the Camp Everglades playground, an equestrian center, and a wetlands preserve with a walking trail.

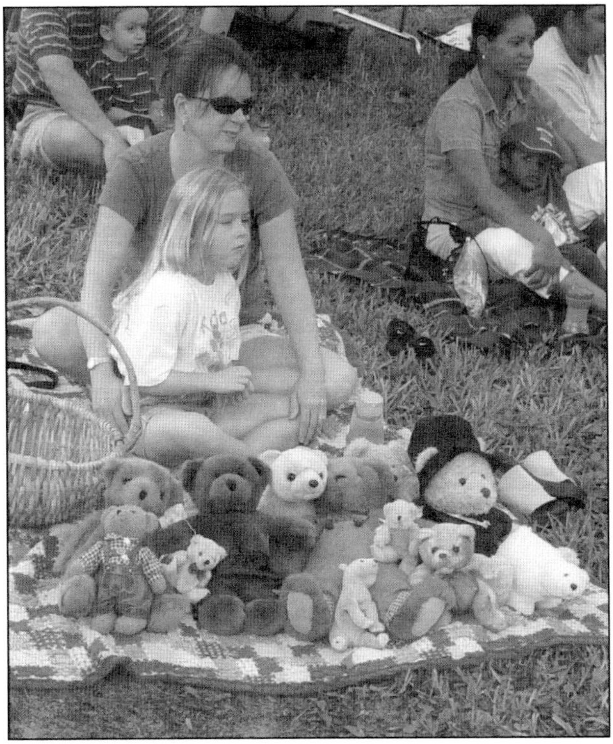

The Helen B. Hoffman Plantation Library holds its annual Teddy Bear Picnic on the first Saturday in May each year. Children bring their bears and a picnic to the library's Reading Garden to listen to stories told by the Broward County Storytellers Guild and march in the Teddy Bear Parade.

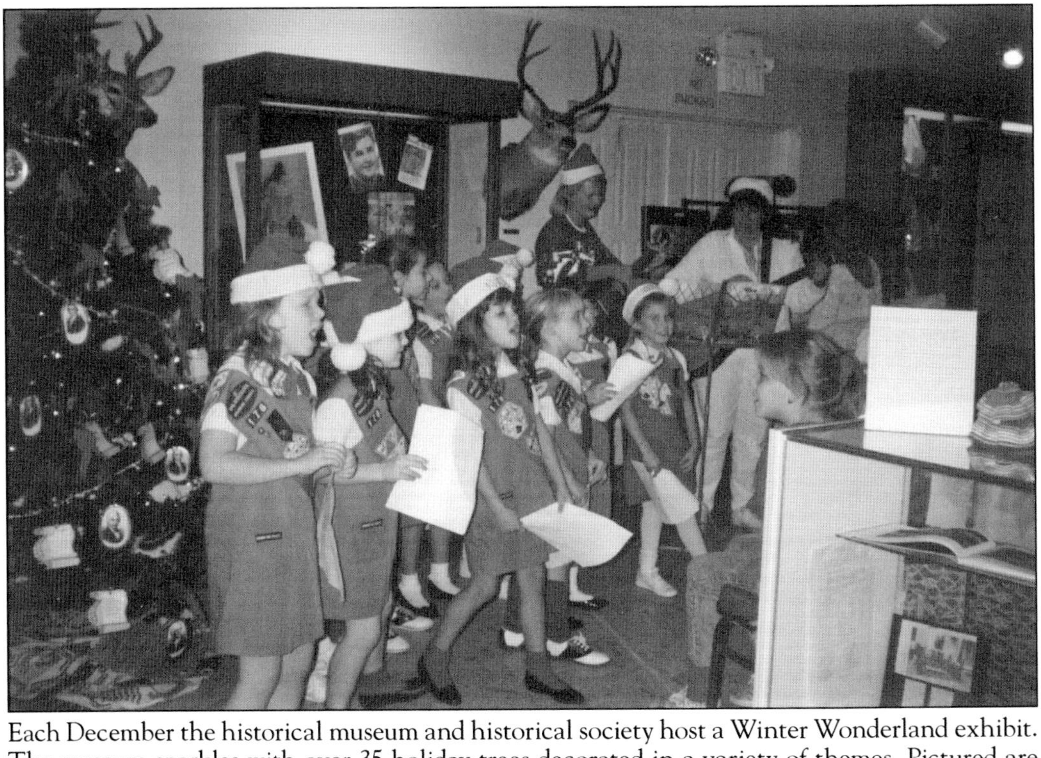

Each December the historical museum and historical society host a Winter Wonderland exhibit. The museum sparkles with over 35 holiday trees decorated in a variety of themes. Pictured are local Brownie Girl Scouts caroling at the museum.

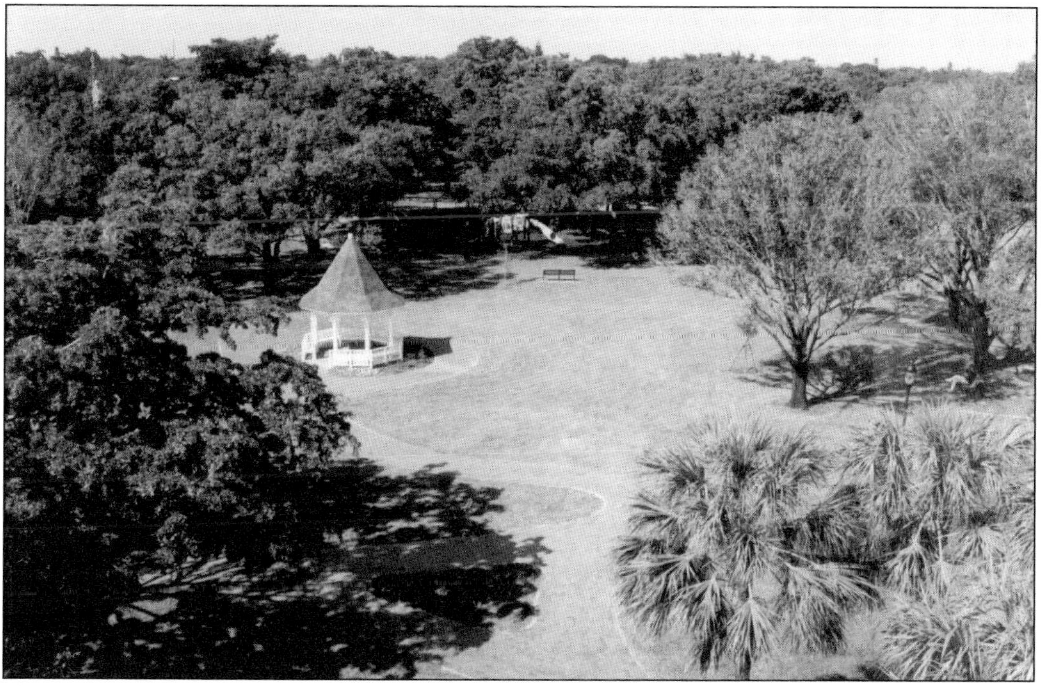

Plantation's Fifth Street Park was renamed Liberty Tree Park during the 1976 US bicentennial celebration. A 45-foot oak tree was planted in the park representing the "Liberty Tree," an elm tree that stood in Boston near the Boston Common in the days before the American Revolution. In October 1989, the Plantation Junior Woman's Club donated a gazebo for weddings and special events. In September 2009, the park was renamed Rae Carole Armstrong Liberty Tree Park in honor of Mayor Armstrong's dedication to parks, trees, and green spaces. She is pictured below participating in an Arbor Day tree planting with elected officials and local students.

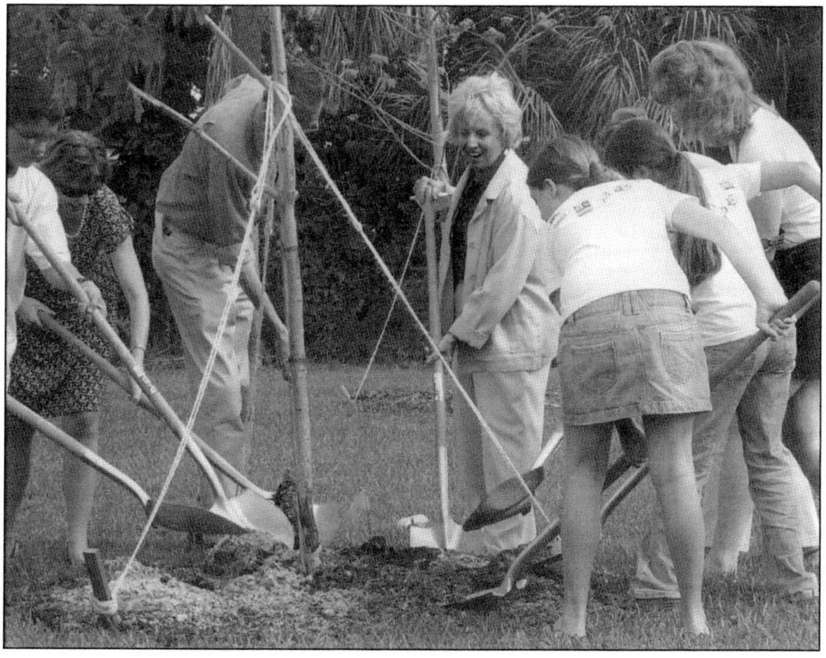

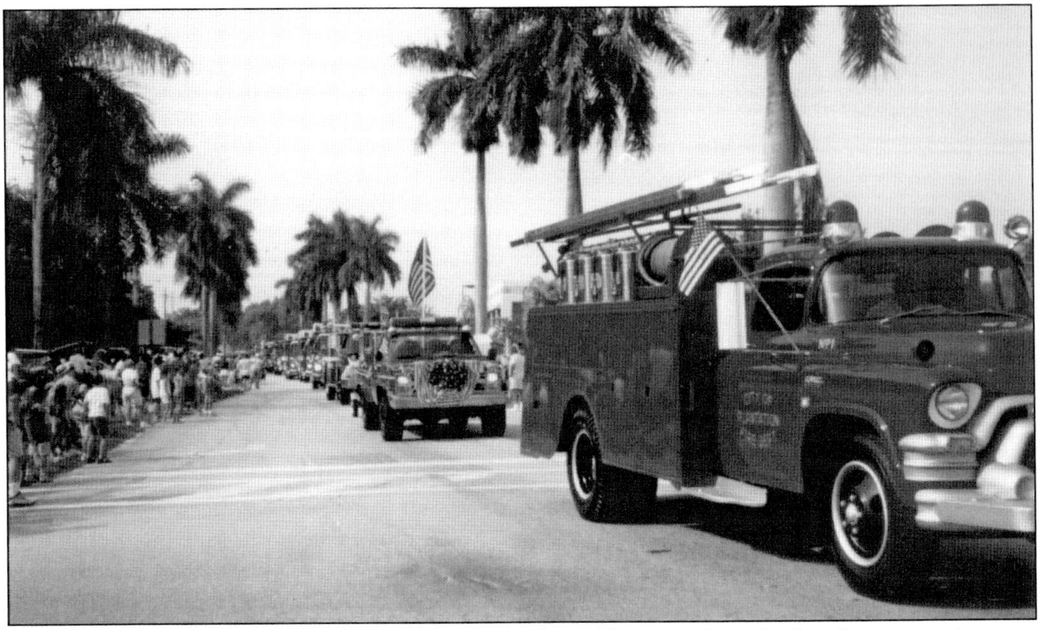

One of the highlights of the city's annual Independence Day parade is the fire department's entry, which includes the majority of the department's fire and rescue vehicles. Pictured above, at far right, is the city's very first firefighting vehicle, Engine No. 1, which now resides at the Plantation Historical Museum. Pictured below at the 1990 ground breaking for the firehouse addition to the Plantation Historical Museum are, from left to right, Agnes Barrett, Betty Crawford, Joan Sidoni, Genevieve Veltri, Kathy Fasting, Rose Scevola, Grace Csoka, and Anneen Longfellow. The new addition to the museum was designed to house Engine No. 1, a GMC front-end pumper purchased in 1956, as well as a large collection of fire memorabilia.

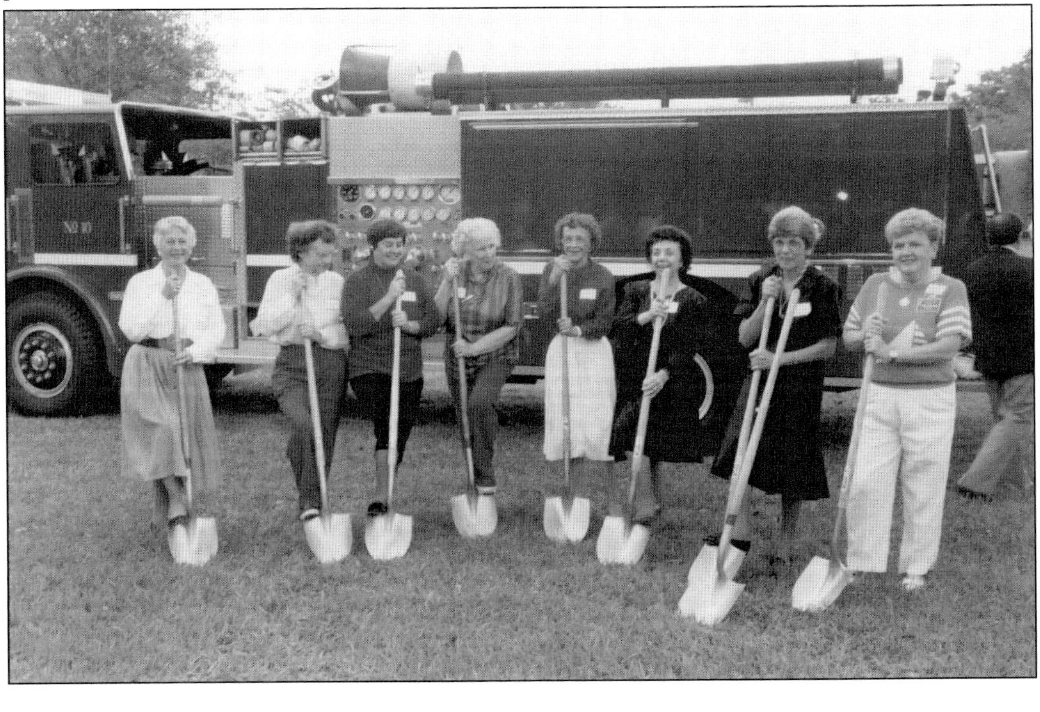

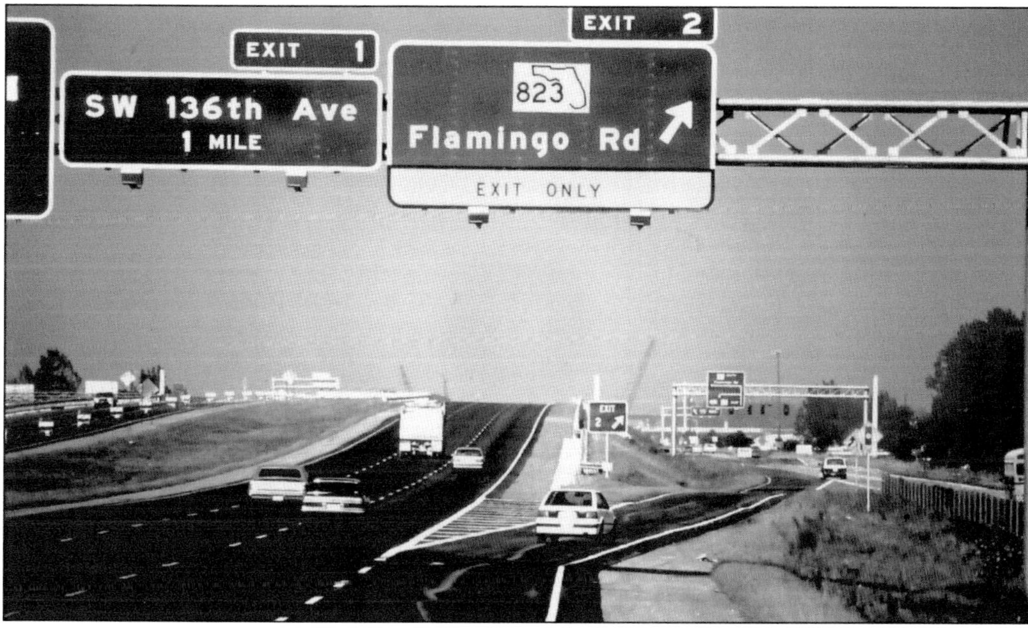

Interstate 595, also known as the Port Everglades Expressway, was conceived in 1969. Construction began in 1984, with the highway opening in stages, and was completed in 1991. Pictured are the Flamingo Road and Interstate 595 intersection and the ribbon cutting for the grand opening of the intersection. Those pictured are, from left to right, (first row) Plantation representatives Gary Clough, city engineer; police chief Morris Meek; Mayor Frank Veltri of Plantation; and police captain Keith Hilgenfeld of Plantation; (second row) Councilman Steven Effman of Sunrise; Fred Reynolds, project manager; Mayor Dan Pearle; Councilman Roger Wishner; Steven Feren; and Councilwoman Fran Klauber, all elected officials of the city of Sunrise.

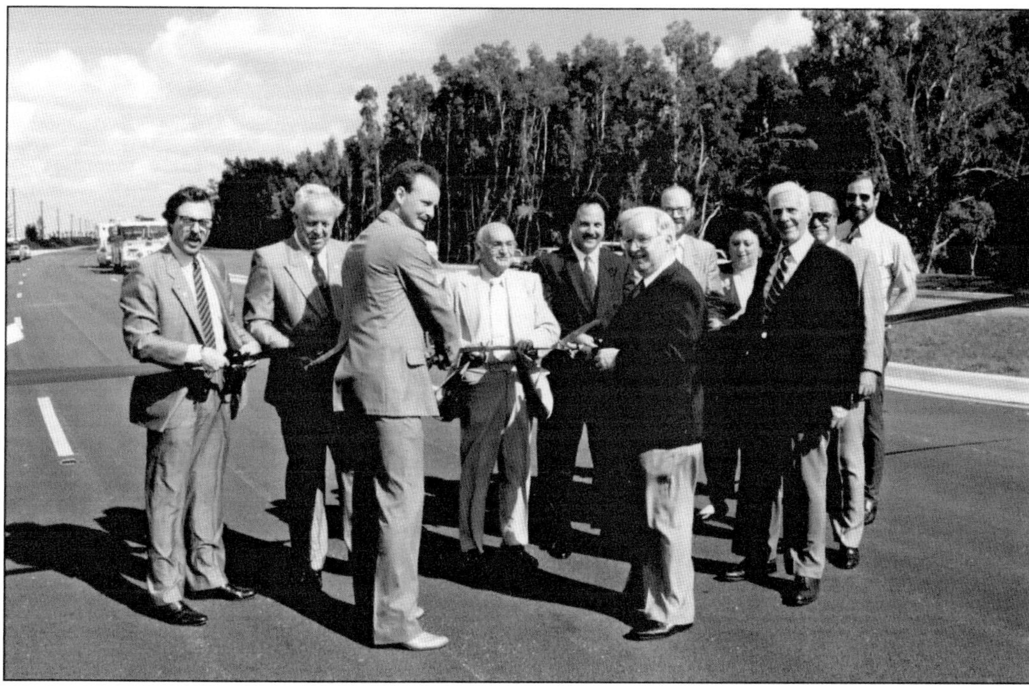

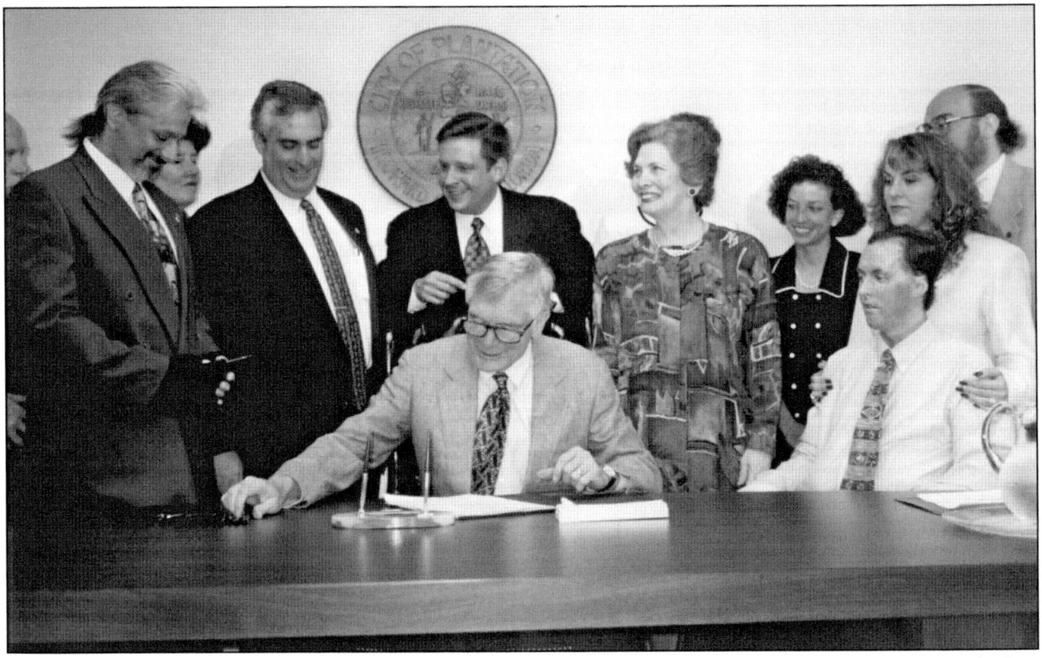

Gov. Lawton Chiles is pictured in 1996 signing the Alu-O'Hara Public Safety Act, named after Joseph Alu and fellow injured officer James O'Hara, officers severely burned in the line of duty. The measure guaranteed that officers would continue to receive health benefits after a catastrophic on-the-job injury.

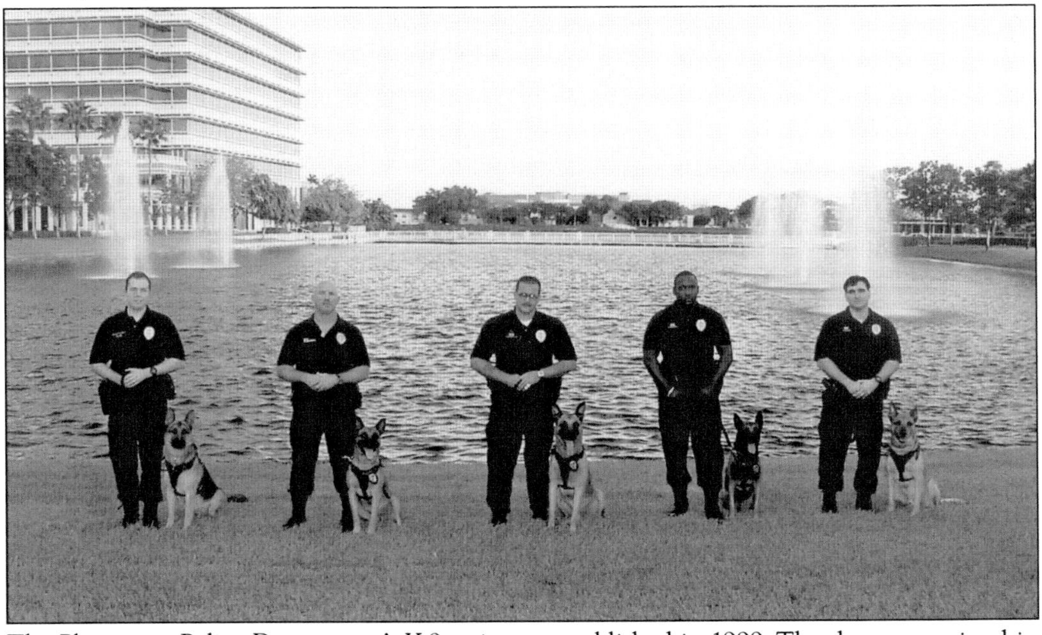

The Plantation Police Department's K-9 unit was established in 1999. The dogs are trained in criminal apprehension and narcotic detection. The K-9 teams are popular guests at school and city events where they demonstrate their skills. Pictured with their K-9 officers are, from left to right, Sgt. Mark Wendt, Officer Ron Massuco, Officer Curt Hampton, Officer Curtis Riddick, and Officer Rob Marek.

The Plantation fire department's rescue division began service in March 1996. Pictured are the "Dirty Dozen," the original 12 members of the Emergency Medical Services Division.

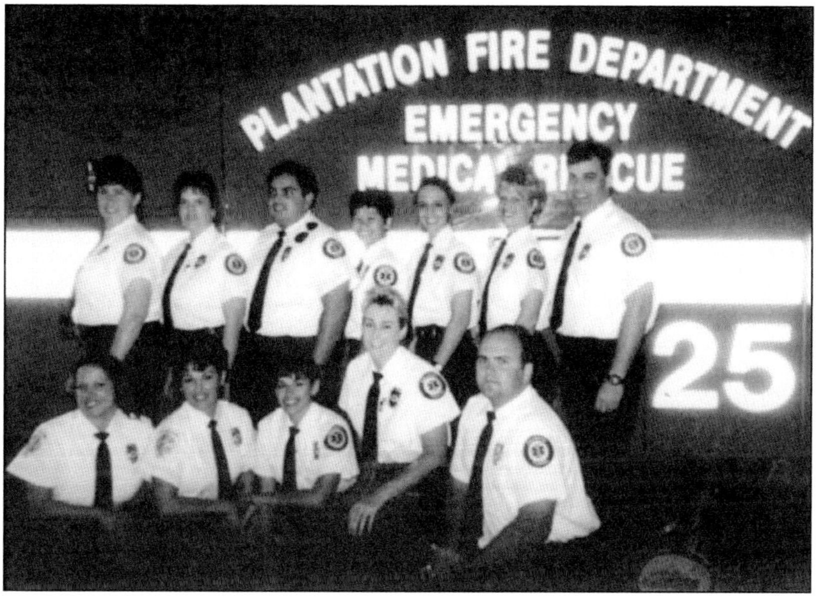

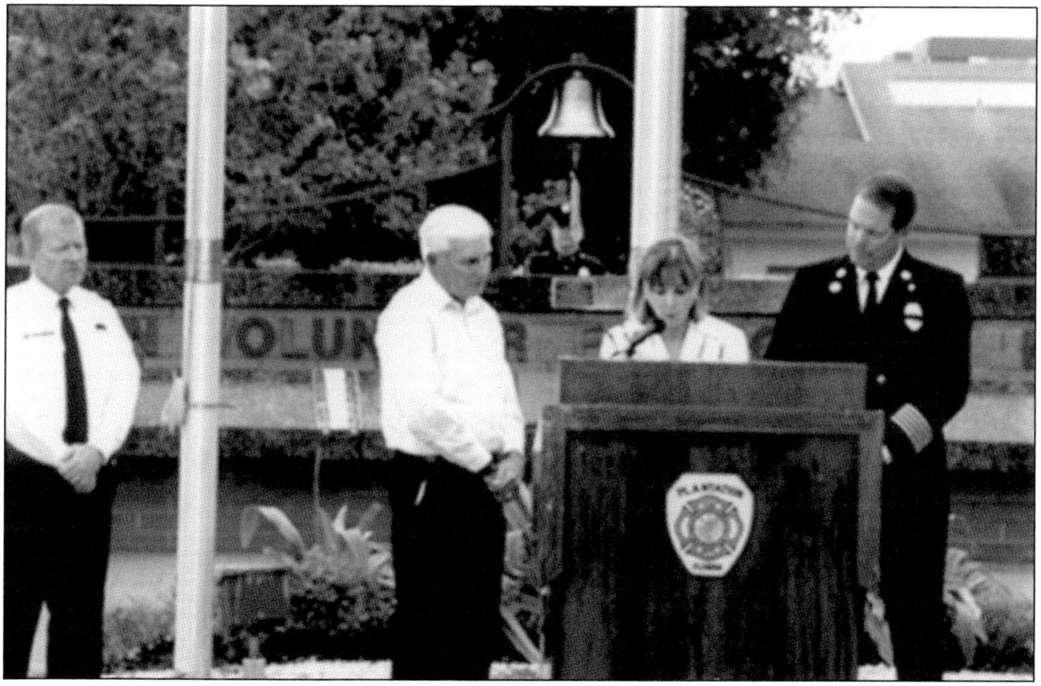

The City of Plantation Fire Department Memorial Bell was dedicated October 27, 2007, in memory of former fire chief and mayor Frank Veltri for his leadership and dedication to the City of Plantation and the fire department. The bell, tuned to the note of "C," tolls the final call to duty at the Plantation Volunteer Fire Association's annual memorial service each October. Pictured are, from left to right, Chris Terwilleger, president of the fire association; Stephen Veltri; Councilwoman Diane Veltri Bendekovic; and fire chief Robert Pudney.

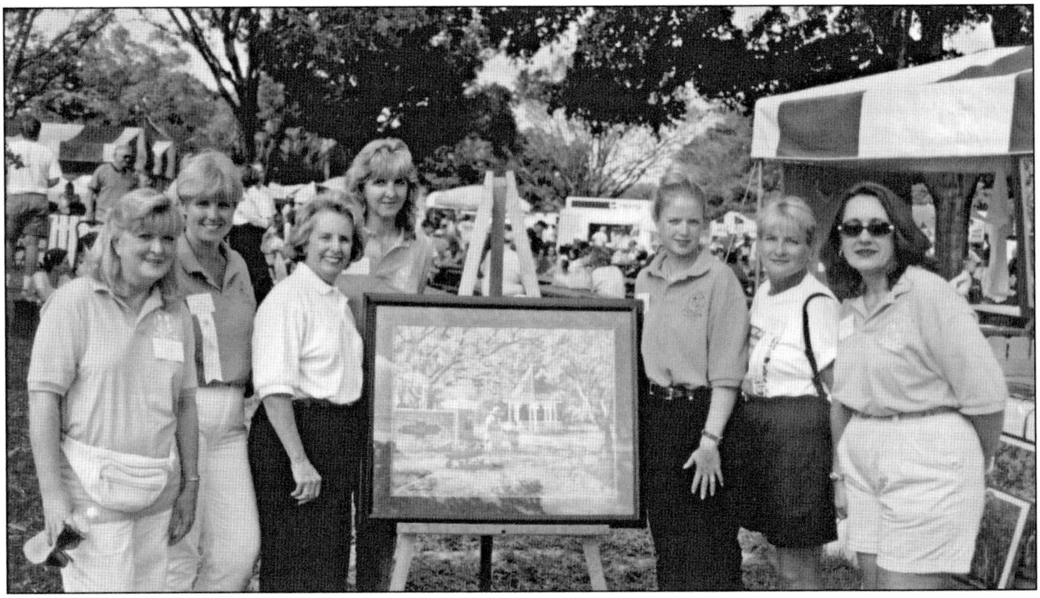

The Plantation Junior Woman's Club's Fall Arts Festival became Art in the Park in 1976. For two days every fall, Liberty Tree Park is home to this popular festival, which features local artists, craftsmen, and sculptures. For many years, one of the highlights was the Art in the Park annual poster. Pictured are Mayor Rae Carole Armstrong and members of the PJWC with an Art in the Park poster.

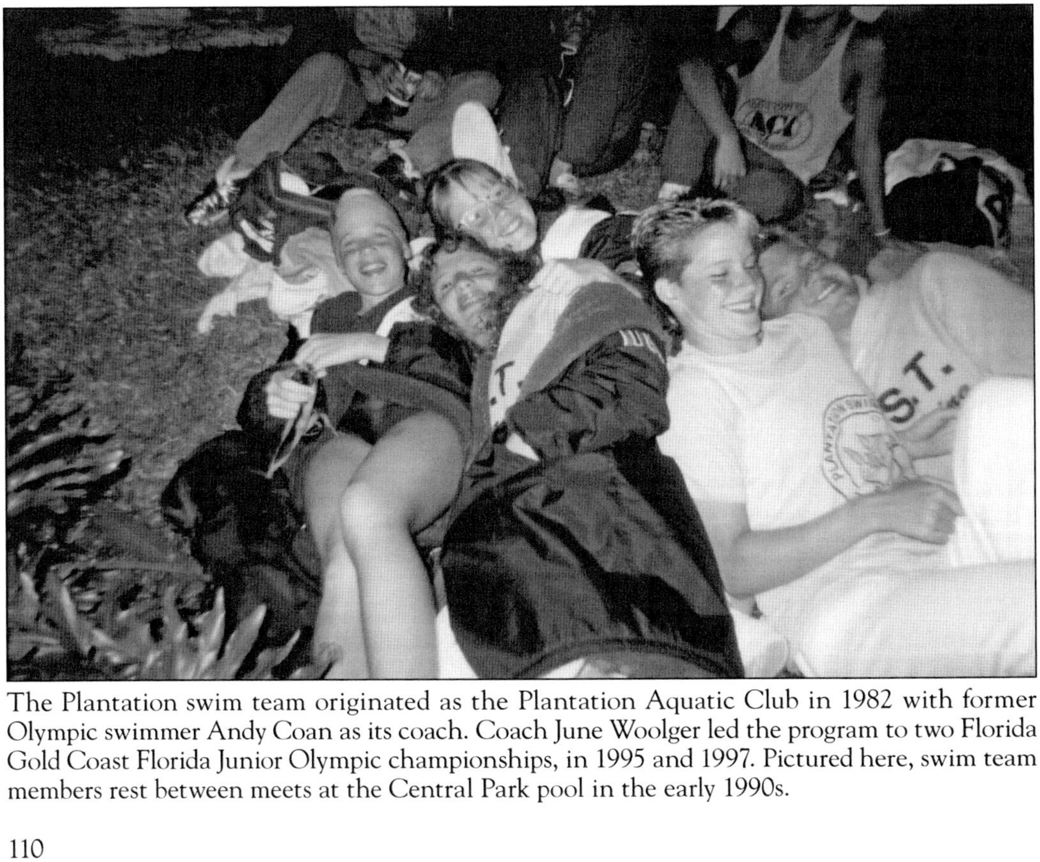

The Plantation swim team originated as the Plantation Aquatic Club in 1982 with former Olympic swimmer Andy Coan as its coach. Coach June Woolger led the program to two Florida Gold Coast Florida Junior Olympic championships, in 1995 and 1997. Pictured here, swim team members rest between meets at the Central Park pool in the early 1990s.

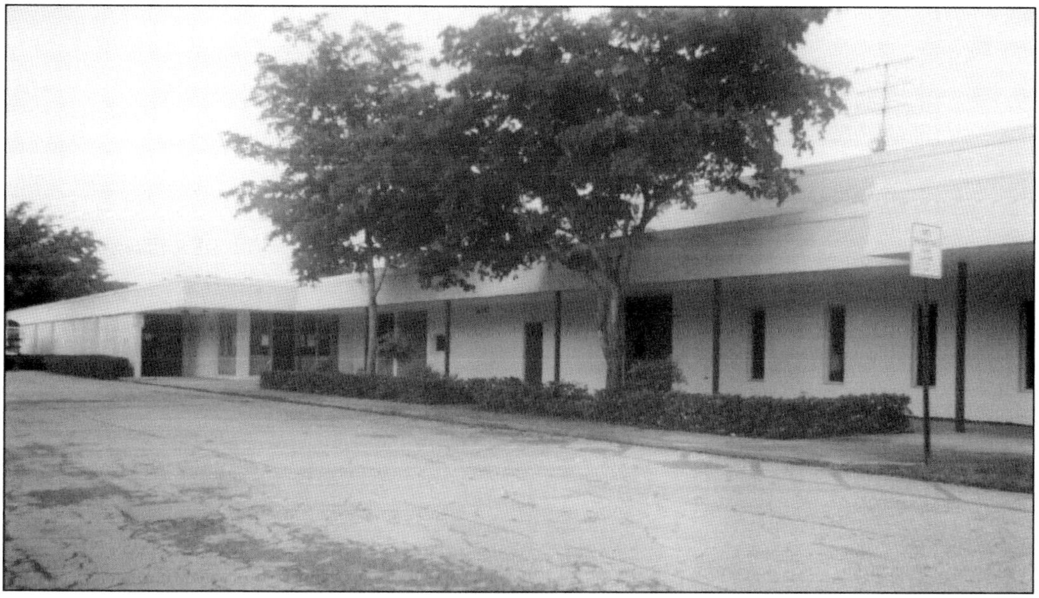

Plantation Elementary School opened in 1965 on Northwest 46th Avenue. After 35 years the school closed, and in 2000 a new facility was opened about one mile from the original on Northwest 42nd Avenue. The city engaged in a land exchange with the Broward County school board and built the Jim Ward Community Center on the original school site in 2002. Pictured here is the front of the original school in the late 1990s.

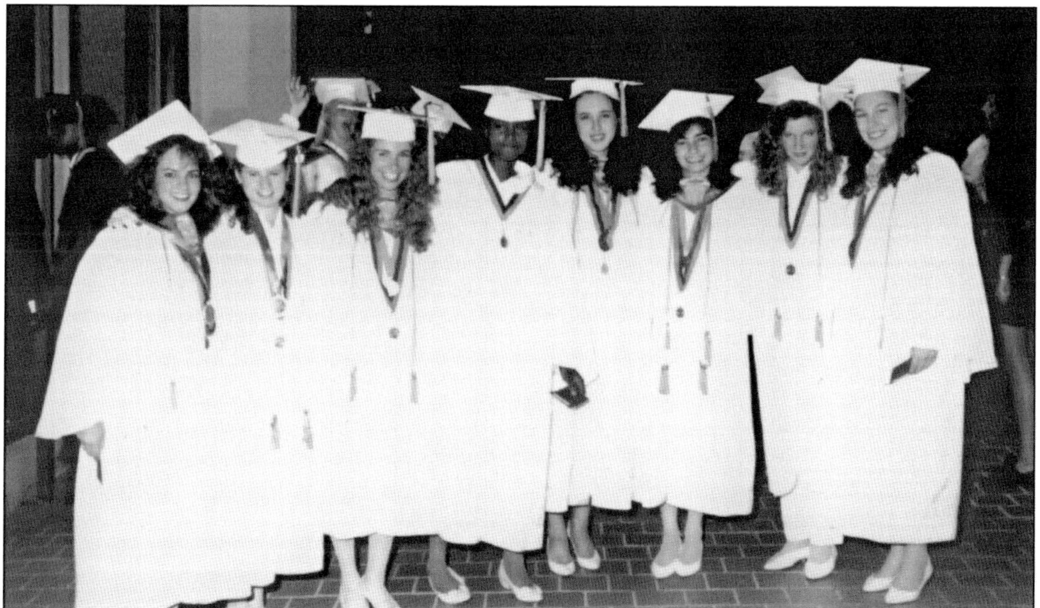

South Plantation High School, also known locally as simply "South" (to avoid confusion with Plantation High), started in 1971 and shared a building with Plantation High School. Plantation High students attended classes in the morning and South students in the afternoon. In February 1972, SPHS students were moved to the school's current campus on the corner of Southwest 54th Avenue and Peters Road. The first graduating class was in June 1973. Pictured are graduating Paladins from the class of 1992.

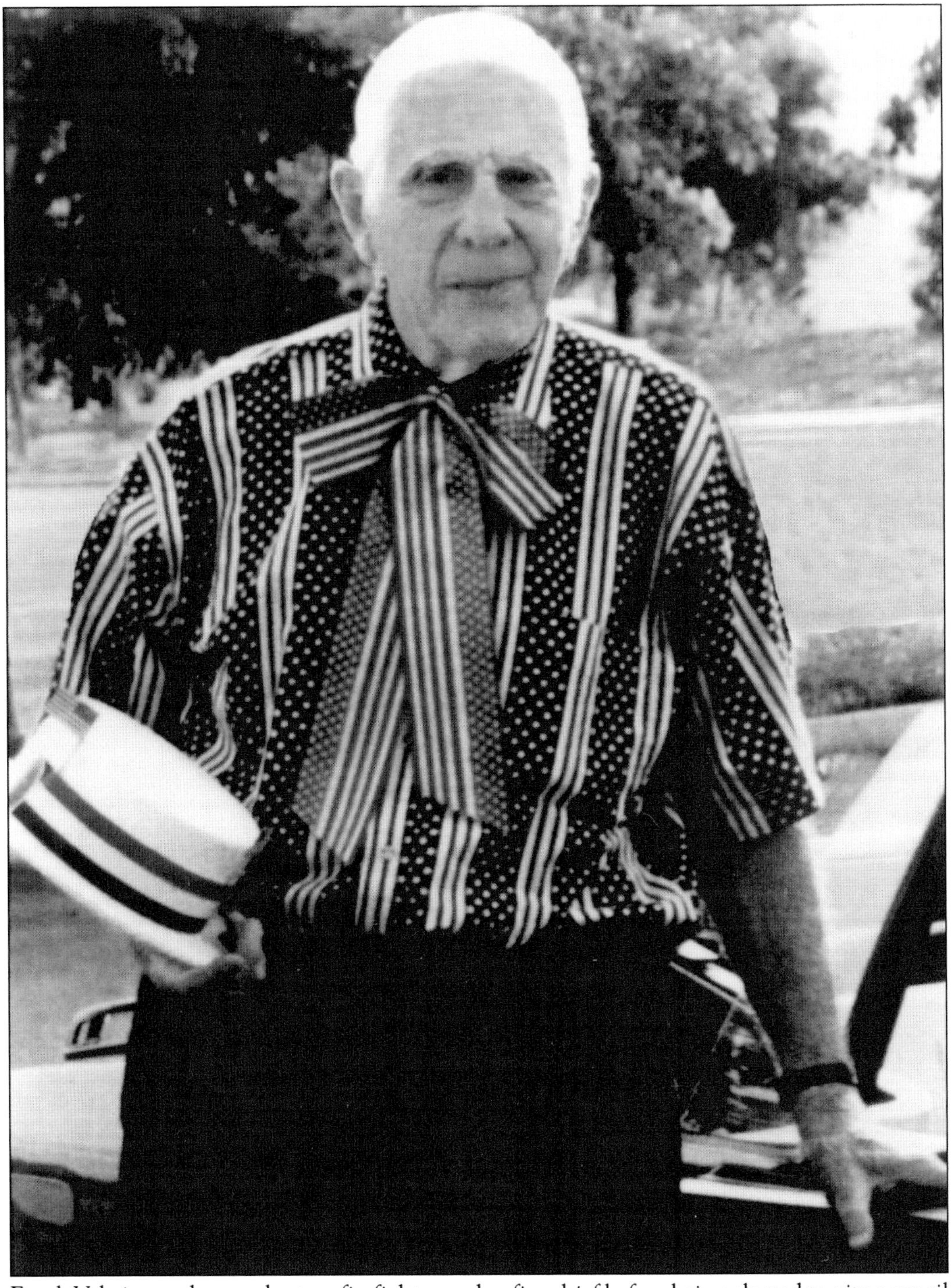

Frank Veltri served as a volunteer firefighter and as fire chief before being elected to city council in 1968. He served as mayor for 24 years, 1975–1999, one of the longest consecutively-elected mayors in the United States. He retired as mayor at the age of 86, but his love of the city, interest in politics, and involvement in the community never diminished. Mayor Veltri is pictured in his signature Fourth of July parade attire.

Eight

THE 2000S

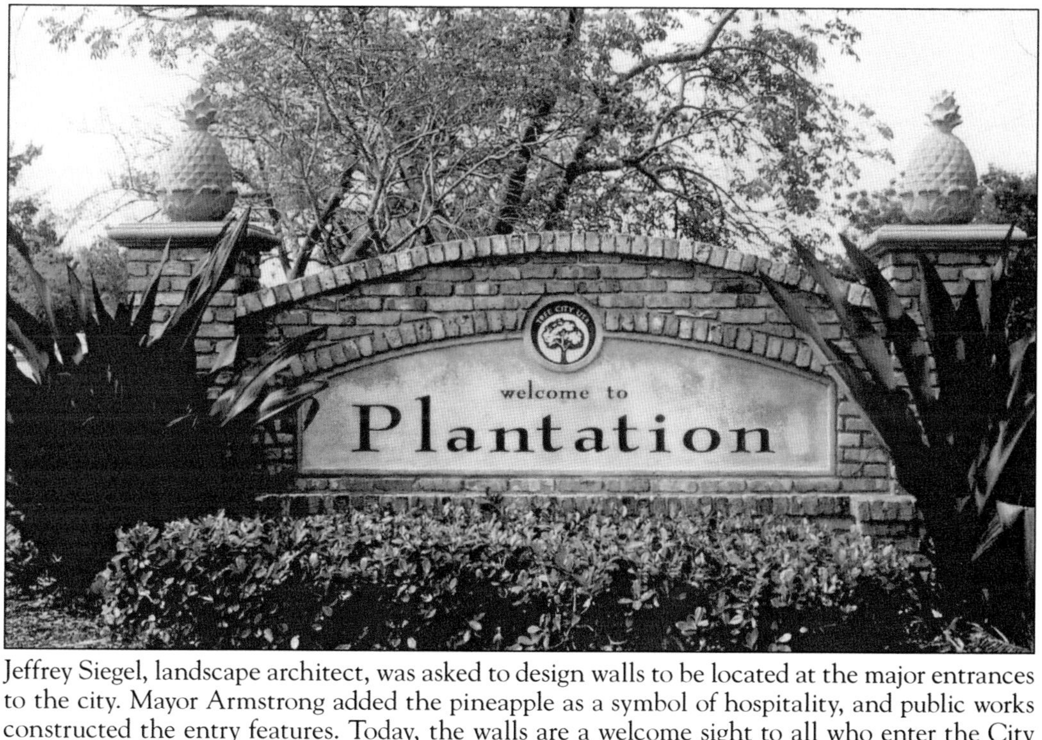

Jeffrey Siegel, landscape architect, was asked to design walls to be located at the major entrances to the city. Mayor Armstrong added the pineapple as a symbol of hospitality, and public works constructed the entry features. Today, the walls are a welcome sight to all who enter the City of Plantation.

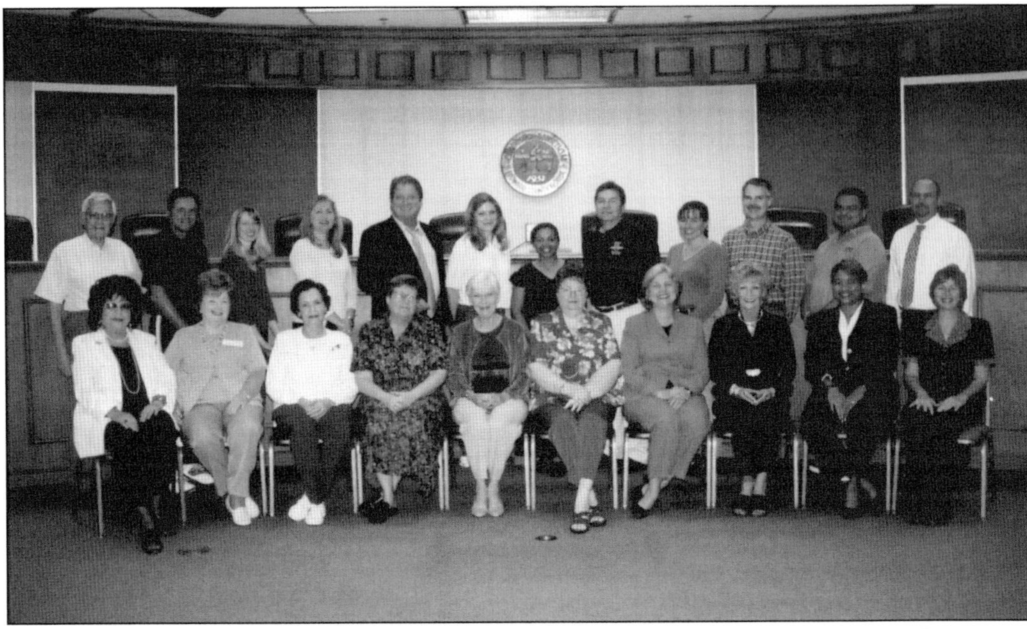

The city celebrated its 50th anniversary in April 2003. The Plantation Anniversary Committee planned a fun-filled eight days of events. Young and old participated in Family Fun Day, History and Cultural Night, and the tennis and golf tournaments. Prior to the celebration's start, there was press coverage for the opening of the time capsule. The 25th anniversary time capsule was donated by T.M. Ralph Funeral Home and memorabilia is added to it every 25 years. In the center of the photograph below, looking into the capsule, are, from left to right, superintendent of facilities Donna Trafford, Judy and Tom Ralph, *Sun-Sentinel* photographer Lou Toman, and his son Phil Toman.

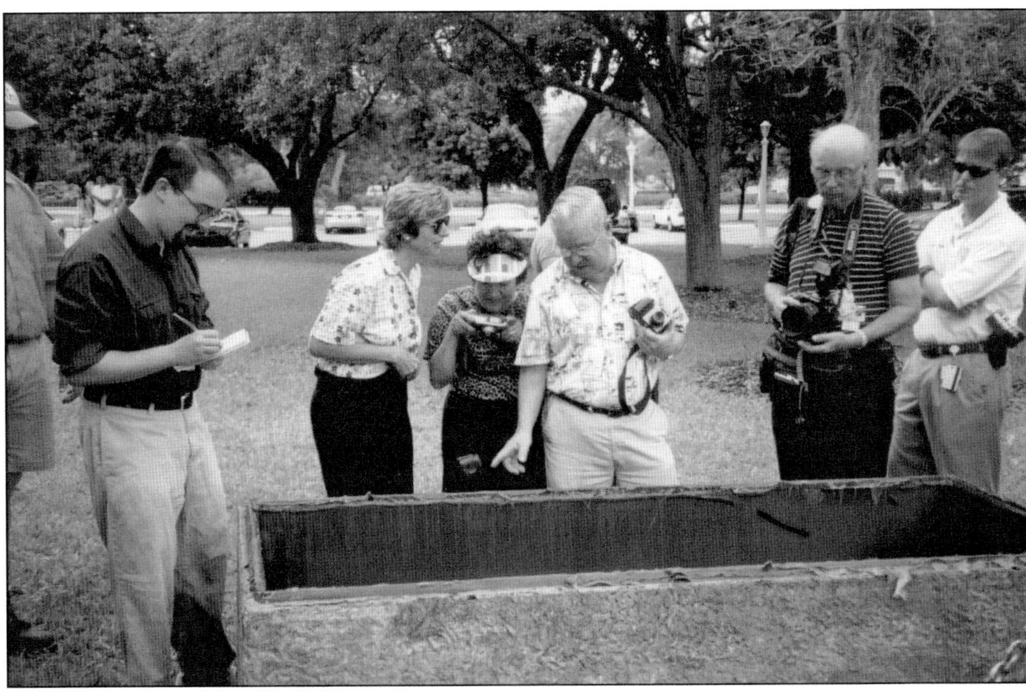

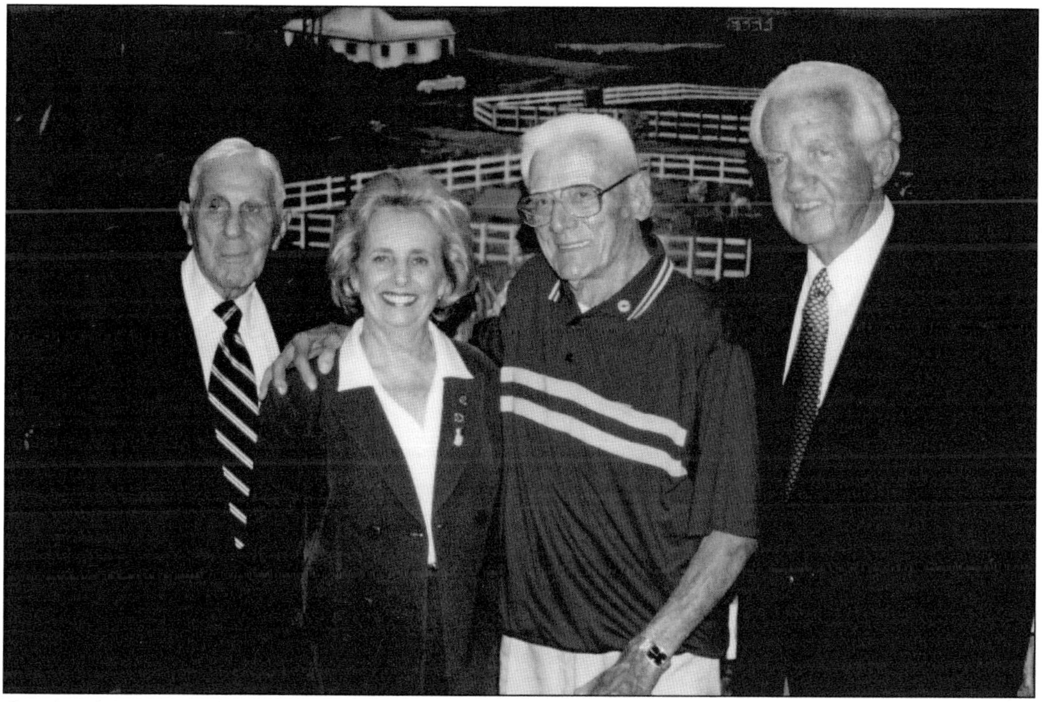

On April 30, 2003, the 50th anniversary ended with a ceremony at city hall. Plantation residents past and present were invited to this historic event. Pictured above are, from left to right, Mayor Frank Veltri, Mayor Rae Carole Armstrong, Plantation's first police chief Hank Donath, and Mayor Jim Ward. As the city was incorporated in 1953, it was only fitting that a sock hop be part of the celebration. Below, parks and recreation staff pose with candy cigarettes at the sock hop.

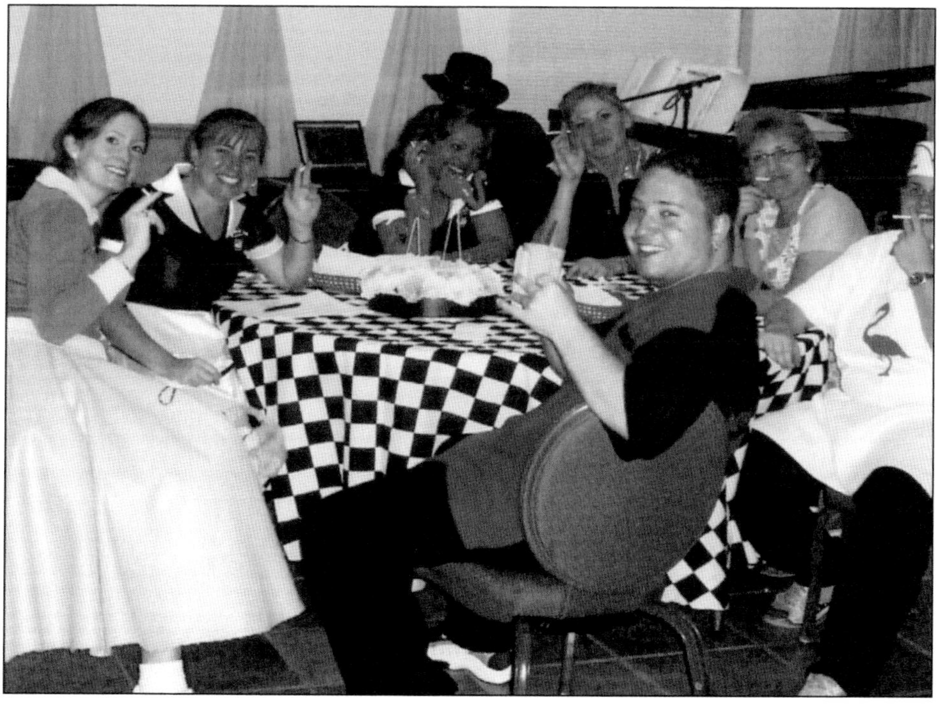

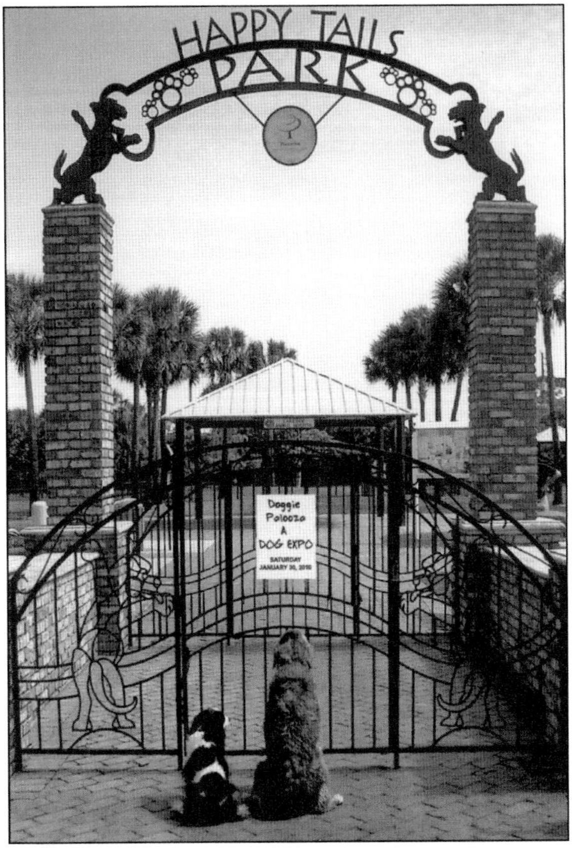

Happy Tails Dog Park opened at Seminole Park on March 2, 2002. The city received a grant from the Florida Recreation Development Assistance Program to build the five-acre park. Happy Tails is home to the popular Doggie Palooza dog expo and is a training facility for the city's police K-9 unit. There are a lot of happy tails wagging daily at this park!

The Jim Ward Community Center opened on January 12, 2002, on the site of the old Plantation Elementary School. Continuing a tradition of recognizing Plantation mayors, the facility was name after Plantation's third mayor, Jim Ward. Pictured here are, from left to right, Mayor and Mrs. Jim Ward, Mayor Armstrong, Priscilla Hawks, Shirley Baker, Kingsley Smith, and Councilman Ralph Merritt III.

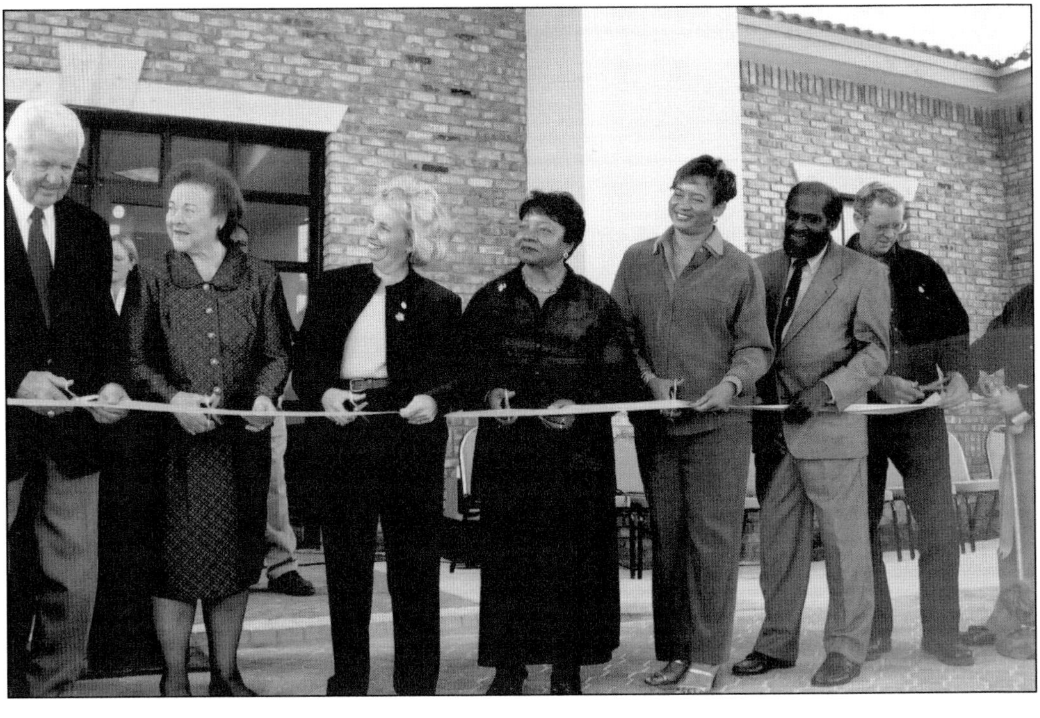

The Plantation Equestrian Center opened on April 2, 2005. Part of the Volunteer Park expansion project, the facility replaced the Plantation Horse Arena on 118th Avenue. Mayor Rae Carole Armstrong and Ron Bergeron of Bergeron Land Development are pictured at right at the dedication ceremony. The new center featured two barns with 96 stalls, three show rings, and two practice rings. Another aspect of the expansion project included a new playground, Camp Everglades, a unique play area modeled after the Florida Everglades. The December 21, 2004, ribbon-cutting ceremony (below) included children from the American Heritage School. The adults are, from left to right, public works assistant director Mike Scott, design and construction director Danny Ezzeddine, assistant parks and recreation director Sharon Kent, associate landscape architect Patrice Sonnelitter, parks and recreation director Jim Romano, Mayor Armstrong, Plantation chamber of commerce executive director Siobhan Edwards, and chief administrative officer Dan Keefe.

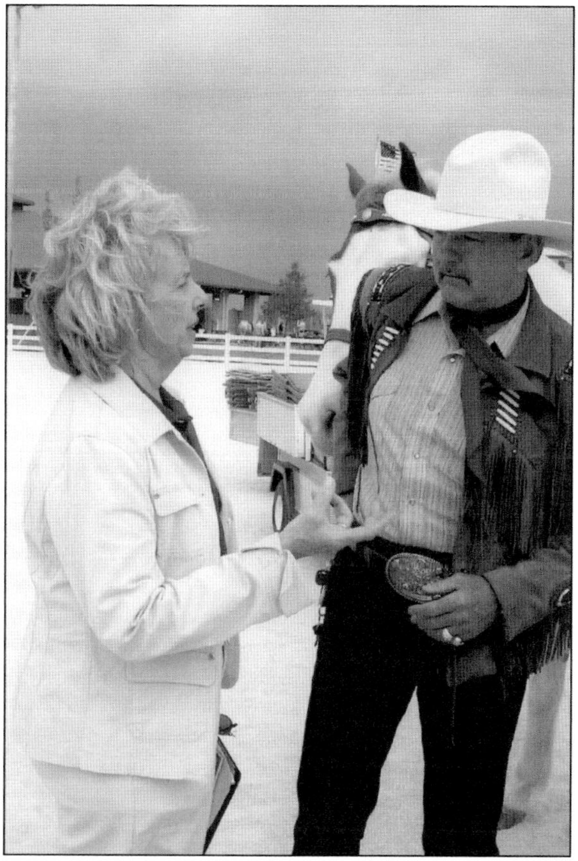

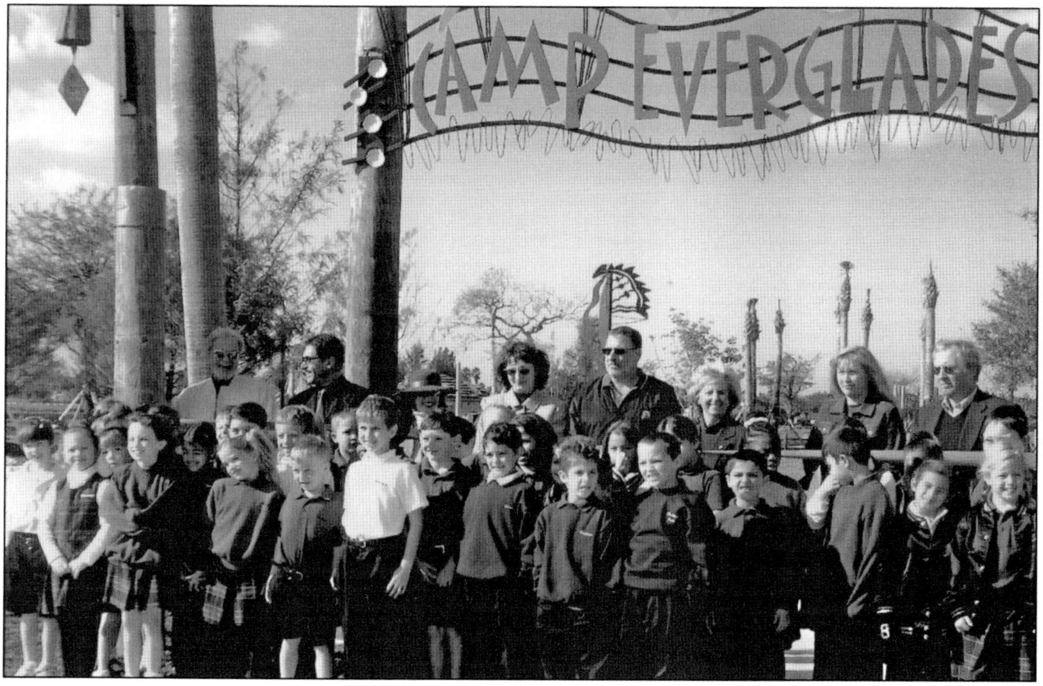

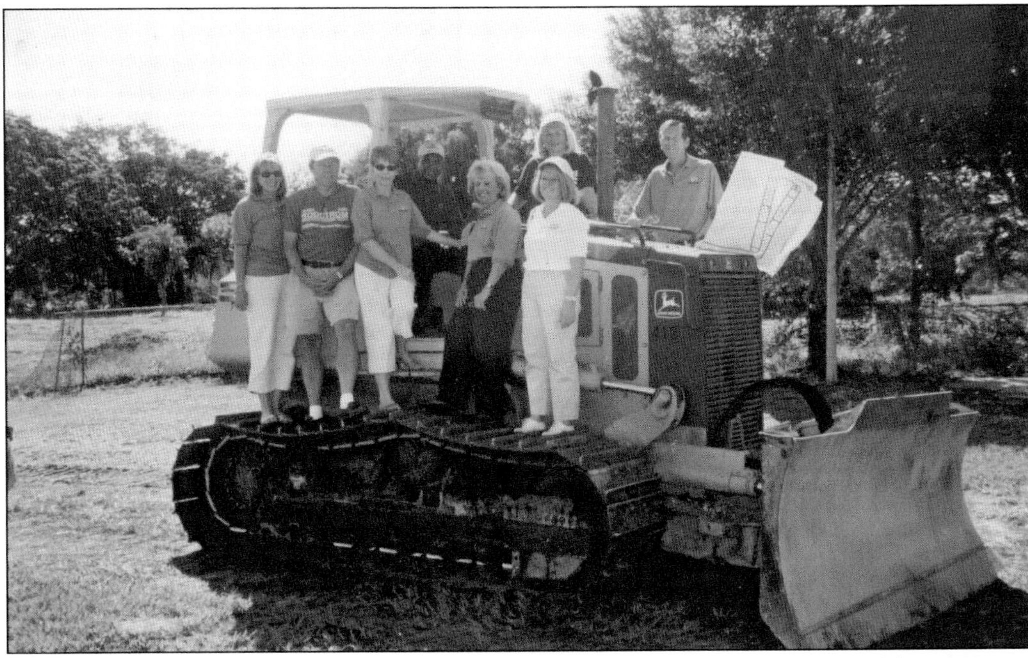

In December 2002, the city purchased the Plantation Golf Course property and hired Hagge, Smelnek & Baril to design a new golf course. Pictured above at the August 28, 2004, Plantation Preserve ground breaking ceremony are, from left to right, (first row) Councilmember Diane Veltri Bendekovic, County Commissioner John Rodstrom, Councilmember Sharon Moody Uria, Mayor Rae Carole Armstrong, and County Commissioner Ilene Lieberman; (second row) County Commissioners Josephus Eggelletion and Lori Parrish, and Councilman Jerry Fadgen. The Plantation Preserve Golf Course and Club were dedicated on April 22, 2006. In 2007, the Preserve's unique linear park that divides the front and back nine holes achieved designation as a Certified Audubon Cooperative Sanctuary. Below is the clubhouse as seen from the Island Green ninth hole.

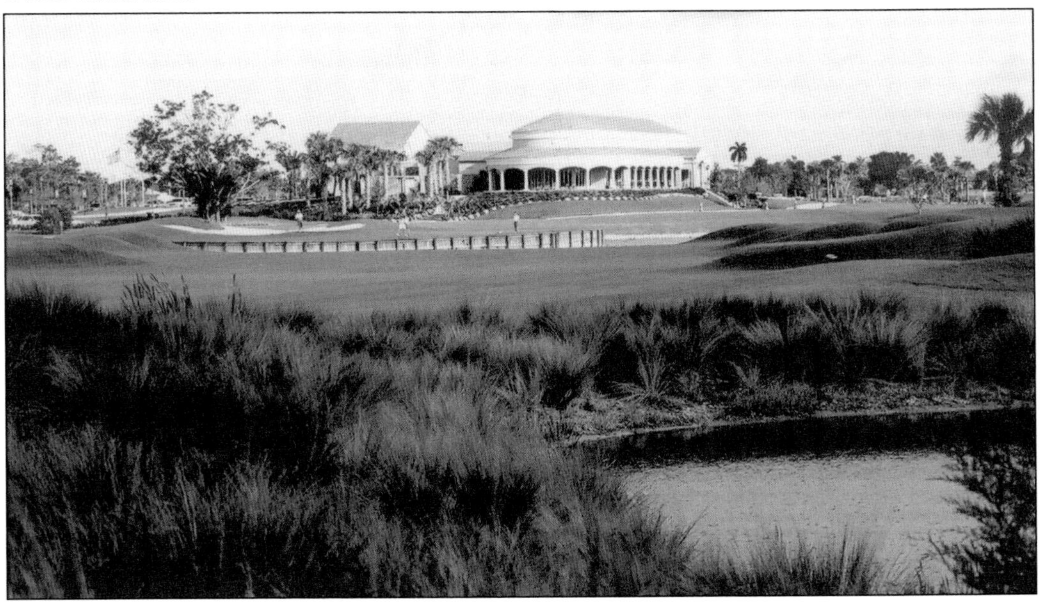

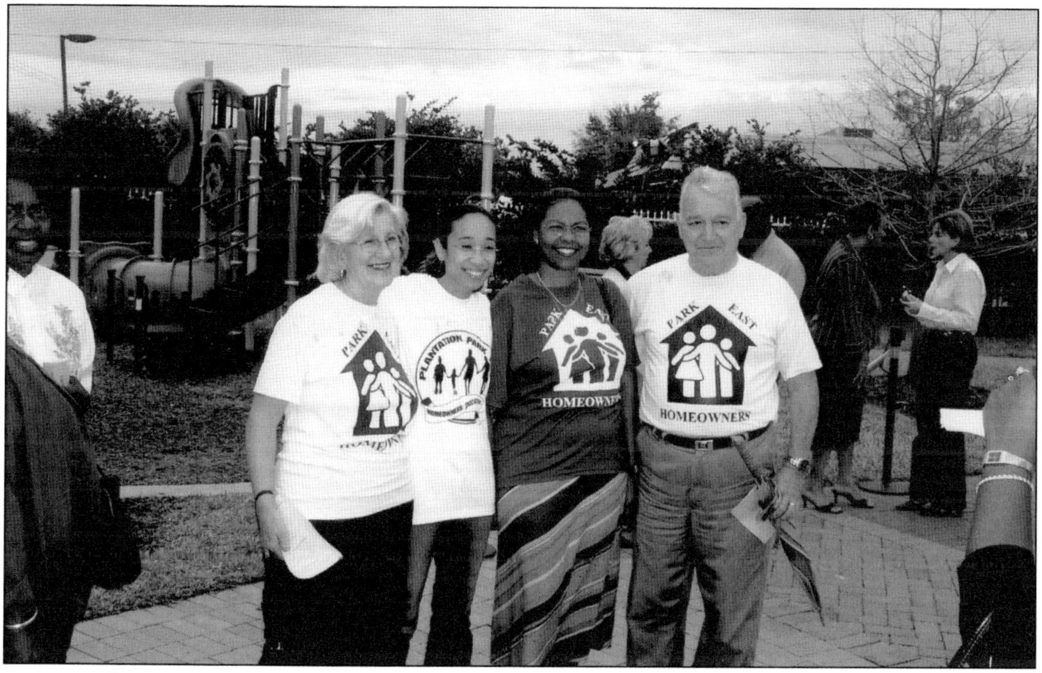

In 2002, the city acquired an abandoned Texaco gas station that serviced northeast Plantation from the mid-1960s through the mid-1990s. Noting the lack of pedestrian walkways and bike paths, the mayor and council, with the help of Plantation Park Homeowners' Association, the City of Plantation Parks and Recreation Advisory Board approved the Park East trailhead designed by landscape architect Jeffrey Siegel. Pictured above are, from left to right, Dolores Stahli, Sandy Gracey, Yvonne Nash, and Rolf Stahli at the February 4, 2006, trailhead dedication. Below, members of the Country Club Estates neighborhood join with Plantation elected officials and staff at the ribbon cutting ceremony of the Country Club Park on March 10, 2007. This 2.89-acre site became the city's 42nd park and included a walking connection to the Country Club Linear Park, a 1.85-mile trail around the Fort Lauderdale Country Club.

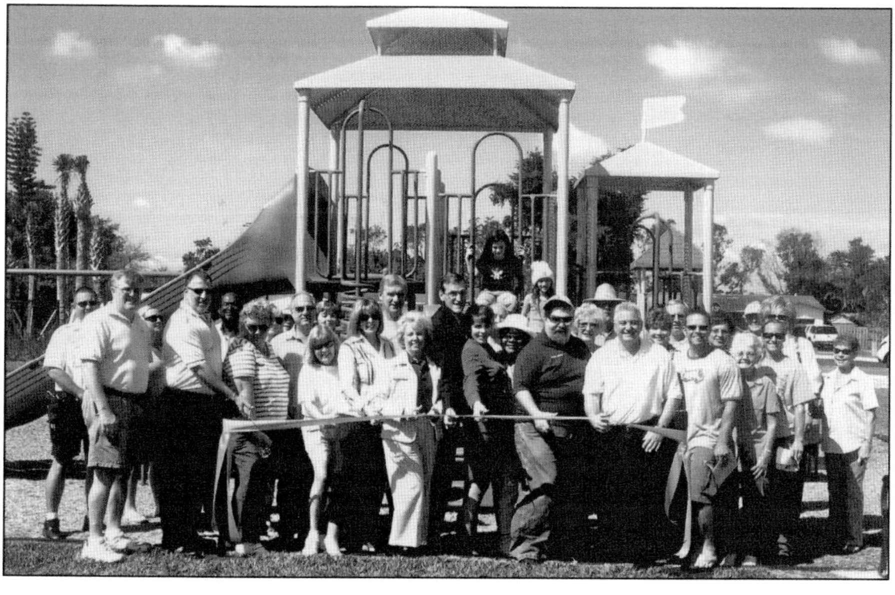

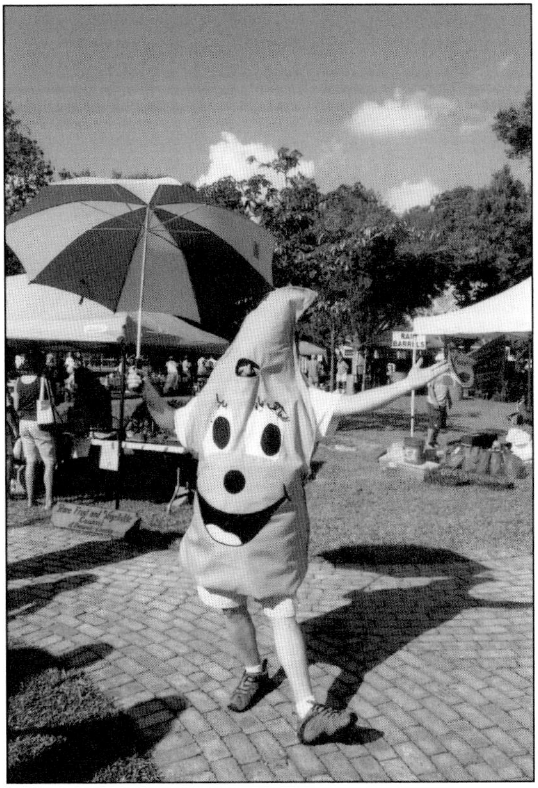

In 2007, the city's landscape department initiated an environmental awareness event at Rae Carole Armstrong Liberty Tree Park. By 2012, the interest in green initiatives, sustainability, and conservation had grown in community participation and attendance. To promote water conservation the city utilities director, Hank Breitenkam, dressed as "Drip the Drop."

Plantation Woods, one of the city's themed parks, opened on June 25, 2010. It is located at Plantation Community Center and features age-specific playground areas and a water splash pad. The park has become one of Plantation's most popular. Here, children enjoy the splash pad at the park's dedication.

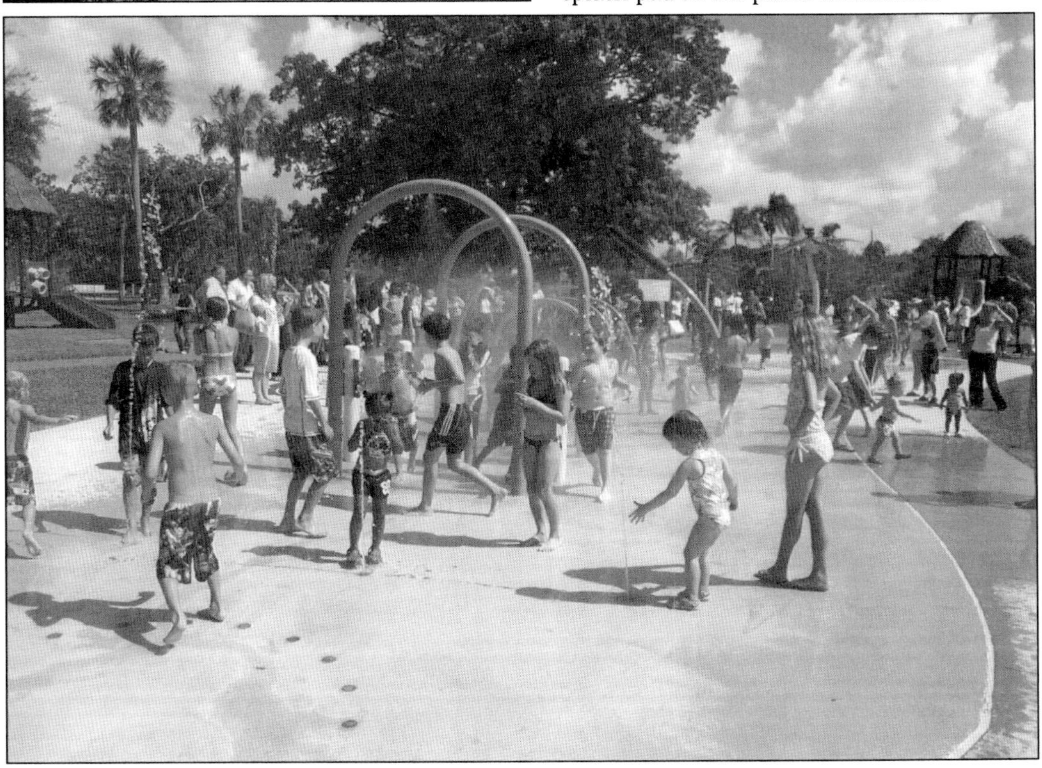

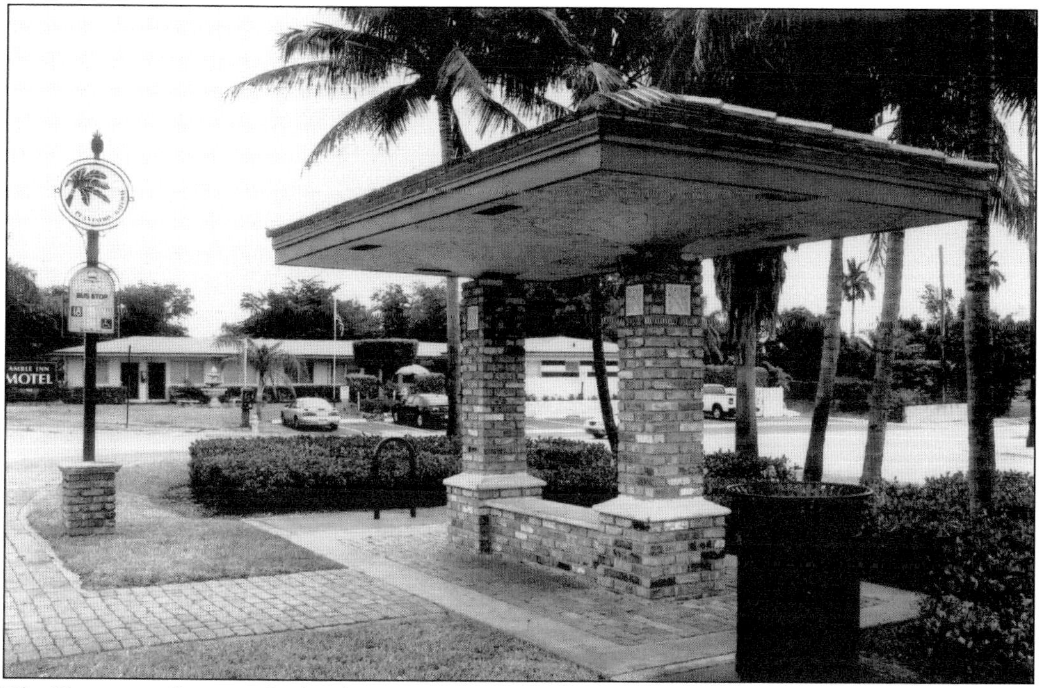

The Plantation Gateway Redevelopment District was created in 2000 after the adoption of the City of Plantation Community Redevelopment Agency Redevelopment Plan. The Gateway Corridor was attained through substantial capital investments and close cooperation with the city and the business community. The Gateway is an economically vibrant business and residential district with public transportation available for all. In 2004, the City of Plantation adopted a conceptual master plan for the Plantation Midtown District. Midtown is a blend of retail shops, corporate offices, medical facilities, restaurants, parks, a regional mall, and residential communities.

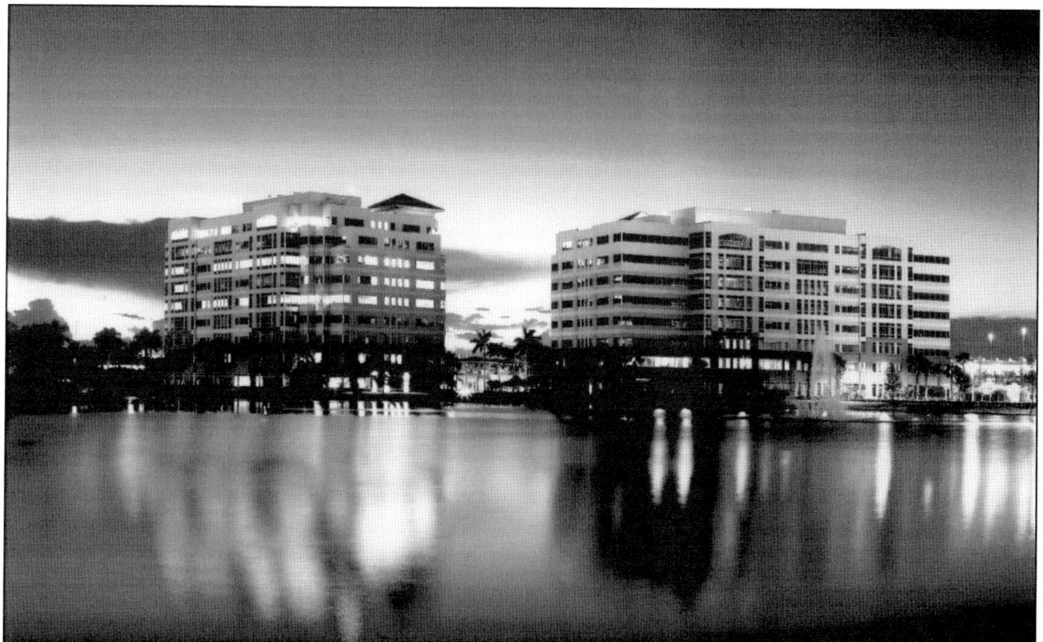

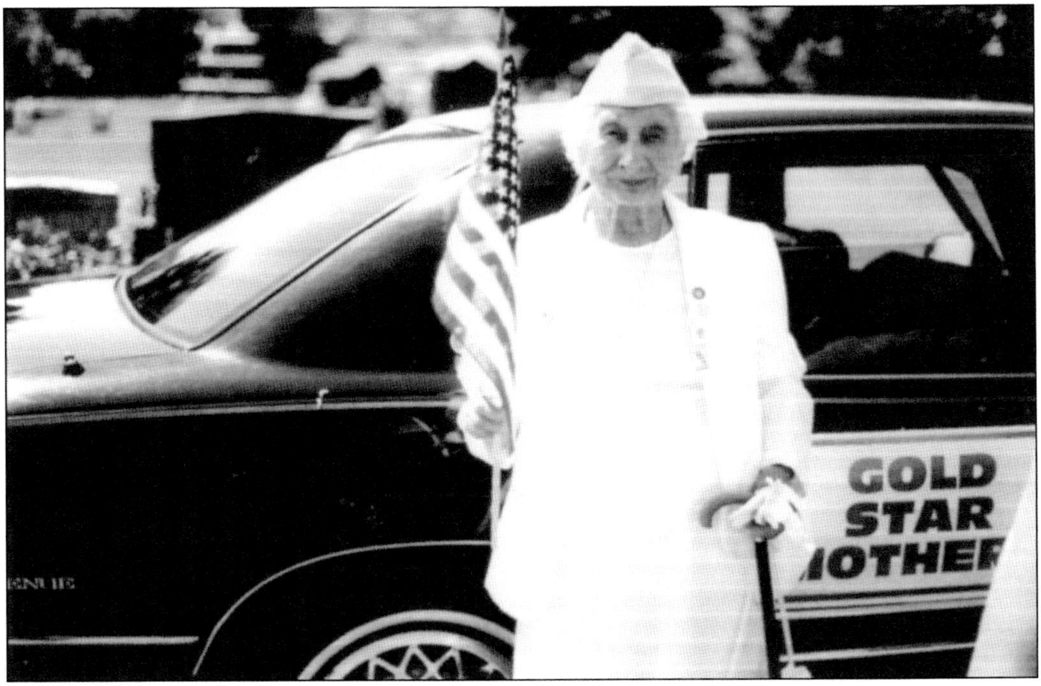

101-year-old Plantation resident Winifred Laflash Lancy was the nation's oldest surviving American Gold Star Mother, a title bestowed upon those who lost a son in World War II. On November 11, 2000, she was invited to attend the National World War II memorial ground breaking ceremony on the National Mall in Washington, DC. The photograph above was taken at the ground breaking. Below, Carl Muscarello, a Plantation resident since 1970, poses with Plantation parks and recreation facility attendant Krista Zawada holding a copy of the *Life* magazine cover photograph taken in Times Square during the Japanese surrender celebration on August 14, 1945. Carl, who claims to be the tall, dark-haired sailor kissing a nurse in the famous photograph, attended the city's Veterans Day service in 2011.

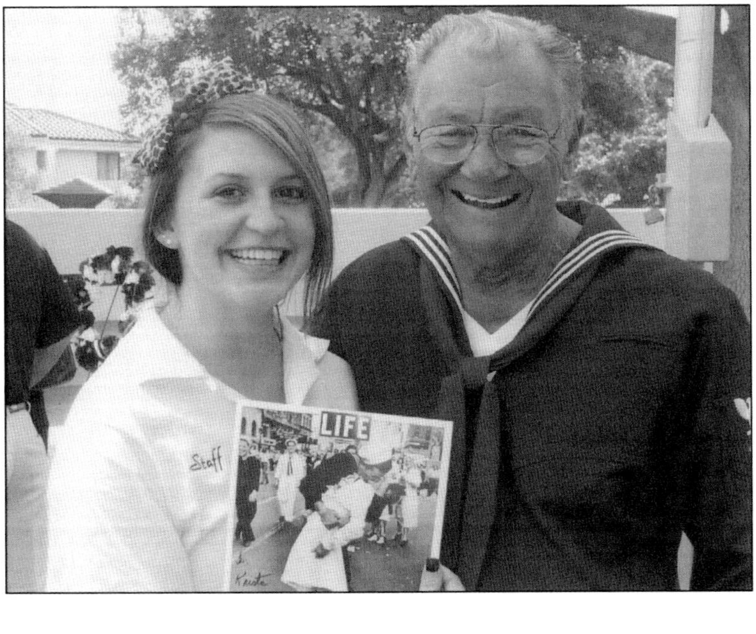

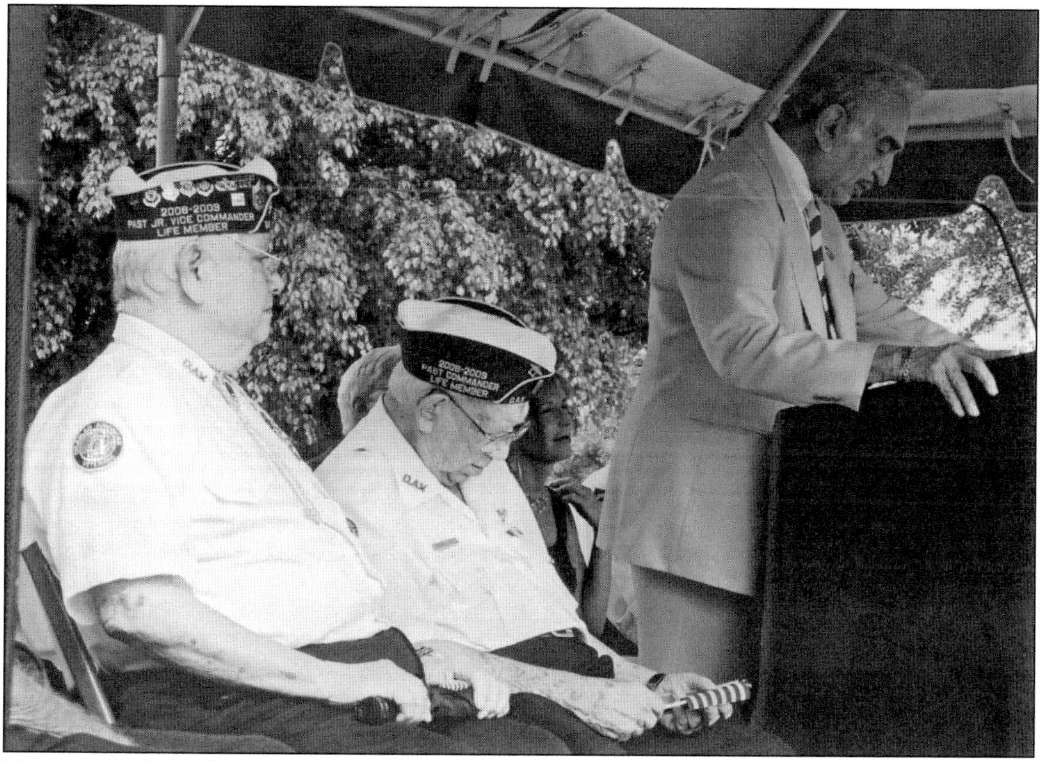

Veterans Park has been the site of the annual Veterans Day and Memorial Day services since 1984. The Plantation/Sunrise Chapter No. 138 Disabled American Veterans and the city have partnered in honoring our armed forces. The residents enjoy patriotic songs, a display of Junior ROTC units, a 21-gun salute, and ending the ceremony with the laying of a wreath. Pictured above is Bill Kling, commissioner of Florida Veterans Affairs, addressing the audience. Below, one of Plantation's first residents, B. Barbara Hoeltzel, celebrated her 100th birthday on December 17, 2000. The Plantation Woman's Club honored her with a party at Deicke Auditorium for family and friends. Pictured are Mayor Rae Carole Armstrong and Barbara Hoeltzel.

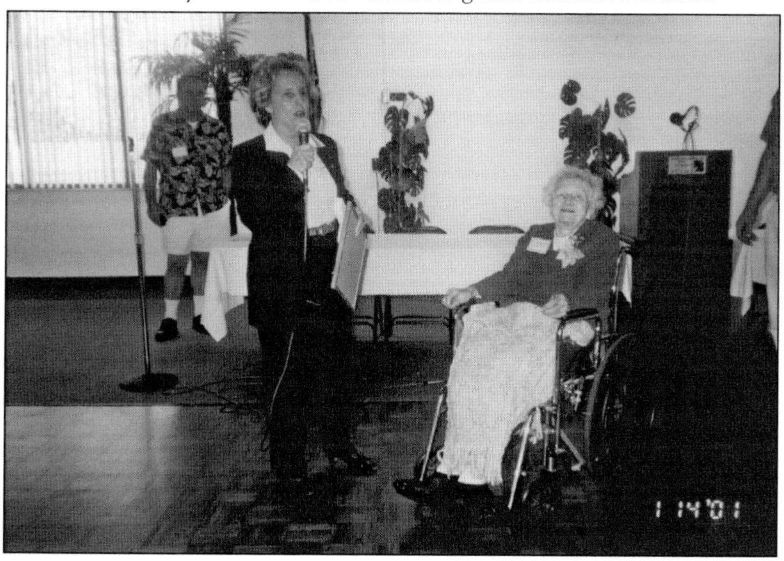

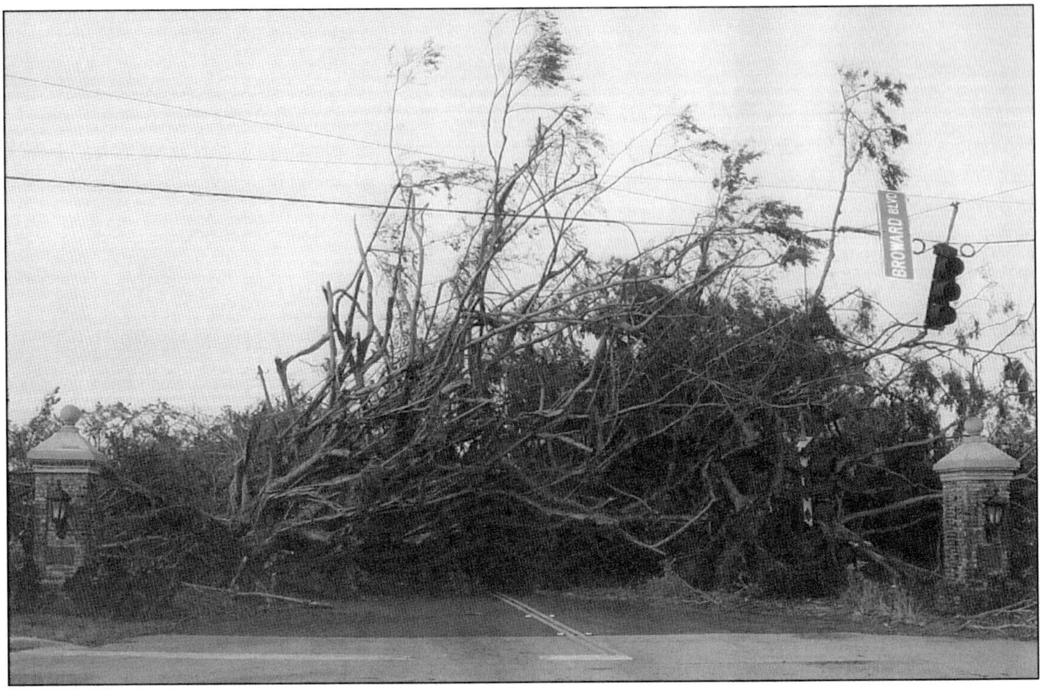

In 2005, Hurricane Wilma wreaked havoc on Plantation's tree canopy, parks, and buildings. Above, North Fig Tree Lane, one of Plantation's signature tree-canopy streets, was just one of the roads impacted by the storm. The city cleared away 750,000 cubic yards of debris, and North Fig Tree Lane was replanted with young oak trees. Below, a team of public works employees clears post-Wilma debris.

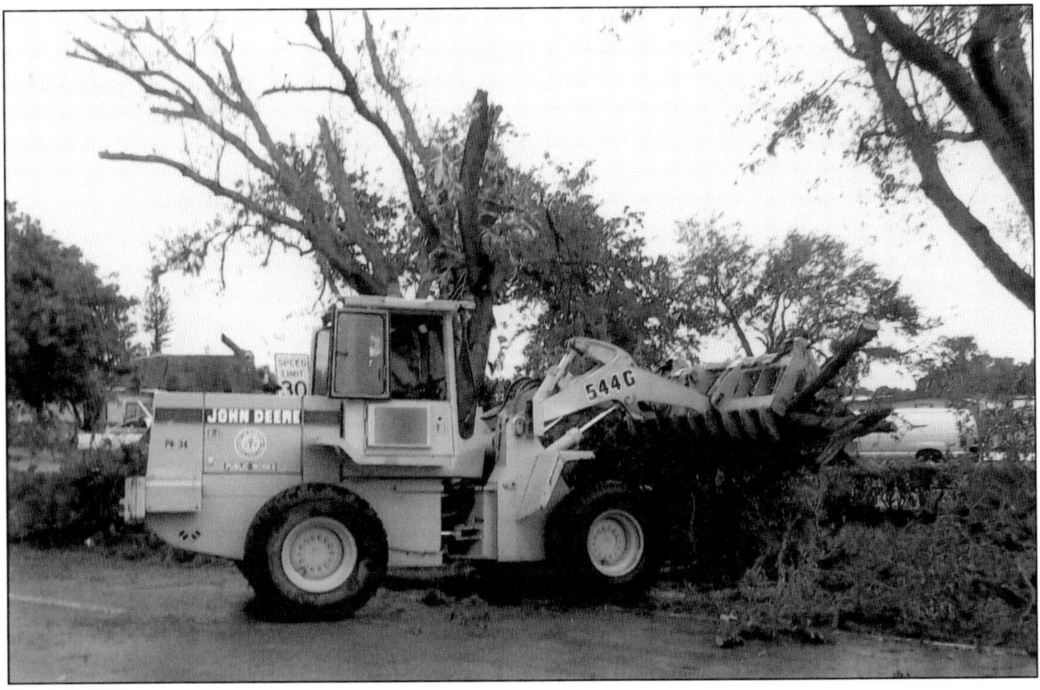

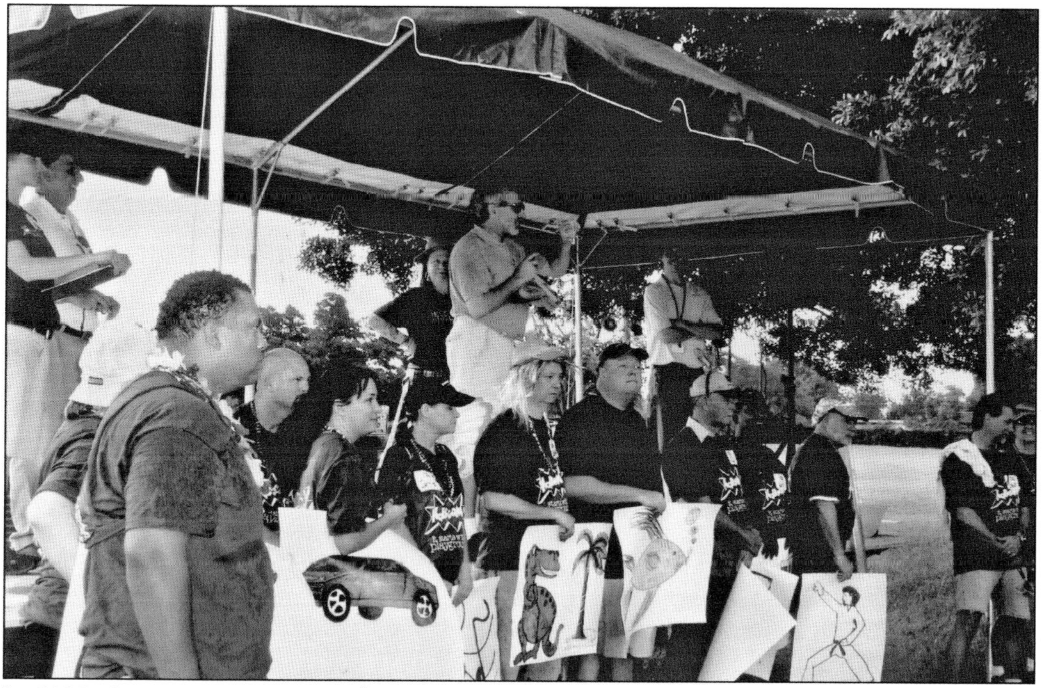

In 2008, the city was awarded a $10,000 grant from KaBOOM, a national nonprofit dedicated to saving play for America's children. The design and construction of the playground in Fig Tree Park was a collaborative effort between the community, Daimler Chrysler, and city staff. The playground was constructed in 48 hours by volunteers and city employees.

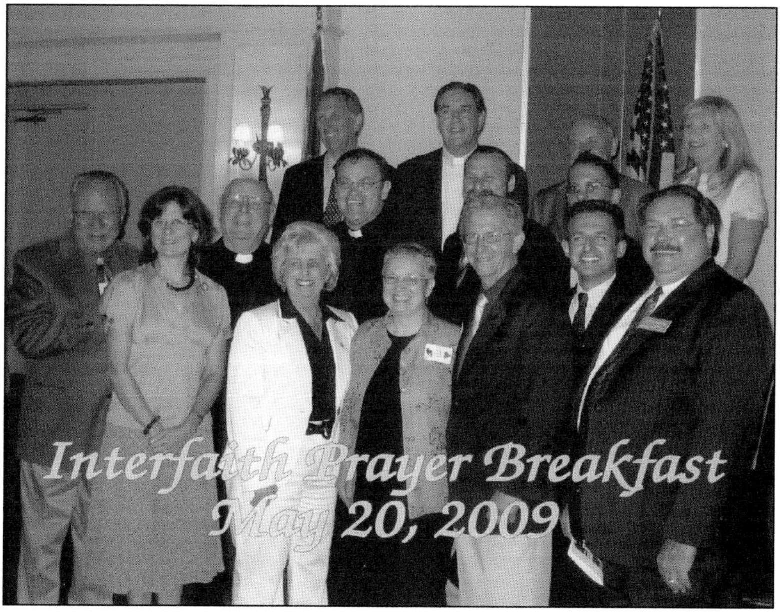

Each year, the Greater Plantation Chamber of Commerce hosts the Mayor's Interfaith Prayer Breakfast. On the first Thursday in May, the National Day of Prayer, religious leaders of many faiths gather together to pray and express gratitude for the city, its residents, and businesses. Mayor Rae Carole Armstrong is pictured with clergy members at the 2009 breakfast.

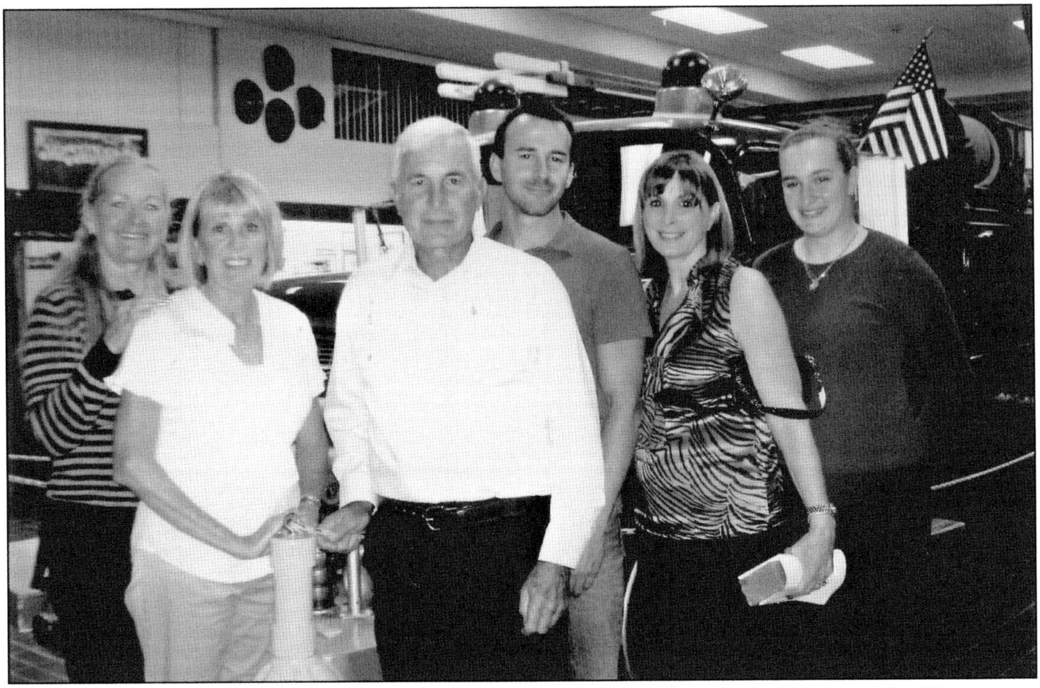

The Veltri family attends the opening of the Genevieve S. Veltri Media Room at the Plantation Historical Museum on September 11, 2008. Pictured are, from left to right, Marsha Veltri, Deanne Veltri Noles, Stephen Veltri, Gregory Veltri, Councilwoman Diane Veltri Bendekovic, and Katie Veltri.

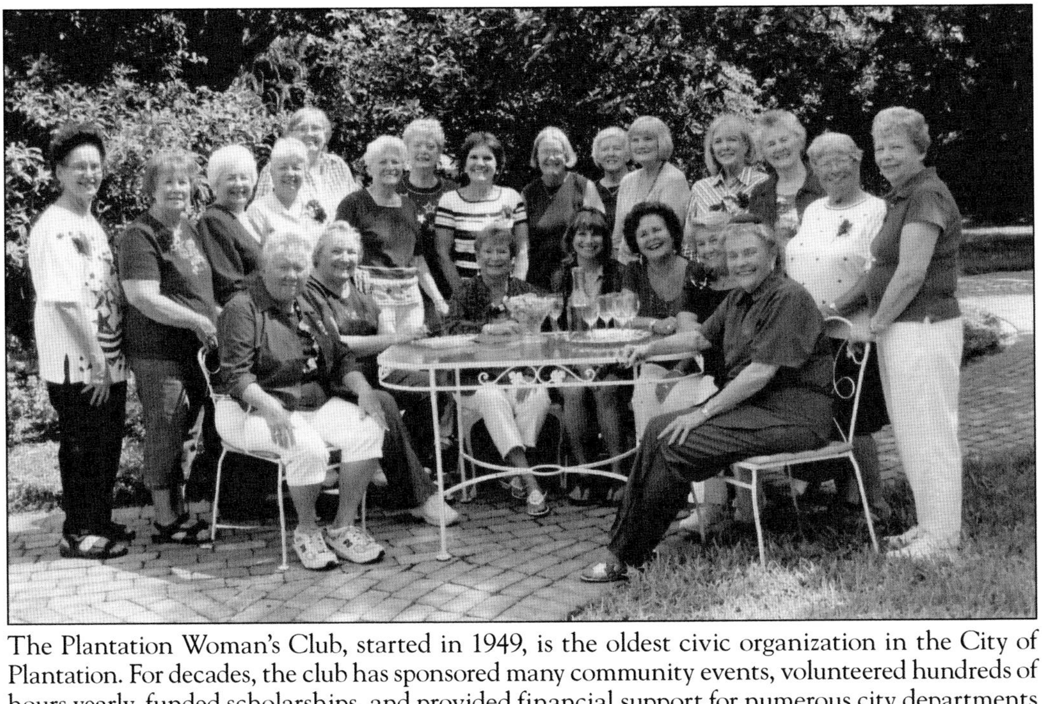

The Plantation Woman's Club, started in 1949, is the oldest civic organization in the City of Plantation. For decades, the club has sponsored many community events, volunteered hundreds of hours yearly, funded scholarships, and provided financial support for numerous city departments and improvements. Pictured are the 2011–2012 officers and chairpersons.

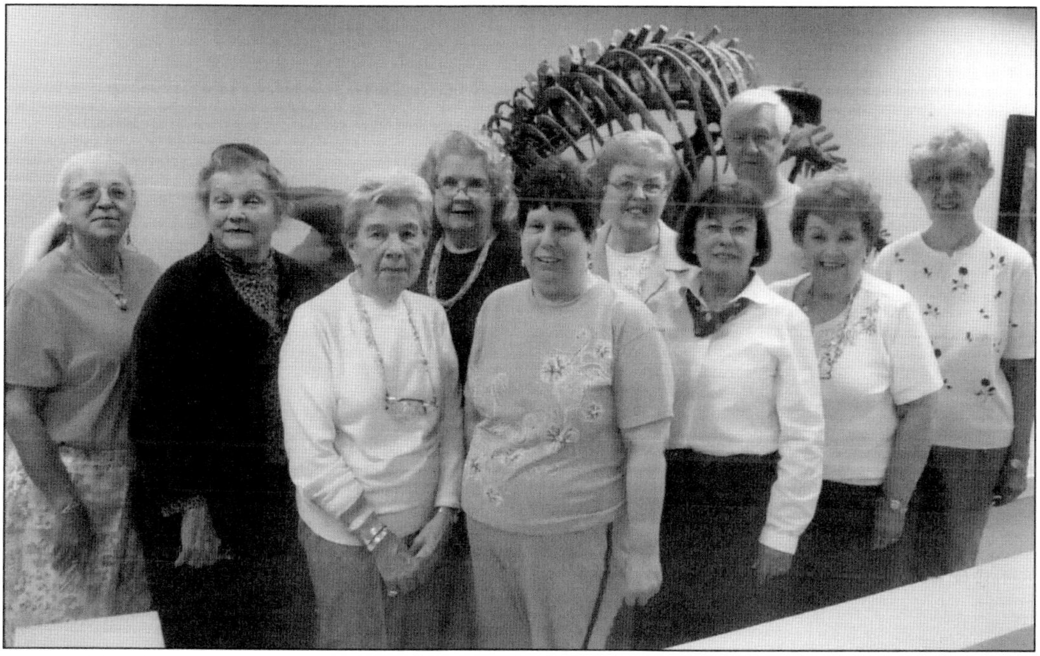

Since 1974, the Plantation Historical Society has dedicated its time and resources to preserving Plantation's history for future generations. The society's generosity has enhanced and supported the Plantation Historical Museum. Pictured are the 2010–2011 executive officers and committee members, from left to right, Cathy Feeney, Betty Cobb, Betty Fitzpatrick, Lillian Ragland, Carol Cotton, Peggy Tingle, Toni Ricke, Sydney Corbin, Shirley Schuler (museum curator and author of this book), and Mary Sliza.

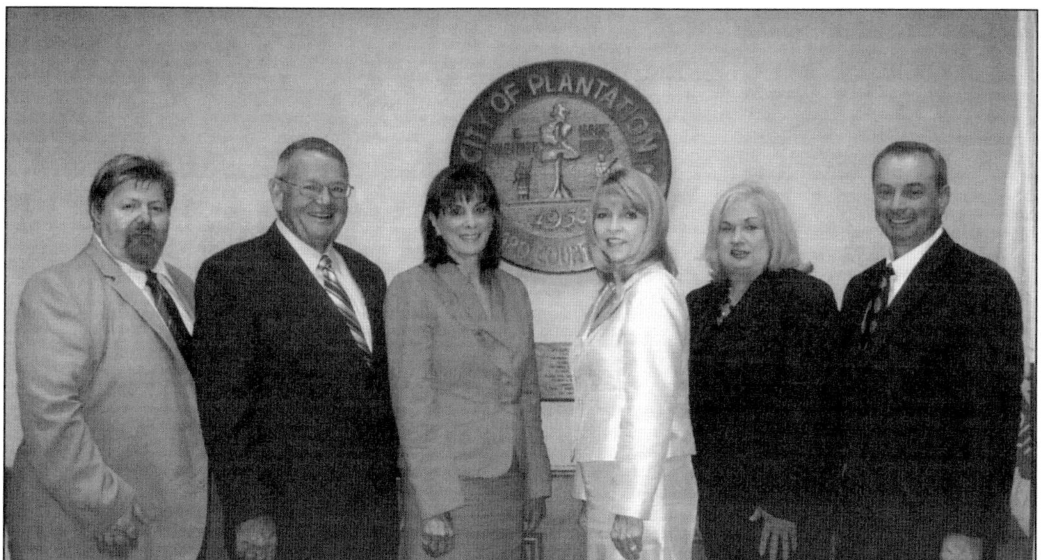

In 2011, Councilwoman Diane Veltri Bendekovic was elected mayor of the City of Plantation. Pictured from left to right are Councilman Dr. Robert Levy, Councilman Pete Tingom, Mayor Diane Veltri Bendekovic, Councilwoman Sharon Moody, Councilwoman Lynn Stoner, and Councilman Ron Jacobs.